WITHDRAWN

IN DEFENCE OF THE MIXED ECONOMY

In Defence of the Mixed Economy

ANDREW SHONFIELD

EDITED BY

Zuzanna Shonfield

Oxford   New York

OXFORD UNIVERSITY PRESS

1984

Oxford University Press, Walton Street, Oxford OX2 6DP

London Glasgow New York Toronto
Delhi Bombay Calcutta Madras Karachi
Kuala Lumpur Singapore Hong Kong Tokyo
Nairobi Dar es Salaam Cape Town
Melbourne Auckland

and associated companies in
Beirut Berlin Ibadan Mexico City Nicosia

Oxford is a trade mark of Oxford University Press

British Library Cataloguing in Publication Data
Shonfield, Andrew
In defence of the mixed economy
1. Economic policy   2. Economics—History
—20th century
I. Title   II. Shonfield, Zuzanna
330.9182'.   HD82
ISBN 0-19-21539-5

Library of Congress Cataloging in Publication Data
Shonfield, Andrew, 1917-1981
In defence of the mixed economy.
Sequel to: The use of public power/Andrew Shonfield.
Bibliography: p.
Includes index.
1. Economic history—1971-   .   2. Economic policy.
3. Industry and state.   I. Shonfield, Zuzanna.   II. Shonfield, Andrew, 1917-1981.
Use of public power.
III. Title.   IV. Title: Mixed economy.
HC59.S493 1984   338.9   83-19488
ISBN 0-19-215359-5

Phototypeset by Wyvern Typesetting Ltd, Bristol
Printed in Great Britain by
Butler & Tanner Ltd,
Frome, Somerset

FOREWORD

THIS book is about public intervention in the modern mixed economy; about how some societies have weathered recent economic storms much better than others; and about what sort of institutions we need to further the dynamic consensus on which to base effective policies. Such a consensus is not an end in itself, but an essential instrument for ensuring prosperity and social welfare in the conditions of impaired growth of the 1980s.

The themes discussed here form the last in a series of studies by Andrew Shonfield about the changing balance of public and private power. The subject was central to his thinking from the 1950s on (see *British Economic Policy since the War*, 1958) and was the topic of his *Modern Capitalism* (1965). Both the present book and *The Use of Public Power*, published in 1982, were devised as a sequel to *Modern Capitalism*, re-examining its assumptions in the altered conditions which have prevailed since the early 1970s. The decision to divide the material into two volumes was in large measure one of expediency. The three chapters at the core of the 1982 book were all but completed at the time of the author's death and so could be published with less delay than the remainder of the material—in drafts, articles, notes and lecture outlines—which required much radical editing. But this division of material in fact adheres closely to the author's original scheme, in which the main text of what is now *The Use of Public Power* was an introductory section—a wide-ranging polemic about the responses of theoreticians and policy-makers to faltering economic growth and to the sporadic signs of rebellion against strong government and steeply rising public expenditure.

What was to follow constitutes, in three parts, the body of the present book (*The Use of Public Power* outlined in its last chapter some of the ideas which go to its making). Part One examines in

This book is part of a series of publications sponsored by the Economics Department of the European University Institute, Florence. The editor wishes to thank the Department, and also the European University Institute, for their support of the study on which the text is based.

greater depth how the Western democracies, and also Japan, coped with the economic strains of the 1970s, comparing policy approaches and identifying the institutions which made the process of adaptation smoother. Among the instruments for managing economic stresses, Andrew Shonfield gives high rank to modern forms of corporatism; because the study of the economic system of Japan yields rich insights into the functioning of an important version of such corporatism, the five chapters of Part Two are devoted to it. Part Three contains a series of reflections on the character of institutional change which would allow modern capitalism to ride the shockwaves of adjustment to new international patterns and to technological innovation, thus making the 1980s less uncomfortable than they threaten to become.

To get the full sense of the direction of the author's thinking, this second book needs to be read in the context of its three introductory chapters, in *The Use of Public Power*. Even so, the implications of this uncompleted work will naturally retain elements of conjecture. But the essential thrust of the message is clear. To thrive, indeed to survive, the mixed economies cannot dispense with a high degree of public intervention. But this intervention must be more selective, balanced and transparent than before.

Although the author felt a deep sense of disappointment about what had happened in the 1970s (in common with anyone who had applauded the vast improvement—at least in the developed democracies—of the period from 1945 to the end of the 1960s over the miseries of the first half of the century), this book is essentially optimistic. His optimism made him emphasize the primacy of national and international institutions over policies—in 1976 he had written of the primacy of politics—in the search for a workable economic system. Some of the potential import of the lessons learnt in the 1970s he only hinted at in writing, though they were prominent in his discussions with friends and colleagues. Among such topics was that of the role of institutions (such as courts and tribunals, some central banks, some international agencies) which are democratically controlled but yet not over-exposed to pressures of single-interest groups; or the possibility of achieving industrial harmony by means of judicious alterations to trade union law followed by an effective use of corporatist discussion; or again, the example of how the small democracies of Northern Europe managed their economies with relative success. The recurring theme of these exchanges was the need to look beyond national boundaries both for models and for solutions.

Ultimately, our judgment about the future depends on how we see the politics of international co-operation. Back in the mid-1970s Andrew Shonfield had identified two aspects of this which would dominate the next decade. A clear commitment to openness in international economic relations was, despite occasional deviations, one of the distinguishing features of the period. But so was the rapid growth of transnational relationships, bypassing the central apparatus of government in a wide variety of ways. This is a development which cannot be fully controlled except by means that are not readily compatible with the maintenance of open national societies. What gave particular cause for concern in view of the countervailing stresses was the withdrawal of the United States from a clear role of economic leadership (as emphasized on p.191 of this book). This was reinforced by the fact that at the turn of the 1970s Germany had still not shown any distinct inclination to lead the European Community countries out of their disappointing performance in the politics of the international economy.

Perhaps because he was aware that editors and readers would have to proceed blindfold, or with only the faint light of remembered discussions to guide them, Andrew Shonfield drafted in the last weeks of his life an outline of the final chapter for the book which he was not going to be able to complete. In this outline he jumped several stages in the orderly progression to the final implications (but this he had done in the last part of *Modern Capitalism* too, although he had then not been writing under pressure). These last reflections, on permissiveness and social authority, answer a few of the questions posed by the readers of the 1982 book; they are summarized here on pp.191-7.

It is a matter for regret that on the very subject which he had intended to emphasize in his closing chapters—the modification of existing institutions and the building of new ones—he left many uncertainties. All sorts of exciting options must remain shadowy and at times equivocal. But if this analysis serves as a prelude to sustained debate about them, the chief object of his writing will have been met.

February 1983   Zuzanna Shonfield

ACKNOWLEDGEMENTS

ON Andrew's behalf I thank a number of friends, colleagues and institutions for exchanges which clarified and enlarged the ideas of this book. In discharging this debt of gratitude I hope to avoid repeating words already used in *The Use of Public Power*, and I therefore have recourse to simple listings of names:

James Billington
Stephen Blank
Alan Bullock
Bernard Cazes
Marcello de Cecco
William Diebold Jr
Ronald Dore
François Duchêne
Jean-Paul Fitoussi
Wolfgang Hager
Arthur Knight
Max Kohnstamm
Arrigo Levi
Kinhide Mushakoji
Kazuo Nukazawa
Hideaki Okamoto
Mancur Olson Jr
Saburo Okita
John Pinder
Kurt Richebächer

Pierre Salmon
Masahide Shibusawa
Niels Thygesen
Takeshi Watanabe
Tadashi Yamamoto

Brookings Institution, Washington DC
Council on Foreign Relations, New York
European University Institute, Florence
Japan Center for International Exchange, Tokyo
Royal Institute of International Affairs, (Chatham House), London
Villa Pamphili Group
Woodrow Wilson International Center for Scholars, Washington DC

Zdenko David, Efisio Espa, Linda Gilbert-Tieri, Sansei Hamagiwa, Dorothy Hamerton, Michiel Tegelaars and Peter Versteeg helped at various stages with the collection and arrangement of data. Bonnie Bonis in Florence and Christine Muirhead in London typed the author's and the editor's labyrinthine manuscripts, often under great pressure.

The Nissan Fellowship generously granted to Andrew in the summer of 1979 facilitated the programme of intensive research, the results of which are written up here in the five chapters on Japan.

I would not have attempted to edit Andrew's papers had it not been for his own systematic encouragement of my efforts to express thoughts on paper. And I wish to thank, now on my own behalf, the following friends who made this book materialize:

Jacqueline Bourgonje, who ably helped Andrew throughout his years at EUI, extended her patience and her good will to me when I took over. Jeremy Schonfield criticized and tidied whenever chaos threatened the whole operation. Leslie Dick's capacity for sharing the excitement of search and discovery made her a most stimulating collaborator during the arduous months of arranging the drafts left by Andrew.

I am very grateful to Niels Thygesen for contributing the Appendix (pp.200–9); this adds a dimension to the text I myself would not have been able to supply. He has summarized the author's views on international monetary relations, using both Andrew's notes and his own records of formal and less formal discussions in which they had both taken part, at the European University Institute and at international conferences, from the mid-70s until the end of 1980.

Bill Diebold, Wolfgang Hager and John Pinder, and also my son, David Shonfield, must surely know that if I express less than adequately my deeply felt gratitude to them it is because I find it impossible to convey in a few lines how much they helped and how that help improved the chapters which follow here. Having encouraged me from the start to salvage Andrew's unfinished texts, they stood by me throughout the operation. All four unstintingly curtailed their leisure-time over much of 1981 and 1982 to add clarity and unity of purpose to my many drafts. Without their help and counsel, and without the critical advice of Bernard Cazes, Ronald Dore, Dharma Kumar, Philippe Schmitter and Ezio Tarantelli, I would not have felt able to complete this task.

To David, Katherine and Pat go my thanks for much encouragement and my appreciation of the good humour with which they bore my obsessive preoccupation with getting the text into print.

Z. S.

The editor wishes to thank the following institutions and periodicals for permission to republish material from articles and lectures by Andrew Shonfield:

Belser Verlag AG, Stuttgart (on behalf of the Forschungsinstitut der Deutschen Gesellschaft für Auswärtige Politik)—'Der Trend zur politisch gesteurten Marktwirtschaft' in *Amerika und Westeuropa*, 1977.

The Executive, Graduate School of Business and Public Administration, Cornell University—'Western Capitalism: A New Balance between Private and Public Power', vol. 4, no. 2, March 1978, and 'Antigovernmental Backlash', vol. 5, no. 1, January 1979.

Futuribles, Paris—'L'avenir de l'économie de marché dans le monde occidental', Autumn 1977.

International Affairs, Royal Institute of International Affairs—'The Politics of the Mixed Economy in the International System of the 1970s' (the 1979 Stevenson Memorial Lecture), vol. 56, no. 1, January 1980.

Revue Economique, Paris—'The VIIIth Plan: Assumptions and Constraints', vol. 31, no. 5, September 1980.

Woodrow Wilson International Center for Scholars, Washington DC—lecture on 'Western Capitalism in the 1970s', 22 December 1976.

CONTENTS

PART ONE

The Mixed Economy at the End of the 1970s

1

CHARACTERISTICS AND CONSTRAINTS

THE nature of the mixed economy defies precise definition. Its complex characteristics are best demonstrated by means of illustration. A mixed economy is one in which prices and supplies of goods and services are largely determined by market processes. At the same time the state and its agencies have a large capacity for economic intervention, which is used in an endeavour to secure objectives that the market would, it is believed, not achieve automatically or not fast enough to meet the requirements of public policy. What is a 'large' capacity for public intervention? Let us in explanation call on an outstanding example of a modern society which was *not* a mixed economy—the United States before Franklin Roosevelt. There, the component of public power was so small and the consequent mixture so thin that it could not function as a mixed economy—like cement mix which has had so much water put into it that it could not be used to hold a building together.

One might almost say, carrying this metaphor a little further, that the opponents of the mixed economy have a preference for dry walls—the building blocks of private enterprise depending on their shape and relationship to one another to keep the structure standing. Indeed, authority for using pre-Rooseveltian America as an ideal type of a *non*-mixed economy may be said to have been given by Arthur Burns, former chairman of the American Federal Reserve, in a notable lecture delivered in 1979 on the occasion of the IMF's annual meeting, on the theme of what had gone wrong with the economic performance of the Western world (Burns, 1979). His answer, essentially, was that its deficiencies can be traced to the advent of the mixed economy, and he fathered the conception of that malign development precisely upon the New Deal of the 1930s.

Three further points will clarify the way in which mixed economies behave nowadays:

First, governments and their agencies may intervene either to accelerate a market process, or to delay it, or to bias the market in a certain direction by means of subsidies or taxes or by direct regulation. Direct regulation is of course very old—almost the favourite business of pre-industrial states. What is novel about its contemporary form is that it attempts increasingly to make some explicit allowance for the social costs of the market process to set against private gains. The opponents argue that the costs of the regulatory exercise are themselves not adequately calculated, and contend that they generally outweigh the social benefits (Weidenbaum, 1977). Whether this argument is right or wrong, the important point is that some calculation of social costs is attempted, and that the outcome of the calculation often aims to even the balance by an addition to private costs.

The second point is straightforward: simply a warning that the degree of 'mixedness' is not determined by the size of the public sector or the proportion of public expenditure to the national income. The Japanese, for example, have much the smallest ratio of public expenditure of any advanced industrial country; yet there is no doubt about the effectiveness or the frequency with which government agencies intervene in the management of the Japanese economy. It is the *function* adopted by the state rather than its mass which counts.

Thirdly, it has hitherto been one of the aims of the mixed economies to reduce the losses of output and welfare which are caused by fluctuations in private business sentiment and activity. This was undoubtedly the aspect of the matter which was most insistently questioned in the late 1970s. It has, for instance, been claimed as one of Mrs Thatcher's achievements to have made 'a final decisive break with the thinking of J. M. Keynes' (*Financial Times*, 15 September 1979, p.32). If this view had been right, in the sense that public policy, notably fiscal policy, now stays neutral in the face of a fall in business activity—which would imply that a recession was accompanied by a drop in net public spending, as tax revenue fell—that would indeed be a large-scale retreat from the mixed economy.

Certainly there is clear evidence of a widespread change in the thinking of the leaders of the major countries of the Western world in their response to the second oil crisis of the 1970s. If one compares their reaction in 1979 with the line of policy to which they gave their collective support after the first oil 'shock' in 1973, one is struck most of all by the absence of any belief in their capacity to limit the consequent damage to the welfare of their own societies. It is worth recalling that in 1974, in the wake of the fourfold increase in oil prices, the main preoccupation expressed by the leading statesmen of the West was how to prevent the consequent fall in our real incomes from inducing a drop in demand and a general slump. They failed. But at least some of them tried hard to offset the secondary consequences of the fall in demand; and all agreed that it would be a good idea to do so.

If we go on to the Tokyo summit conference in July 1979 and recall the tone of what was decided there, we obtain a sense of the intellectual distance traversed in the previous five years. What the leaders of the mixed economies of the West and of Japan agreed was that there should be no attempt whatsoever to cushion the shock to their economies of the rise in the cost of energy: incomes had to be reduced at once and there was no hint of any counteraction to moderate the effect of this upheaval on the level of business activity in our economies. That meant, other things being equal, that unemployment, already high by post-war standards, would have to rise further. The key point in the communiqué issued at the end of the Tokyo meeting was that each country was adjured to pursue its own appropriate economic policy to achieve 'durable external equilibrium'. There was no recognition of the kind that followed the first oil shock in the early 1970s, that since a collective deficit of the rest of world with the oil producers was inevitable, separate decisions, each aiming to eliminate a national deficit, would cause still more collective damage.

It is worth noting that the marked change which has taken place in the attitude of policy-makers cannot simply be attributed to changes in the composition of Western governments. The new doctrines had penetrated very widely well before Mrs Thatcher and President Reagan appeared on the scene. Even among the smaller advanced industrial countries there was a greatly weakened will on this occasion to sustain internal demand and the employment deriving from it. When the Swedes beat a retreat from Keynes—or as perhaps they might prefer to say, from Myrdal— that surely signals a climacteric!

The protagonists

It is, however, too often mistakenly thought that the big change which brought this system into being was all, or mainly, to do with Keynes. There were other powerful formative influences, including the contributions made by the socialists and planners.

The socialists were concerned above all with the control of what they called 'the commanding heights' of the economy; and their solution was to nationalize them. In the event, the socialist governments of the post-war period have been able to 'command' precious little from the eminences they captured, or which had been captured for them. Whether it was that the economic landscape of the second half of the twentieth century had changed, so that the newly nationalized industries like coal and steel no longer counted as much as before, or whether the original analysis was mistaken, does not matter too much for our present purposes. The significant result was that governments were left with a large stock of productive assets in their possession and with direct responsibility for employing and managing a large number of industrial workers. It has indeed proved more difficult for non-socialist governments to get rid of these assets and transfer them to private control than it was to put them into the public sector.

In many countries this issue may, in fact, have lost some of its original ideological edge. There was, for instance, a notable absence of excited argument surrounding such events as the effective transfer of large parts of the French steel industry to public ownership in the 1970s, or the similar fate of the great bulk of Swedish shipbuilding. For both of these governments, whose politics were clearly and consciously right of centre, nationalization was treated just as an obvious expedient to be employed as a means of safeguarding the future of an important national asset during a period of poor business and commercial difficulty. In this context, those who point to the current activities of the British Conservative government would do well to recall the heroic attempt of an earlier Tory administration under Edward Heath to put the firm of Rolls-Royce, which was losing a lot of money, into bankruptcy. More recently, the modifications of the first great burst of denationalization rhetoric following the 1979 Conservative election victory suggested that this government too, in common with others which are in the business of running a mixed economy, was in the end moved by the fact that a large-scale industrial enterprise has to be thought of in terms of its function as a long-term national asset. Simply washing one's hands of all responsibility for it and handing it over to the highest bidder, regardless of his provenance or his intentions, will almost certainly turn out not to be practical politics.

This is not to predict that the Thatcher government will fail to dispose of *any* of the business assets at present in public ownership—they may well be able to sell shares in enterprises such as aerospace and airways to a lot of (small) investors, probably with a minimum effect on the conduct of management. All that is being postulated here is that judging by the record of this and other countries, it will not be easy to bring about a significant change in the ratio between publicly-owned and private assets. When the object is to get rid of those assets which do not make a useful contribution to public revenues, the matter is difficult indeed. Governments, whether of the Right or of the Left, do not enjoy having to call on taxpayers to make good the losses that are periodically made by the big businesses which they own, and a person who happened to be deaf would find it difficult to detect the difference in their behaviour; the main observable distinction lies only in the kind of painful noise that they make about it.

This brings us directly to the second group of people who have been so important in forming the mixed economy—the planners. Their influence on this question of the ownership of important industrial assets derives in part from a clear trend in the second half of the twentieth century towards the increasing concentration of business, which is noticeable in nearly all Western-style countries. The result in the medium-sized countries, as well as more obviously in the smaller countries, is that activity in a particular industrial field is in many instances dominated by one or two, occasionally three, major enterprises. It is hardly necessary to give examples; all of us could think, in each of the big European countries and in Japan, of half a dozen important industries running from chemicals through to electrical engineering where this holds good. And the pattern is even more marked in the smaller countries, though of course with fewer significant firms.

The consequence of this process of concentration is that these big firms are thought of in the guise of 'national champions', and the issue of public or private ownership is less important than the fact that they are clearly seen to be controlled in order to safeguard national interest. That interest is itself rarely defined; indeed the question of whether a firm is or is not truly a 'national champion' is usually only brought up when there is the possibility of ownership passing into the hands of a foreign national. In practice both parties, the government and the big private enterprise, are expected to engage in a 'mixed' style of decision-making when questions affecting the long-term future of the industry concerned are under consideration. To term it 'mixed' rather than 'joint' decision-making is not, however, to suggest that there is a formal commitment of any kind to submit a certain category of decisions to the government for approval. It is more a matter of habitually recognizing that common interests exist, though the degree of involvement of the representatives of the public side will vary greatly from one case to another.

Paying for displacement

This 'mixed' decision-making, which is sometimes dignified with the title of indicative planning, is conducted with more or less vigour in different countries. It is notoriously vigorous in Japan and France. For quite a long time it has been taken for granted by the smaller West European countries, for whom looking after the health of a 'national champion' has traditionally been a major aspect of foreign policy, as well as of the conduct of domestic affairs. Until recently it may have been thought that the United States was an exception to this style of behaviour, but the massive rescue operation mounted in 1979 to save the Chrysler Corporation has made this a hardly plausible view. Of course the Americans might be surprised to hear Chrysler referred to as a 'national champion'; they would no doubt point out that they already had two other rather successful champions in the same industry. But that would be taking the business of championship too literally—as if it were a variation on something like a medieval form of jousting. The simple point is that many Americans, for historical and also, partly, for well-established ideological reasons, feel that they need a minimum of three large motor firms in order to serve the public interest. It is not, either, simply a matter of making sure that there is adequate competition in the motor industry: there is more than enough of that coming from outside, and likely to continue to do so. In the event the American authorities endorsed the view that three automobile companies 'of their own' were what was needed.

The experience of Chrysler, and the sense of outraged shock conveyed by American commentary on the affair, is merely a case of a lag in recognition. There was, naturally enough, a deep reluctance on the part of the US citizens to put a great American corporation in the same category as various European lame ducks. Bigness in a nation has certain advantages, but it does sometimes succeed in swamping the national perception of what is obvious to smaller people.

When the matter of protecting large investment, private or public, is considered in the broader context of the evolution of the public purpose in the Western democracies during the past quarter of a century, there is nothing here that is worth puzzling over. The fact is that the governments have been saddled with responsibility for securing a rising minimum of welfare for their citizens, and for preventing situations in which any one community within the nation (for example, an economically backward region) is substantially worse off than the average.

The issue of regional policy and its implications for the management of the economy offer a particularly clear illustration of the typical compulsions of the mixed economy as it operates today. It has come to be almost an article of faith in Europe that a national society is unhealthy if a large disparity in the economic performance of different regions within the country is dealt with by shifting more and more people from the old established centres to areas of geographical advantage. This is not solely a matter of sentiment about the destruction of familiar places and institutions, or concern for the personal discomfort of those who are uprooted. The state, and through the state the average taxpayer, is necessarily involved in the financial consequences of this displacement of people, and the effect is often costly. The state generally has a large investment in the social infrastructure of existing commmunities, and this infrastructure has absorbed increasing amounts of investment during recent years, as public welfare services have advanced. There would be new social investment to be paid for in the places to which people move—new and probably more expensive social investment, because of the costs of congestion which are typically associated with these rapidly expanding, affluent centres of business activity and employment.

At the very least, then, the state has an interest in seeing that public investment produces a high return and does not have to be written off prematurely. So, regardless of the ideology of the government in power, it is impelled to intervene; and its intervention in such cases is designed to prevent market forces at work in the private sector of the economy from fulfilling their normal function—for the labour market, if left to its own devices, would no doubt respond efficiently to the rewards and penalties offered by businesses looking for the optimum location for the conduct of their activities.

This is but one example among many of the way in which the state finds itself under a compulsion to intervene in the market economy, with the aim of securing a desirable distribution of the resources for which it is responsible. To some extent this formulation, with its emphasis on the degree of responsibility assumed, begs a number of questions. But this is in order to emphasize the other aspect of the matter, which is that the state cannot confine its concerns exclusively to the expenditure of the actual sums of money with which it is entrusted in a given budget year. In a mixed economy it has to think about the overall efficiency of the deployment of national resources, if only because the size of the amounts which will become available for the purpose of pursuing the public interest—whether directly, through such activities as education, or indirectly, by means of income transfers to people like old-age pensioners—depends on the efficiency with which capital and labour are deployed throughout the economy.

Many examples show the state intervening with the intention of frustrating, or delaying, the operation of market forces. But it may, and does, equally intervene on occasion to anticipate market forces. This could be the case, for example, in the market for energy, where the government might raise the price above the current market level because the latter does not adequately discount the probable future scarcities and costs of particular resources. By the time the free market catches up with a full awareness of the facts, it may be rather late to start investing in the more expensive forms of energy production. The government may, therefore, deliberately set out to raise the price of energy in order to accelerate the market process, leading potential investors to apply their capital to this purpose in preference to others.

It is not necessary to lengthen this list of possible ways in which governments may set out to influence, or to frustrate, market forces in a mixed economy. The essential point is not whether their judgment happens to be right or wrong in any particular instance, but that they cannot evade a share of the responsibility for certain economic decisions, private and public, with strategic consequences for the use of national resources—including above all the nation's resources of manpower.

2

THE CHECK TO PUBLIC
EXPENDITURE

THE prevailing mood of the late 1970s in the Western industrial countries, and also in Japan, was notably sceptical of the ability of governments as economic managers. Specifically, there was widespread doubt about their capacity to manipulate the levers in a way that would ensure that the economy kept expanding at the steady pace which had been enjoyed, with only a few interruptions, during the first quarter of a century following the Second World War. And the governments themselves were not encouraging; the politicians in charge appeared to be suffering from a certain loss of nerve.

This was particularly marked in their changing views about the acceptable size of public expenditure. During the 1960s and early 1970s there had been an extremely rapid advance in public spending throughout the Western capitalist world, caused, in great part, by the enormous expansion of social welfare of all sorts. The growth of social welfare, capturing a steadily increasing share of the national product year by year, had of course been in progress for some time before this, in most Western countries ever since the end of World War Two. But what happened from the early 1960s onwards represented a clear acceleration of the trend. Indeed if it had not been for the simultaneous, and equally widespread, decline in the share of defence expenditure in GNP throughout the West, the burden on the taxpayer of public spending to support the greatly extended social responsibilities assumed by governments would have been significantly larger.[1]

As it was, government expenditure in the OECD group of countries rose from a little over one-quarter of GNP at the start of the 1960s to around one-third in the early 1970s. These are median figures, and Japan, which has an unusually low ratio of public expenditure, reduced the totals. The broad picture in the advanced industrial countries of Western Europe and North America is that in *all* of them government took—either for its own purposes or to pass on in the form of transfer payments—between 30 and 40 per cent of the gross national product by the early 1970s. In 1972, just before the great inflation, the Europeans were not greatly different from the Americans (whose government took a little under one-third of GNP) in their public spending habits. Among the Europeans themselves there was a clear tendency for the northerners, especially the Scandinavians, to be ahead, with a ratio approaching 40 per cent of GNP. The United Kingdom, Germany and France bunched at around 35 per cent of GNP. The southerners, in the Mediterranean area, held at a significantly lower ratio.

The subsequent slump distorted this picture, as public spending on relief and on wide-ranging efforts to stimulate the economy increased sharply while the national product fell. There had never before been pump-priming on anything like the scale of 1974–6; nor, it is fair to say, had there been a slump of anything like these dimensions since the advent of the post-war welfare state in the Western world. The slump distorted the 'picture' rather than the pattern of public expenditure. The point was made by Charles Schultze, at the time chairman of the Council of Economic Advisors, when he usefully recalculated US budget expenditure on a non-cyclical basis. By eliminating the identifiable effects of the business cycle on the level of government spending and on the size of the national product, Schultze and his co-author Emil Sunley pointed to the fact that the share of government, federal as well as state and local, remained on this 'base-line budget', just short of one-third of GNP (Owen and Schultze, 1976, tables 8–2, p.328 and 9–1, p.373, and pp.401 ff.). Some of the very high figures for other OECD countries would probably be similarly reduced if a corresponding 'base-line' calculation were applied to them, to eliminate the effects of the mid-1970s slump and the strenuous efforts to spend our way out of it.

But even after making allowances for the special circumstances of the mid-1970s, the essential questions remain: Was the greatly accelerated expansion of the public sector which we have experienced in the past two decades part of a secular trend? Is it likely in the longer term to involve a decisive change in the relative weight of market forces in our societies—a great enlargement of public, at the expense of private power?

Trends in Europe and the US

The novel feature of the second half of the 1970s is that a number of nations which have been among the most dynamic and expansive designers of social welfare programmes embarked on a deliberate policy of curbing the impulse to improve by spending more. The new mood took a grip particularly in the established citadels of social democratic politics in Northern Europe—in Germany, Britain and Sweden. All three decided, though the reasons deployed by each were different, that the welfare state was becoming over-extended. In the British case the eventual outcome was a cut-back in real terms of the absolute volume of publicly financed welfare. This was not because the British welfare services were larger than elsewhere but because the other sectors of the national economy which supply saleable goods were less productive than in other countries. In Britain the productive base required for sustaining the expanded welfare programmes had been found to be too narrow; and its narrowness expressed itself in a particularly vulnerable balance of payments—a failure to earn enough abroad to cover the country's purchases of foreign goods and services.

The German and Swedish cases were different, in the sense that there was no direct imperative imposed by the balance of payments. The forces making for a curb on public social expenditure were in these two cases less obviously urgent and compelling than in Britain, though perhaps just as profound. They had to do with the governments' judgment about the limits of the taxable capacity of the nation—a factor which was already influencing the views of the Swedish Social Democrat government before its defeat at the polls in 1976—and, in Germany, with the secondary effects of rapidly expanding public expenditure on the long-term productive capacity of the economy. By the mid-1970s, the Germans had come to fear that the resources pre-empted by the public sector would, in one form or another, be subtracted from investment needed for the renewal and enlargement of industry's productive capacity (Germany, Council of Economic Experts, 1975/6).

This points to a further factor which curbed the growth of public expenditure in Western Europe at large, the coincidence of the great expansion of publicly provided welfare with an extraordinary wages push at the end of the 1960s and in the early 1970s. The later phase of this exceptional pressure on wages was clearly prompted in many countries by the anticipation of equally high price increases and the desire to compensate for them in advance. However faulty the economic logic of a wages policy of this kind, the motives of the trade union leaders who make such demands are clearly compensatory rather than predatory. The first wave of extraordinary wage claims had been differently motivated: labour had aimed to capture a larger share of the real national product at the expense of other claimants. And in this the wage-earners of Western Europe were very largely successful.

The upshot was that in a wide range of countries, including all the major European industrial nations, the share of profits was sharply cut by a scissors movement of increasing wages on the one hand and increasing public expenditure on the other. It has now become a matter of stated public policy in most of these countries to reverse this process, to increase radically the share of profits and hence the volume of profit-financed investment. Again, it was, interestingly enough, the social democratic governments of Germany and Britain that took the lead in this endeavour.

It is worth observing, further, that some curb on the growth of government spending was implicit in the new phase of wages and incomes policies adopted in the latter part of the 1970s by the social democrat nations in Western Europe. In the first phase of an incomes policy, the bargain typically involves the government in the extension of certain public welfare policies of particular interest to the trade unions, in return for restraining their wage claims. This is likely to require an increase in public expenditure in the short term. The core of the trade union bargain, however, is some form of commitment from the government that tax concessions will compensate wage-earners, in part or in whole, for wage increases forgone. Sometimes this bargain is fully explicit, as in Britain in 1976 when Denis Healey, the Chancellor of the Exchequer, attempted to make his budget concessions on income tax conditional on future trade union action to limit wage claims to a stated figure. More often the bargain has rested on a tacit understanding between the trade unions and the government. In either case the arrangement for limiting wage demands compels the government to limit public expenditure which has to be financed by taxation falling on wage-earners' incomes. If it avoids higher taxation by incurring an increased public deficit which translates itself into higher prices or higher interest rates, the government simply holds back the recovery of investment. Such action frustrates the central purpose of the incomes policy, which is to engineer an expansion of output without inflationary price effects.

Now, it will be argued that most of these incomes policies were a transient political phenomenon, which is related to a particular kind of business cycle in which the Western world became entangled in the mid-1970s through the inefficiencies of its economic policies. But even though the experiment did not last in this particular form, all the signs are that a number of countries, notably those like Britain with a vulnerable balance of payments and a powerfully organized labour movement, will have to persist in—or return to—the effort to hold down money wages by means of a contractual agreement between the fiscal authorities of the state and the trade unions. The effect of these incomes policies in the conditions of the late 1970s, while governments were engaged in an effort to nurture a sustained rise in profits, was to impose a slight brake on the continued expansion of the public sector, at any rate on the scale and pace experienced in the relatively recent past.

Charles Schultze has pointed out that the increased share of the American GNP absorbed by public welfare programmes has been largely due to three causes. First, the introduction of new forms of assistance such as Medicare and food stamps; secondly, legislation to increase the scope and raise the level of existing welfare programmes; and thirdly, the marked rise in the number of those eligible who actually claim their benefits. All this, he argues, amounts to a once-and-for-all development. 'By now virtually everyone is covered by social security, and for the average retired couple benefits have already been raised to over 60 per cent of earnings just before retirement' (Owen and Schultze, 1976, p.357). The proportion of eligible people claiming the benefits to which they are entitled simply cannot go up very much further.

Any further necessary enlargement, for instance to ensure uniformity and general availability of services, will in fact have almost certainly already occurred. It is only those accountants who are wholly preoccupied with the distinction between what does and does not figure in the public sector's financial statements who fail to observe the fact.

The management of the economy

The high point of confidence in the effectiveness of government economic power was probably in the early and middle 1960s, during the successful US experiments of the Kennedy years with a 'full employment budget' and the British Labour government's launching of its National Economic Plan. The coincident, though very diverse, failures of American and British economic policies in the late 1960s and early 1970s have largely contributed to the reaction against 'fine tuning' in the economics profession. It so happens that the cultural dominance of Anglo-American economics has been a potent force in setting the more optimistic expectations of governments in the earlier post-war period. The accident of the débâcle occurring in these two particular countries was therefore all the more influential.

It was to some extent the exaggerations of some of the exponents of 'fine tuning' at the earlier stage which subsequently brought Keynesian techniques of short-term demand management into disrepute. The reaction helped to give currency to an extreme anti-interventionist school of economic policy. This school argued that since the behaviour of the economy was in fact determined by predominantly monetary factors, which were not controlled by the fiscal policies of the state, intervention by government designed to achieve short-term changes of direction was almost bound to be ineffective in the long term and very likely to be damaging, too. On the other hand, changes in the money supply, which do affect economic performance, would, unless they were very infrequent, be harmful. The policy prescriptions emerging from this school of economists who came into prominence in the 1970s amounted, in political terms, to a general exhortation to governments to keep their hands off—and let markets, unhindered, do their beneficent work.

Very few, if any, were willing in the event to obey this precept to the letter. But the new doctrines, and even more the political rhetoric which went with them, did undoubtedly help to reinforce an inclination widely evinced in Western industrial countries to reduce the *ambit* of government economic intervention. Typical consequences of this mood were, first, the general departure from fixed currency parities in the early 1970s and the adoption of floating exchange rates. Secondly, there was a tendency to accord greater independence of action to central banks in their dealings with ministries of finance and other departments of government.

In this matter Germany and the United States have set the tone. Both have powerful central banks whose independence is guaranteed by law. To a large extent the constitution of the post-war German central banking system was directly modelled on the US Federal Reserve System, and like it was designed to express the doctrine of the separation of powers, applied to financial policy-making. In most other Western countries central bank policies had after World War Two been increasingly integrated into those of governments: political decisions were in the last resort to take precedence over technical monetary considerations. Indeed effective co-ordination of national policies, and particularly national economic planning, was believed to depend crucially on an institutional relationship which guaranteed the political subordination of the central bank.

The pressure for a reversal of this post-war settlement is a subtle process and makes itself felt in such a form as the influential international club of central bankers which meets monthly at Basle. And the insistence on the separation of powers principle has been considerably reinforced by the fact that the leading exponents of the doctrine in financial management—the USA and Germany—were also much the most powerful members of the international financial system of the 1970s, at a time when other nations had become far more dependent on their goodwill to secure the external financial support which they need more frequently and on a larger scale than in the past to sustain their domestic economic policies.

It is typical of the politics of economic policy-making in the late 1970s that there was a heavy emphasis on the commitment of governments, often very reluctantly given, to money-supply targets. In this cult the Americans and the Germans again played a leading part. The political significance of this kind of target is that achieving it is primarily the responsibility of the central bank, operating through the money market. A government can of course affect the outcome by its fiscal actions. But if a central bank disapproves of, or dislikes, some aspects of government policy, it has at its disposal—after the adoption of a money-supply target—an additional and powerful means of influence. It may, in the extreme case, see itself as having a licence to use the money market to frustrate the government.

Moreover, an influential current of opinion has emerged in Western countries which argues in favour of an even more drastic separation of financial powers, through the establishment of an autonomous agency of exceptional authority to act as the overseer of government financial policy. This is in fact a programme for the institutionalized distrust of government.

There are a number of reasons why governments have become vulnerable to this kind of attack. For one thing, certain scientific deficiencies have become apparent in the theories underlying the short-term management of the economy. In particular, there are uncertainties about the extent of the time lags affecting measures aimed at inducing an economic expansion or contraction. What is clear is that the time taken for such measures to work their way through the system varies with different circumstances. But the uncertainties led many governments to argue, during the later stages of the strong recession of 1974–5, against intervention to stimulate visibly flagging economies, on the ground that by the time the proposed stimuli took effect, the recovery of world demand would already be in progress.[2] Thus inadequate understanding of time lags made governments cautious and justified a policy of abstention, at a time when vigorous intervention was required to help the economic recovery along.

Another factor was the evidence of a built-in tendency for rising price expectations to accelerate sharply during periods of high pressure of demand, with no corresponding mechanism to secure an automatic reversal of the process in periods of slack demand. On the contrary, the momentum of the earlier price expectations continued, in certain circumstances, even after the economy had turned sharply downwards. Again, the effect was to make governments more hesitant to intervene with measures of pump-priming in a recession than they would have been in the 1950s and 1960s.

To some extent the failures of government intervention reflect a wider phenomenon: the blunting of the traditional instruments of economic policy with the emergence of mass affluence and large-scale public welfare from the early 1960s onwards. The responses to the old-style pressures of unemployment and reduced economic activity proved to be different when a substantial floor of real income (with welfare payments in many countries generally indexed against price rises) had been guaranteed to the great majority of the population. It is to be observed moreover that the economy is not only less responsive to downward pressures; governments have found during the latest business cycle that people who have acquired personal assets and have the habit of saving do not react so readily to the encouragement to spend more. Cuts in consumer taxes, easier credit, and the various attempts pursued in different countries to induce the mass of consumers to spend the economy out of the slump must be judged a flop. The new class of affluent consumers, it emerged, had other matters on their minds, which lent themselves less readily to manipulation by the technicians in the ministries of finance and the central banks.

Finally, national governments operate nowadays under the constraints of a much more obtrusive international environment. Apparently rational acts of policy which make good sense in purely domestic terms, like changing an exchange rate or moving the rate of interest up or down, are regularly swamped, and often frustrated, by their effects on the movement of funds through the international financial market. The consequence is that the room for manoeuvre of an individual country, even a big and important country, acting on its own is considerably reduced.

Friedman's fallacy and Hirschman's 'voice'

The call for the limitation of public power, through the political elevation of the central bank or some other independent agency to impose discipline on the politicians, is part of a more general anti-government pro-market polemic. Professor Milton Friedman, who is probably its leading exponent, deployed the argument with great vigour in an *Encounter* essay (Friedman, 1976) and his text usefully elucidates the underlying thinking of the movement which came to prominence in the 1970s. Its first characteristic, to which Friedman's oratory is highly attuned, is a penchant for categorical simplification. Thus he starts out by refusing to allow any distinction at all between an economic transaction between a buyer and a seller in a market place and a political transaction involving a citizen and some person or organization, actually or potentially, wielding public power. He insists that the competition for votes by politicians corresponds exactly to the competition for custom among entrepreneurs in the commercial market: after an election is over, the successful politicians use their acquired control over public goods for purposes of their own self-aggrandizement.

No allowance is made for the fact that it is by common consent wrong to sell one's vote and generally regarded as a crime for a candidate to buy a vote as part of a personal bargain, i.e. that, in fact, the whole process is intended to be radically different from a market transaction. The underlying assumption of democratic politics is that a voter is motivated by something besides the aim of maximizing his personal advantage through a deal with a candidate. Friedman seems to think that this is impossible. At any rate, all that he perceives in the political relationship is an inferior kind of economic transaction—a species of long-term service contract without a break clause.

Given these premises, it is little wonder that he concludes that the average citizen who depends on the political process to provide him with desired public goods is inevitably duped. He sets out to be a consumer and succeeds in being a victim. But let Friedman speak for himself: 'The fundamental difference', he notes, 'between the political market and the economic market is that in the political market there is very little relationship between what you vote for and what you get. In the economic market you get what you vote for.' This is partly because the men engaged in purveying public goods are driven entirely by 'their private interest in seeking to extend the scope of their power, importance and influence' and we foolishly enter into a bargain with them, which binds us, like an indentured servant, to obey their behests during extended periods of time between elections. More fundamentally, the great advantage of the economic market, according to Friedman, is that transactions are taken one at a time and are individually subject to the buyer's free and untrammelled acceptance or rejection.

Now the latter assertion seems to be based on a strangely unrealistic view of the common run of transactions in a society in which most of us are involved in a great variety of service contracts, which can only be broken suddenly at considerable inconvenience; in which many goods are provided in a small number of standard forms, designed to meet the putative tastes of large and homogenous blocks of consumers; and in which the services, on which we spend an increasing proportion of our incomes, are frequently offered to the consumer with very little effective choice at all. It is small consolation that if one does not like the bus on which one is invited to travel, one is free to walk or to hire a taxi; nor is one much comforted in a moment of deep dissatisfaction with the telephone service by the knowledge that one can, after all, send a telegram instead. The general point is that oligopolistic modes of economic conduct are deeply embedded in advanced capitalistic societies; they are not an incidental aberration of an otherwise fully functioning competitive market system. In some measure, we, the consumers, have chosen to make it so. But it is then highly misleading to argue as if we still retained in our daily lives the untrammelled freedom and total authority of a shopper who, when buying ties, looks around for a pleasant pattern— Friedman's actual example of the apotheosis of the free consumer.

There are a great many forces making for the severe restriction in the number of producers in any given market and for a strong effort by each of them to carve out some privileged piece of terrain where it has a built-in advantage as a seller. These forces are most evident wherever there are increasing economies of scale in production or where the process is constricted by the physical limitations of an increasingly crowded society. Beyond that there are the conveniences on the side of the customer which he derives from having a continuing relationship with a big and well-equipped enterprise for the supply of services on which his comfort depends. What most of us want when we make a choice in these matters is the assurance of regular, reliable service, if possible with a responsiveness on the part of the supplier to modest variations in our needs. The supplier for his part is eager to enter into a long-term engagement with his customers, because that allows him to plan his business more efficiently. Predictability is a benefit sought by both sides. Moreover, the service element is often an important component of the package which a consumer chooses to buy when he acquires a costly durable consumer good, such as a car or a central heating system.

Ignoring the fact that much of what we actually buy as consumers comes in sets, rather than as individual items, Friedman enlarges on the contrast with the political process which, as he sees it, consists of one enormous package delivered once every so many years—whenever elections take place. Now, this is a deceptively narrow view of what politics is about. It is also misleading as a guide to economic transactions. Albert Hirschman, in his *Exit, Voice, and Loyalty* (1970), brilliantly describes the actual economic situation by examining the terms 'exit' and its opposite, 'voice'.[3] He defines 'exit' as the ultimate decision *not* to buy or sell something. In contrast, he describes 'voice' as a persuasive means of altering the content of a proposed transaction. He concludes that, in practice, 'voice'—which is essentially the use of political methods—is much more pervasive in economic bargaining than the conventional analyses of economics would lead us to believe. Indeed, he remarks, the decision *not* to buy or sell is the extreme case: we resort to it only after we have tried the alternatives of persuasion and discovered that they do not work. In other words, most of the time we are *not* buying ties. Hirschman himself, commenting in a 1973 article on his earlier work on this analysis, added that since 'voice' is an entirely new category for economists, our thought processes are not properly attuned to it and it will take some time to uncover all the situations in which the importance of 'voice' has been underrated (Hirschman, 1981).

Friedman's gross underestimate of the prevalence of the political mode in business life, together with the misunderstanding of the character of political transactions, provide the general basis on which he builds his argument for a drastic reduction in the supply of 'public goods', with the aim of forcing the public sector back into something like the modest role which it occupied before the advent of the welfare society. He concedes that there are certain matters—his example is the conduct of war—which must be a government rather than a private decision. But 'the problem is that we have extended the political market beyond things of that kind and to the kind of things where it is possible for each person to get what he votes for. . . .' The question then is: Is the purchase of a tie from an existing range in a shop characteristic of the likely demands to be made on the market economy in the future? Or is it rather the case, as the evidence of the last forty years strongly suggests, that there are an increasing number of services, running through education to public transport to hospitals, which we want and which are only likely to be efficiently provided by a collective act of will, requiring a political mode of decision? Experience surely suggests that the areas of exceptionally dynamic demand include a number of such services; and there is no indication of a prospective change of trend in consumer demand which is likely to halt the advance in collective provision. As will be shown later (pp. 177–85), this still leaves scope for the competitive process. But there is a widespread sentiment that most services of this kind ought to be subjected to close public supervision and control. The final responsibility must be political, accountable to a court other than the market.

The rebellion against high public expenditure

This leads to an important distinction that needs to be made about the character of the various kinds of activity on which the greatly increased sums of public money are expended. First there are some functions, like those of the armed services, which must be performed directly by the state. Secondly, there are others which may or may not be financed by the state but which must, in any case, be subject to a large measure of public control. Hospitals and other collective medical services are obvious examples.

A third category consists of straightforward transfer payments to individuals suffering from some recognized disadvantage—extreme poverty, old age, poor health, and so on. Such payments are the most rapidly growing part of public expenditure; they have expanded very greatly in recent years in all the advanced capitalist countries. This is not mere coincidence. The underlying sentiments which led to the great advance in social welfare provision during the 1960s and early 70s were no longer those of the traditional charitable impulse which aimed at ensuring that no one fell below a certain minimum standard of existence. The new objective of social policy, confusedly identified at first but made increasingly explicit, was that people should not, in so far as possible, be disadvantaged by accidents over which they have no control. The guiding principle for this new endeavour was thus closely related in a number of fields to the conventional insurance principle. Some countries decided that all citizens should have the benefit of a full-scale health insurance, regardless of whether they were wise enough or rich enough to buy it for themselves. A similar decision was made about old age pensions, with the addition of the further principle that the level of these pensions should be high enough to avoid a drastic reduction in living standards on retirement.

Now, there is no inherent reason why the state itself should be financially responsible for comprehensive national insurance of this kind. It might simply pass an ordinance which made it compulsory for all citizens to insure themselves in the prescribed ways. In that case, the change would not be viewed as a dangerous advance of government power at the expense of the private market, any more than compulsory car insurance is.

However, the difficulty was, and is, that many Western societies have a very uneven distribution of income (OECD, 1976, ch. 5 and annex II), and quite often those people most exposed to the risks to be covered by social insurance of various kinds are least likely to be able to provide it for themselves. In such cases the underlying aim of the advance in social policy would be frustrated. Governments have in practice found that they had to tackle the problem of gross inequality of incomes in order to arrive at their social objectives. They had to subsidize the non-insurers, who happened to be the people most in need of insurance. The point is that the more equal incomes are in any society, the more nearly the public provision of social transfer incomes is likely to approximate to a straightforward commercial insurance scheme. The entire programme becomes in that case a means by which people arrange to equalize their *own* incomes over a lifetime, setting aside part of their income accruing during the period of high earning power to spend it in old age or in sickness or unemployment. This is the characteristic Swedish pattern, where there is a fairly even distribution of income over the great majority of the population; and it perhaps explains why social welfare policy has not been a significant issue in the hard-fought politics of Sweden in the later 1960s and the 1970s. The analysis of voters' views in these Swedish elections gives no hint of any serious questioning of what is probably the most extensive welfare system in the world; and it would surely be wrong to interpret the defeat of the Social Democrats in 1976 (by a marginal shift in a small number of votes) as a popular rejection of it.

This is not at all the social pattern of the United States; here heterogeneity and high rewards for individual initiative produce great unevenness of personal incomes. The remedy proposed in the 1960s—a sudden dash for equality under the Great Society programmes—was supposed to lead to the establishment of a more reliable basis for the welfare society. Among other devices to this end, the Warren Supreme Court in the 1960s (as A. E. Dick Howard, 1977, has pointed out) used the 'equal protection' clause of the Constitution to considerable effect. The Burger Court of the 1970s, weighted with President Nixon's appointees, tended to recoil from this endeavour. Does this, as Howard suggests, reflect a change not in the day-to-day weather, but in the climate of American public opinion? The evidence available, and this includes the decisions of the Burger Court itself, does not point to the prospect of a reversal of the established rights which emerged out of the reform movement of the 1960s—the right to equal racial treatment and to the equal apportionment of political power—but to a certain check in the active pursuit of the ideal of comprehensive social equality.

New approaches to welfare

None of this of course disposes of the question as to why public spending increased so rapidly from the mid-1960s onwards. One plausible explanation is that programmes of welfare spending were formulated on the basis of expectations about future prosperity which mechanically extrapolated the recent past. In the event the demands on the public services by individuals who were less prosperous than had been expected were that much greater, and total national resources were less. Certainly, if output and employment had continued to rise in the 1970s as they had in the 1960s, the proportion of the national product represented by public expenditure would have been significantly less.[4] (One of the factors in this would of course have been that, in absolute terms, welfare spending would decrease if there were fewer unemployed to support.)

Even so, that would perhaps only have delayed the perception of a problem which was becoming irksome. Just how irksome was it felt to be? Surely, as suggested earlier, some point is reached when the creeping process of the advance of public expenditure involves a radical change in the balance of social and political relationships. How close was this point and how much concern was there about the prospect? The evidence on this matter is uncertain; all that can be said with assurance is that the public reaction varied, both in motivation and in symptoms, between the different countries of the Western world.

These differences in national experiences and attitudes are worth exploring further. They should help to shed some light on where and to what degree the advance of public power in the management of the economy aroused resistance which made it that much less effective. By the second half of the 1970s the share taken up by public expenditure in the OECD group of countries amounted on average to over two-fifths of total output. Assuming that there is a limit beyond which this share can only grow further on the basis of a drastic reordering of established views about the rights of citizens to decide how to use the bulk of their personal earnings, then many of these countries were clearly approaching it.

In fact, the share of public expenditure (in terms of current prices) continued to increase for the remainder of the decade. In the most advanced and richest welfare states, like Sweden and the Netherlands, it rose above 50 per cent of the national product. And the rate at which it increased in these liberally spending, most heavily taxed countries, was steeper than elsewhere.[5] The pace of the advance, in these years of relatively slow growth of personal incomes, was remarkable. In Sweden, for example, the share of public spending in GNP in the course of the 1970s increased by 13 percentage points (OECD, 1980, *Sweden*, p.2). We have explained elsewhere (Shonfield, 1982, p.xix) that although some of this resulted from the effort to counteract the effects of the slowdown by increasing public spending, the main element in this expansion lay in the open-handed welfare programmes—consisting chiefly of income transfers to the most disadvantaged—which had been planned under more favourable economic circumstances. 'Disadvantage' came to have a much more widely encompassing meaning in the 1970s, and such generosity in redefinition can be costly, especially at a time of high unemployment.

It is clearly perverse to see this expansion as simply a manifestation of the irresistible urge towards bureaucratic self-aggrandizement, which some critics have purported to identify as the common cause of the rising public expenditure in Western society. Aaron Wildavsky advances this explanation of recent history in terms of a larger generalization; in his version it covers all ages of bureaucratic man. 'Summing up the system of incentives in central government spending, addition is easier than subtraction. . . . Earlier it was defense, more recently it has been social welfare, soon it will be something else' (OECD, 1980, p.17). But were the driving force always the same, i.e. bureaucratic politics, then one would surely expect the preferences of bureaucrats to be reflected, to some degree, in the *forms* of rising public expenditure. At the very least one might expect the choice to point towards activities which permitted some scope for the exercise of initiative and power. If the aim is always to expand, then the logic of the process suggests that enlargement would be guided by the selection of places in the system offering a springboard for further expansion. Assuming that bureaucrats are guided by some form of strategy involving the occupation of key positions which would permit them to exercise an influence on the future shape and size of the activity, you would not expect them to devote their efforts most enthusiastically to the rather mechanical business of making transfer payments.

A point that is worth making is that an increase in public expenditure for welfare purposes is not necessarily seen everywhere as an addition to public power at the expense of the private individual. Income transfer payments, for instance, if they are automatic and if their eligibility is determined by a transparent set of rules involving the minimum of bureaucratic discretion, cannot in themselves be considered to make the apparatus of government any more powerful. It is in fact a peculiar doctrine (though part of a longstanding ideological tradition belonging to one version of economic liberalism) that financial relations between citizens and their government are, except in a small minority of transactions, a zero-sum game. The justification of this doctrine is an overwhelming scepticism about the capacity of democratic institutions to make rational choices between alternative courses of action which accord with the desires of the majority.

One's first impulse would naturally be to guess that the cult of the political zero-sum game, between citizens and government, would catch on most readily in societies where the weight of public expenditure was especially heavy and the rate of increase particularly steep. But such a bald prediction does not stand up to what happened in practice. If the voters felt seriously uncomfortable about the burden which had gradually weighed down their shoulders the reversals in the fortunes of political parties showed, at least in Sweden, little evidence of having originated in the backlash.

There was one important revolt among the Scandinavian and Low Countries group—that of Denmark in the early 1970s, after it had been subjected to an extraordinarily rapid increase in direct taxation. The doings of Mr Glistrup and his Anti-Tax Party provided plenty of drama at the time for a normally staid country. The rebellion was for real: the Anti-Taxers managed to topple longstanding political alliances, as well as the governments which had come to depend on them. The fiscal reforms which followed moderated the rate of increase in the Danish tax burden; however, by the mid-1970s public expenditure, at over 45 per cent of GDP, still had a characteristically Scandinavian look. And, after the Danish incident, there was until the American rebellion at the end of the 1970s no evidence of the contagion spreading abroad, or indeed of overwhelming discontent at home in Denmark. As we have said in an earlier context, the decisions taken late in the 1970s in a number of Western countries to cut back the share of public spending in GNP were the direct result of a 'generally recognized national need for coping with a long-term budgetary and balance of payments problem'. But they were not primarily political, except for the arguments 'about who should sacrifice what' (Shonfield, 1982, p.xx).

The United States and the UK stood out as exceptions. Here, in spite of the fact that public expenditure accounted for a smaller share of the national product than in Scandinavia or the Netherlands, the reaction against its growth became in the 1970s a political issue of major proportions. Moreover, while in the UK there was an admixture of expediency about the backlash, the Conservatives claiming to offer the voter policies designed to make good the shortfall in British economic performance, the US position was strongly ideological. When the people in the United States set themselves the task of cutting back government power in almost all of its civilian manifestations, by withdrawing the financial resources which sustained its exercise, they saw themselves as harbingers of a new freedom. Their campaign was in the true spirit of the zero-sum game between public and private interests. Denying funds to government was only the first move in reducing its capacity to regulate economic activity or to intervene in commercial transactions between one citizen and another. The aims were large and the mood that of a crusade—as reflected in the language used by the spiritual mentors of the reaction against government, from Milton Friedman to James Buchanan. Our concern here is however less with a critical assessment of the theories deployed by the intellectual leadership of the movement than with the way in which the latter impinged on the process of policy-making.

How strong a backlash?

The promulgation of Proposition 13 by a 1978 referendum of the citizens of California is a direct example of how current political theory affects popularist political action. Prior to the Republicans' electoral victory in 1980 it was the American anti-government movement's most celebrated achievement. The Proposition was not in itself revolutionary: it simply imposed a limit on the amount that could be levied in property taxes by the state and other local authorities in California—1 per cent of the 'fair value' of the property. Its significance was however powerfully symbolic. Property taxes had increased very fast over a long period and constituted a substantial proportion of all the tax revenue of public authorities in the state. There was no means of replacing them; so governments at local and state level were forced to cut back their spending, and keep it cut. Furthermore, in 1979 additional legislation reinforced the limit on government spending in California, introducing a permanent restriction on *real* public expenditure per head of the population.

Because in practice the drastic curb on public spending was not without its inconveniences, local authorities tried to mitigate the discomforts to their constituents arising from straitened budgets by having recourse to the device of charging 'fees' for certain public services. When such a 'fee' is collected at the same time as other regular tax payments, it may be difficult for a citizen to detect the practical difference between it and the earlier system of giving this item a place in the ordinary budget. The difference becomes even more tenuous when buying the service—and paying for it by 'fee'—is made compulsory. Moreover, other services, notably those to particular groups of people who qualify for special care because they are deemed to be less capable than the average of looking after themselves, cannot be handled in the same way. Not surprisingly, the poor were among the chief sufferers, especially people belonging to immigrant racial minorities, of whom there are many in California (*Economist*, January 1980, pp.18ff.).

To some, small, extent the effect of this out-of-tax cutting was to shift the emphasis from smaller (local and state) government to big government. But that was no more than a temporary distortion caused by the fact that you had to begin somewhere. The clear aim of the US rebels was to attack the very citadel of US government taxing power in Washington. The ultimate objective, which was spelled out with great polemical force by James Buchanan who had inspired and nurtured much of the thought which went into the movement over a period of years, was a constitutional convention of the states composing the American Union which would bind all future US governments to limit in a precise way their power to spend public money.[6]

The proponents of this form of budget limitation believed that governments were in any case prone to overspend and that the devices provided by Keynesian demand management offered them an irresistible opportunity to indulge themselves; moreover, each further bout of self-indulgence tended to become a permanent feature of government behaviour. But in form, at any rate, the proposal was a straightforward prohibition on government to meddle with the business cycle during the downward phase. There was nothing to prevent it from cutting down public expenditure and running a surplus while the economy was moving up. It was the 'beneficent' effect of business recession which needed to be reintroduced and carefully preserved.

The point chosen for this particular attack on government expenditure was shrewdly selected. The conduct of anti-cyclical demand management by governments, most especially in the United States, had not been a success. It was also clear that the mistiming of government, and central bank, actions and the misinterpretation of trends in the economy had tended to add to inflation. Against this background, the movement for imposing a legal limitation on the US government's ability to engage in deficit spending, on the lines of the Buchanan proposal, attracted an impressive measure of support from part of the academic community and from respected persons who had held the responsibilities of public office.

It is impossible to provide conclusive proof for the contention, but the evidence available suggests that a proposition of this kind, if it had been put forward in other Western countries, would not have achieved anything like this response from national élites. Indeed the very fact that no such idea found its way into the serious political debate of West European countries (with occasional rare and transient exceptions, such as Morgens Glistrup in Denmark) or Japan is a persuasive indication. The American supporters would no doubt counter by saying that they were merely carrying the flag for a wider movement which would manifest its presence abroad later on. If so, this would argue a remarkable electoral passivity on the part of the leaders of opinion in countries with a long democratic tradition, such as Sweden and the Netherlands, where the volume of public spending as a proportion of the national product was, as we have seen, half as high again as that of the United States. It is on the whole more likely that the reasons for the difference lie elsewhere—at least in part in the well-established attitudes towards public endeavour. Certainly the conventional rhetoric on the two sides of the Atlantic, and the two sides of the Pacific, was markedly diverse.

But how far is the rhetorical style an accurate guide to the realities of popular feeling and its ultimate manifestation in electoral decisions? In view of the Republican victory in November 1980 the question might appear superfluous—at least when applied to the US. There is no doubt that particular taxes (notably property taxes which had risen fivefold since the 1950s) and individual items of expenditure (notably welfare payments to the 'less deserving poor') aroused hostility. However, it is by no means clear how deeply rooted the rebellion against high public spending is: of the ten referenda held at the time of the 1980 election on the issue of setting California-type limits to the taxation powers of state governments, only four were successful (*Economist*, November 1980, p.29). It seems that when voters are faced with the prospect of losing the *particular* benefits which they derive from the expenditure of their state governments, a considerable number of them demur. And a number of surveys conducted in the US during the 1970s, including the period when the campaign for the limitation on public expenditure was gaining strength, produced answers from a variety of majorities affirming that the government 'should do more' on several issues where public action on an increased scale was plainly going to be expensive (Lucier, 1979).[7]

So perhaps what is being expressed is a desire not for less public expenditure, but for more efficient spending and above all, as we have said in another context (Shonfield, 1982, p.99) more *choice* as to what we buy for the taxes we pay. Such options are among the themes of the final chapter of this text (see pp.177–86 *passim*).

Notes to Chapter 2

1. For example, US national defence and foreign expenditure as a proportion of GNP declined by nearly 4 percentage points between 1960 and 1975, from 9.5 per cent to 5.7 per cent (Owen and Schultze, 1976, p.328).
2. See for example the pronouncements of Denis Healey, British Chancellor of the Exchequer, in 1975 and early 1976.
3. For those without easy access to Hirschman's subtle discussion of these concepts, the following condensed definitions may be of use. 'Exit': a form of protest which consists in the consumer withdrawing his custom from a supplier of unsatisfactory goods or services, and perhaps switching to a substitute one. 'Voice': the articulation of objections by the consumer within a continuing relationship with a supplier, with the aim of getting more satisfactory goods or services. A consumer association or a parent association in a school are typical expressions of 'voice'. [*Ed.*]
4. Heclo (1976, p.31) quotes evidence (Beck, 1976, p.17) that 'general government expenditure' as a proportion of GDP, measured in *real* terms, had in fact gone down in a number of countries, when the figures are corrected for the much greater price rise in the public sector. The comparison is between 1950–2 and 1968–70: according to Beck's evidence the UK is among the countries where the ratio dropped markedly—here it went down from around 31 per cent to just over 25 per cent. By contrast in Sweden it went up from 23 per cent to 33 per cent. The median change for US, Canada and eleven European countries (all included in Beck's data) is a drop of just under 1 per cent.
5. This was the trend up to the second half of the 1970s, according to the important statistical analyses undertaken by the OECD (1976 and companion volumes) which, for the first time, put the highly variegated data about public spending on a comparable basis. Note that these figures show that from the mid-1950s on the different groups of countries have, in broad terms, stabilized their position in the league table of public expenditure (OECD, 1976, table 15). After the high-spending small country club in the North of Europe, comes the group of large European states—France, Germany, Italy and Britain—with a well-established though rather less generous welfare tradition

than the small countries. Their percentage of GDP going into public expenditure in the mid-1970s was in the low forties. After them comes the United States which has consistently had a lower proportion of public spending, though the rate of increase in the post-war period was in line with that of the European large country group, with the American proportion rising to 35 per cent by the mid-1970s. Canada, Australia and New Zealand have also held their (rising) public expenditure share somewhat below the OECD average. Finally, and much lower down, is Japan with a public expenditure ratio in the mid-1970s of 25 per cent.

6. Buchanan's argument was that the existing system had the effect of artificially lowering the price of public goods by comparison to private goods, and so provided an unending incentive to increase the share of the former—unless this was prevented by constitutional law. The proposed constitutional amendment would simply impose on governments the obligation, in all but the most exceptional circumstances specified by law and therefore subject to judicial decision, to balance budget expenditure against tax revenue. The theory was that if the power to borrow were removed from governments, they would be forced into retreat (Buchanan and Wagner, 1977, p.103).

7. The following comment by William Diebold Jr on the complexities of American attitudes on restricting public expenditure is relevant here:

We have [in 1982] not only the proposal for a constitutional amendment for a balanced budget and many more examples of state and local 'capping' of expenditures in various fields, but also the sense that has been publicly expressed by liberal leaders that the whole budget making and fiscal process is 'out of control'. The focus of the argument about 'the new federalism' on what is paid for by the federal government and what by the states or what is not financed at all further complicates comparisons with Europe.

3

THE CHANGED CONTEXT OF ECONOMIC PLANNING

THE arguments about social equality and about the advance of the public sector in the capitalist mixed economy have, as we have seen, become intermingled and confused. To add to the confusion, it so happens that some socialists who have been among the most active proponents of the extension of social welfare have also been advocates of transferring more of industry to public ownership. This has by no means been true of all socialist parties. Indeed, two of the leading, and most successful, social democratic parties in Western Europe, the German and the Swedish, have set their faces firmly against this course. In any case, while there is widespread scepticism about the efficacy of partially nationalized industry, full ownership by the state is not, on the evidence to date, seen as necessarily more efficacious; indeed in some cases it is visibly less so.

What is, however, not in doubt is that there is a growing number of economic decisions, with long-term implications, which need to be subjected to regulation of a deliberately co-ordinated rather than competitive character. The need for co-ordination applies to all categories of enterprise, those publicly owned or in mixed private/public ownership as well as the fully private ones. In these decisions, which are typically those which involve high uncertainty and risk with social implications, the public authorities will unavoidably play a leading part.[1] The most obvious are, firstly, risks to the natural environment (pollution, etc.) and secondly, risks to the man-made environment (affecting regional policies, urban redevelopment, etc.).

The third type of risk in which the public interest is involved is implicit in almost any very large-scale commitment of resources—whether private or public, and often a combination of both—to an investment project which is both indivisible and has a long lead-time from commencement to the stage of production. The social significance of this kind of undertaking is partly a matter of 'opportunity costs': if this is done, then something else has to be given a miss. Future jobs and living standards will, if the project is large enough, be significantly affected by whether the investment risk is or is not well-judged.

It should be understood that even in cases where the initiative and capital stem entirely from private sources, the expression of the public interest is not going to be viewed as an unwelcome intrusion by government into a domain which by rights belongs exclusively to private enterprise. The traditional assumption that private enterprise always resists government 'interference' is no longer true. Indeed, already in many European countries the private sector is anxious to share some of the big risks with the public sector. Large-scale private enterprise has found, especially during the period of rapid advance in social welfare provision since the late 1960s, that it is subjected to rising costs for social and environmental purposes. At the same time the risks associated with investment in projects involving advanced technology, which often require the commitment of big blocks of capital, and a long wait before returns on investment are realized, are on the increase. The 'entrance fee' for introducing new technology has escalated alarmingly (*Financial Times*, 28 January 1977, p.17).

If the costs of innovative projects rise at the same time as the returns on capital tend to be reduced by the need to meet additional social and environmental expenses out of profits, then this could be a deterrent to many kinds of expenditure which on other grounds may be judged to be advantageous to the community. And this points to a more general consideration about the relationship between private sector investment and the public interest. It sometimes happens that the commercial judgment on an investment of high social or political importance is based on the market rate of discount of certain risks, which make the proposition relatively unattractive. This has been notoriously the case in the exploitation of energy resources in the United States. The Congressional Budget Office, in considering the future of the energy programme in 1976, applied itself to this difficulty. The higher levels of energy output required might be dangerously delayed, if, as the CBO put it, 'near term technical and economic risks will be such as to inhibit private investment . . . in time to increase domestic production'. Its conclusion was that securing the extra output would involve 'considerable budgetary costs', in the form of subsidies ('commercialization incentives') to cover the difference between the rate of discount applied to the commercial risk and to the political risk (US Congressional Budget Office, 1976, p.287). The proposal illustrates a trend which will, it seems certain, induce even those governments, like that of the United States, which have an ideological preference for the strict separation of the private and public spheres to engage in future in a more active and systematic collaboration with business management.

A more familiar reason for the increased intrusion of public policy into long-term economic decisions is that the cost of economic activities for which government is directly responsible—that is to say public consumption and investment—amounts nowadays to a substantial proportion of the national product (between a fifth and a quarter in most industrial countries), and what is done with them over the long term has important consequences for private business organizations which are trying to take an intelligent view of the appropriate allocation of their resources. Defence, education, health services, the bulk of public transport and telecommunications—most of these things have an extended lead-time between the point of decision and the production of public goods and services. Central and local government agencies are together responsible for the even larger share of total fixed investment, especially in housing. The tempo of business activity and the level of employment are profoundly affected by government decisions about capital expenditure. Unless the private sector is made cognizant of the government's long-term commitments and aspirations, it will itself be deterred from making its own longer-term investments.

Public authorities will of course be compelled to continue to intervene in situations when private business embarks on policies which reflect the built-in oligopolistic and monopolistic features of our society and ought to be subjected to systematic surveillance on behalf of the public interest. The alternative of the elementary anti-trust procedure—which simply breaks up the offending enterprises—is not always available in such cases. It is worth observing, in any case, how often in recent times the American device of settling an anti-trust action with a 'consent decree' (involving a promise to fight rather than embrace one's neighbours in future) has in practice been the means of securing for the government the status of a *continuing supervisor* of the investment and marketing decisions of certain key corporations.

All in all economic planning is not, then, irrelevant, nor the illusory technique that critics like Hayek (e.g. in his January 1976 article) have claimed it to be. In particular, indicative planning, far from being an irrelevant or anachronistic technique, as some critics have asserted, is of the essence in the management of contemporary economic problems. By economic planning is meant a systematic effort to co-ordinate the decisions on investment in the public and private sectors, and to do so on the basis of explicitly stated objectives often set some years into the future. The content of such economic planning has been changing in recent years: it is much less concerned with the earlier ideal of comprehensive economic management, the manipulation of all the large aggregates of economic activity. Rather, it concentrates on a limited number of functions, normally implying some measure of public financial involvement, which are to be pushed through because of their long-term significance for future economic growth or society in general.

French and German plans of the late 1970s

In order to illustrate this approach to planning, it will be useful to examine the features of recent French planning and compare them with the characteristics of German longer-term management of the economy. In the past those responsible for French planning used to make much of what they saw as its 'unique' features. In recent years, notably during the 1970s, they have recognized that the French Plan, for all its special features, belongs to a family of policy-making instruments shared by a number of other countries. This is at least in part due to changes in the character of French planning itself (France, VIIIth Plan, 1979), though it also reflects a wider international phenomenon of changes in the style of policy-making in a number of advanced industrial countries. The French government had limited the objectives of its planning exercise, making it altogether more selective in the range of national objectives to which it was applied; this found a particular expression in the *Programmes d'Action Prioritaire* (PAPs) introduced in the VIIth Plan, 1976–80. On the other hand, other nations (even some of those which had little doctrinal sympathy for the idea of a collectively planned economic effort purporting to perform some of the functions that should be fulfilled by the spontaneous action of market forces) came to see the usefulness of formulating medium-term public policies on the basis of a carefully constructed and consistent set of assumptions about the future. Once it was clear, to the French as well as to the others, that a national plan was not a long-range prophecy about the changes in the economic environment and the response of the public and private sectors of the national economy to them, the planning activity itself acquired new adherents—some of them in unexpected places. Germany, for all its anti-planning rhetoric, became adept at it.

One of these German planning efforts of the late 1970s, the celebrated German Four-Year *Finanzplan* of 1978, is a useful means of focusing attention on certain problems which are central to the French VIIIth Plan and which the Germans, in a sense, anticipated. If it is thought fanciful or even eccentric to go looking for a yardstick for current French economic planning across the border in Germany, a careful reading of the condensed document presented to the Bundestag, with its 'projections' of the main variables in the national economy 1978–82 (Germany, *Finanzplan*, 1978), will quickly demonstrate that the Germans were addressing themselves to basically the same range of problems as the French in the VIIIth Plan, and doing so in an unashamedly interventionist spirit. The great differences in the approach to policy-making at the turn of the 1970s decade were between Britain on the one hand, and France and Germany on the other, rather than between the French and the Germans.

The convergence of France and Germany derived in part from the limitation on the range of planned intervention by the French authorities. The VIIth Plan's whole conception—a 'methodological break'[2] with the past—had been of a medium-term policy which was not comprehensive: the insistence that the government's commitment was solely to the PAPs and to no more than that set the tone of the new approach. (It could be argued, in fact, that what was really new was not so much the approach itself as the recognition that the older pretensions to a comprehensive form of concertation, covering public and private activity, had already been outdated.) It was in practice largely a plan about the spending of public funds. On the German side, there was the gradual recognition in the second half of the 1970s, following the ephemeral recovery of 1976, that the private sector acting on its own was unlikely to achieve the profound structural changes in the economy required to return it to full employment and a high level of productive investment. The slackening of Germany's invest-ment effort pre-dated the recession of the early 1970s and had become a source of serious concern to economic policy-makers.[3] Accordingly, when the 1978–82 *Finanzplan* was launched, the government was at great pains to explain that this was not a short-term effort in economic pump-priming designed to meet a business downturn. The emphasis was all on the sustained character of the governmental commitment to supplement deficiencies in private demand, most especially in the field of business investment, by the input of additional public funds, including a wide range of discriminating investment subsidies to public and other enterprises.

Of course the rhetoric of the German and French endeavours remained different. The Germans set out their economic policy problem as part of a fiscal analysis, as if the main issue was to secure orderly budgets. On the other hand the French planners, as is notorious, have spent much of their effort in recent years trying to persuade their colleagues who are in charge of the annual budget to take the longer-term economic objectives laid down in the National Plan seriously. The VIIth Plan may indeed be seen as having been to a large extent an attempt to reinforce the powers of persuasion of the planners in this sense.

The German Plan of 1978 started out with the advantage that it represented a conscious and dramatic turn-round in official thinking. As the Annual Report of the German Council of Economic Experts emphasized, the government and practically the whole of the official economic establishment, including the Council itself, had up to that point been firmly attached to the doctrine of 'neutrality' in financial policy; they insisted that no attempt was to be made to use fiscal means to raise economic activity above the level set by market forces (Germany, Annual Report, 1978). To reinforce the credibility of the German operation, the financial planners set out in detail the reasons why they had concluded that there would be a deficiency of market demand during the subsequent four years and obtained from parliament the acceptance of a significant enlargement of the budget deficit during that period. The point was made, once again by the Council of Economic Experts, that if the aim was to change business expectations sufficiently to induce the private sector to increase its investment and engage more workers, then a large-scale and *sustained* commitment by the financial authorities was essential.

How far could the French in 1980 proceed in a similar fashion? The Germans were in fact very successful in using the stimulus of public finance—an increase of net spending equal to one per cent of GNP in one year—to induce a substantial increase in private investment. But this was at the cost of a sharp deterioration in the external balance of payments. Indeed, a deterioration of this kind, moving the German external account from an apparently chronic surplus into deficit, was one of the objects of the *Finanzplan*. Here France in 1980 had much less room for manoeuvre. Moreover, the businessmen, whose expectations the planners needed to change in order to raise the level of French investment, knew that this was so.

On the other side, it is arguable that the French budget was in much better shape at the beginning of the 1980s than the German budget had been when the Germans undertook the massive expenditure of public funds in 1978—with a deficit of less than 2 per cent against something over 3 per cent for Germany at that time. So it may be said that although one side of the so-called *Carré Magique*—the balance of payments—was relatively weak and therefore inflexible, another one of its sides—the budget balance—could, in principle, be manipulated by the planners to secure some expansion of demand and activity.

One difficulty with this line of reasoning is of course that these two sides cannot be treated as independent variables; an enlarged budget deficit would almost inevitably have an adverse effect on the balance of payments. Indeed it could be argued that the more convincing the 'demonstration effect' of a commitment to a medium-term increase in the budget deficit (in the German style), the more pronounced would be its influence on the exchange value of the franc. And that outcome would be likely to be accompanied by a higher rate of inflation. Thus the third side of the *Carré Magique*—the control of inflation—appeared to be vulnerable too.

However, the fourth element of the *Carré*, which is defined by wage and salary incomes, looked distinctly more favourable. French wage rates in the second half of the 1970s rose consistently less than would have been expected on the basis of earlier trends. Moreover this does not seem to have been simply the effect of economic recession, since in 1979 when economic activity began to revive, real wages continued to be held down. The thinking behind the VIIIth Plan seemed to be based on the expectation that French wages would prove to be fairly inelastic in respect of a further moderate increase in demand and activity. New entrants into the labour market, expected to average over 200,000 a year in the early 1980s, would in any case keep the supply of labour plentiful.

Could a combination of wage moderation with a high level of savings, sufficient to offset the inflationary effect of an enlarged budget deficit, give France the opportunity of pursuing the strategy of employment expansion fuelled by public investment, which the Germans carried through in the late 1970s? A calculated risk of this kind seemed to underlie the strategy of the VIIIth Plan. Without it the planners would have found themselves paralysed by the constraints of the *Carré Magique*, much as the British economic policy-makers believed themselves to be despite the greater ease which North Sea oil gave to the UK balance of payments.

The answer to the question falls into two parts. First: Yes, there probably was at this point in time some additional scope for publicly financed investment based on increased public borrowing at home and abroad, and there is little evidence that such borrowing would have the effect of 'crowding out' private investment in the conditions of the early 1980s. Second, and harder to determine, is whether this enlarged input of public money would then be translated in time, as it was in Germany in 1979, into a revival of private business investment. Plainly, this will depend in part on the scale of the public sector input. France, for the reasons already given, could not, without very grave risks, embark on a massive operation in deficit financing, comparable with that of the Germans in 1978.

This is where the distinctive character of the French approach to economic planning is relevant. The French planners proposed to make up for the smaller volume of public investment by selecting the points of entry of this public money into the economy with purposeful discrimination in such a way as to maximize their effect. Instead of the massive German impact effect of the late

1970s, the French VIIIth Plan sought out the places in the economic system where the multiplier effect in terms of additional employment in the medium-term was likely to be greatest—and also obtained at the lowest cost in terms of inflation and/or the weakening of the balance of payments. The vast exercise of putting more than a hundred of the most promising '*variantes*' through the DMS model,[4] one of the most ambitious exercises in measuring the trade-off between vastly complicated policy options which has ever been undertaken, was designed primarily to serve this purpose. Among the useful results which emerged from this laborious process, extending over many months of computer time, was to bring into especially sharp prominence the difference between the short-term and longer-term effect of devices designed to raise the level of employment. It allowed the policy-makers to identify and reject ineffectual measures (such as indiscriminate cuts in the working week) which promised immediate rewards in terms of extra jobs but were disappointingly prone to handicap the capacity of employers to sell in competitive markets.

The French alter their formula

There are some special problems involved in the management of a discriminating stimulus to investment during a period when economic growth slows down and the general propensity to invest is accordingly low. In such circumstances an investment subsidy which is not highly specific in its application to particular purposes risks being used to replace privately financed investment expenditure rather than to create a net addition to the stock of productive capital. It is of course unlikely to be a complete one-to-one replacement; the point is that the net benefit, in a period when the anticipated incremental rate of return, i.e. the marginal efficiency of capital, is low, could be significantly less than the gross public expenditure devoted to the investment incentive.

As Bela Balassa has observed, the trend in French planning since the late 1950s has been away from selective intervention, with an increasing emphasis on 'general policy measures aimed at encouraging investment, technological change, and exports and promoting industrial concentration'. He proceeds to argue forcefully that this is the direction in which French economic policy ought to continue to move in the future, avoiding 'selective measures aimed at assisting particular sectors, subsectors and enterprises . . .'—largely for the reason that government planners have not evinced a particular talent for picking out the most promising enterprises to back with public money and have quite often been wrong in their judgments (Balassa, 1979). It is hard to quarrel with Balassa's general argument that the decline of the old style of French interventionist planning has been correlated in time with the increasing success of the French economy. (It might be harder to show that the correlation expressed a general rule, in the face of the evidence coming from other countries, notably Japan.) But it is worth observing that this account of the long-term trend omits altogether the experience of the second half of the 1970s, covered by the VIIth Plan. It was not only that the planners were once again highly selective in their targets, singling out the *Programmes d'Action Prioritaire* for special financial support, but also that they made most particular use of the large nationalized undertakings (*Grandes Entreprises Nationales*—GENs[5]) as the major instrument for their purpose. For better or for worse, these public enterprises accounted for some 60 per cent of the total increase in productive investment during the VIIth Plan, roughly double the proportion of investment for which they were responsible in the VIth Plan.

This is an important change which has a bearing on the difficult problem, almost certainly common to the VIIIth as well as to the VIIth Plan, of making sure that investments for which finance is available on attractive terms are actually made during a time when the marginal efficiency of capital in general is low. The extent of this problem during the period of the VIIth Plan is brought out by the fact that the whole group of large nationalized undertakings accounted for only 25 per cent of total productive investment in 1979—and for a smaller proportion of total production. The VIIth Plan appears in this regard to have had a very timely success. Had the planners continued and reinforced the trend described by Balassa, total productive investment would have been very much lower in the second half of the 1970s.

It might still be argued by critics of the Balassa persuasion that this public investment effort was ill-judged and wasteful, though there is no factual evidence that the programmes of construction which vastly enlarged the French telephone system or the investments in nuclear and other energy installations (the two main forms of public investment) failed to add to the stock of useful capital at the disposal of the French people. The general point that is worth making however is that even on the worst assumption about the relative efficiency of this kind of operation, it took place in the context of a particular period when the opportunity cost of the labour and the domestic products employed in investment was very low indeed, in some instances approaching zero. This is characteristic of a time of high unemployment, low demand, and factor prices fairly inflexible in a downward direction. It follows that if, as seemed likely, the early 1980s were going to be another period of slow economic growth, a replay in some measure of the middle years of the 1970s, the VIIIth Plan would have again depended on the successful promotion of investment in the GENs.

That is not to say, however, that there is much prospect of securing during the period ahead the marked counter-cyclical effect which was achieved by the nationalized undertakings during the VIIth Plan. As was noted earlier, this effect derived from a huge increase in the *share* of total productive investment by the GENs, which served to offset the weak investment effort of the private sector. To repeat that trick—if one is assuming a return of something like the economic environment of the mid-1970s— would require another very large jump in the incremental share of new investment by the GENs, starting from an already high level. There is no inherent reason why this should not be done, though it would appear that the VIIIth Plan was realistic in its assessment of the limits of the growth of public enterprise investment, at any rate in the circumstances of French politics operating in 1980. If the trend of the VIIth Plan had for example been simply extrapolated into the VIIIth, this would have implied a significant change in the balance between the private and public sectors of the economy.

One might of course argue that it is a proper function of public authorities to create useful capital assets during a slump, when the private sector's propensity to invest is low, and to sell off appropriate parts of the additional productive capacity (at a profit) during the next boom. But such an approach would require a much less doctrinal approach to the subject of public ownership than is in evidence so far in most of the European countries. An exception should however be made in favour of the more rational approach to the problem of a few countries which have benefited from sophisticated social democratic leadership, such as Sweden and Germany. It is noteworthy that no one raised any questions of an ideological character about the vast sums of money which the German *Finanzplan* of 1978 devoted, in the form of investment subsidies, to publicly owned transport and in particular the deficit-ridden German railways, which were singled out for especially favourable treatment.

Effects on productivity

A more general question which needs to be addressed to the French VIIIth Plan's prescription for the unemployment problem of the 1980s is whether it took a correct reading on the long-term trends affecting productivity and working hours. It is striking that the doubts about productivity trends which figure so largely in the recent American debates on economic policy receive so little attention in the French planning documents. True, the productivity performance of most of the European Community countries (with the exception of Britain and Italy) since the 1973 boom has been far better than the American.[6]

However, there are significant differences even among these relatively successful economies, notably between France and Germany. The fact that French labour productivity increased more rapidly than the average of advanced industrial countries of the OECD during the period of rapid economic growth up to 1973 does not appear, on the basis of this later evidence, to be a good reason for projecting a similar relative performance into the period of slower growth in the 1980s. Indeed, the limited data available for the 1970s suggest that French productivity tends to be more vulnerable to a slowdown of economic activity than German productivity.[7]

There may have been special reasons for Germany's exceptionally good performance in the 1970s. But the question which immediately concerns us is whether it is reasonable to suppose that French productivity will recover its earlier rate of growth in the 1980s if the general economic environment is again unfavourable. This is the assumption made in the initial outline of the Plan scenarios by INSEE (1979) and followed in the later formulations of the Plan. There is at least a possibility that the factors underlying 'Okun's law'—that changes in the rate of growth of output and of productivity are correlated—may be applicable to periods of longer duration.

It may be, of course, that there are more fundamental forces at work in Western economies, which, for instance, have been responsible for holding back the growth of productivity in the United States even during the period of its rapid expansion in the late 1970s. No one has fully explained what factors may underlie this change of trend in the United States and in some other countries. But one of the adverse influences on productivity is the effect of greatly increased energy costs on the structure of production: some of the potential for labour-saving innovation existing previously is not realized because it involves unattractively high energy expenditure. The argument may, in the context of the VIIIth Plan, be carried a stage further. It is quite probable that a substantial part of new investment expenditure will be devoted to the task of economizing that very scarce resource, energy, rather than to the traditional objective of increasing the output of a given amount of labour—labour having become relatively plentiful and (possibly) relatively cheap.

If a deeper tendency of this kind were at work (and it would be surprising if it were entirely absent in a period when the total volume of investment is more limited than in the past and likely to be especially directed towards immediate cost-saving) then a number of consequences would follow. With a slower rise in labour productivity, a higher level of employment could be more easily maintained. On the other hand, returns to labour in the form of real wages would increase less, and no doubt sharpen industrial conflict over the competing claims of wages and profits.

Without attempting to predict the outcome of such sharpened competition for income, it did seem unlikely in these circumstances that there would be a positive response to another of the proposals of the VIIIth Plan: to reduce normal working time, in order to increase the supply of individual jobs. This seems in any case a not very promising expedient during a period of relatively slow economic growth. The long-term trend in the Western industrial world from 1950 onwards of a reduction in the number of hours worked per year has been accompanied by a steady and substantial rise in material living standards, only interrupted in the middle 1970s. The rate of reduction of working time, as well as the absolute number of hours worked, varies greatly from one OECD country to another (OECD, 1978, table 5, p.41). The evidence does not suggest that French workers have been among those who have been most ready to take the benefits of increased productivity in the form of reduced working hours, rather than in more direct material benefits.

It seems reasonable to suppose that large and powerful labour organizations with a capacity to control their own members (as well as to bargain effectively with employers) are necessary to secure sustained and systematic reductions in working hours, such as for example the Germans and the Swedes have achieved, amounting to more than 8 per cent per decade over a quarter of a century, twice as fast as the rate of decline in other advanced OECD countries. This is not to say that a powerful trade union movement is a sufficient condition for the rapid reduction of working hours—the British case alone would refute that proposition—only that it is probably a necessary condition. In other words, strong collective discipline on the side of the workers is normally part of this kind of bargaining about the way in which the benefits of increased productivity are to be allocated.

In this respect the relative weakness of French organized labour, which is partly reflected in the modest increase in real wages during the recent period, is probably a disability. Labour market forces, which appear to act more powerfully in France than in several other advanced industrial countries to make wage-earners responsive to changes in overall demand, also have the effect of making their behaviour less responsive to the behests of collective labour organizations. The normal behaviour of individuals when they are faced with a slower rate of increase in wages than they anticipated, or desire, is to try to reorganize their leisure time in such a way as to secure more work. If they are also offered more leisure time, the odds are that they will be that much more active in seeking additional work.

The broad conclusion is that if the chosen means of raising the level of employment is to be organized work sharing, a country will need rather different institutions from those possessed by France. On the other hand, it may well be that, even without a significant reduction in working time, the level of French employment may become somewhat higher than that envisaged by the VIIIth Plan. Productivity, including productivity in the services sector which is expected to continue to expand, will not rise as rapidly as the planners have envisaged. There may be less additional wealth and rather more jobs.

Implications of new approaches to planning

Some aspects of France's new approach to economic planning bear an interesting family resemblance to a major administrative innovation of the 1970s in the United States. This was the new Congressional budget exercise, which had its first run in the 1976/7 budget, and most especially, the institutional innovation of the Congressional Budget Office (CBO), established at the start of 1975. It was a new effort to bring coherence into the often conflicting objectives of the US legislature. From the outset, the institution's first director, Alice Rivlin, emphasized the long-term purpose of her agency which has been lavishly equipped with professional expertise:

> I see as one of our major missions getting the Congress to look at the multiyear implications of what it is doing, and to think five to ten years ahead about where it wants the country to go and then translate this back into immediate budget decisions.

And she commented:

> If national planning means that the Congress and the Executive are seriously looking at alternative futures for the federal government and alternative futures for the country as a whole, then obviously we need to do that and the CBO seems a step in that direction (Rivlin, 1975, p.30).

In fact the making of such long-term projections is laid down in the Congressional Budget Reform Act of 1974 as one of the functions of the CBO which it authorized to be established. At first congressmen had not been much interested in this aspect of the new procedures which they had created. The officials concerned with the running of the agency expected that a change would come, when the bargaining for national resources grew more intense and developed into an argument about the competing priorities for the future of the nation. But, even at the early stage of the experiment, it was worth noting its implications for the wider process of integrating the disparate elements which have in different and sometimes contradictory ways determined the shape of the US economy.

Also in 1975 (the year which had seen the birth of the CBO) the two bills with which the name of Senator Hubert Humphrey is associated, the Humphrey–Javits Balanced Growth and Economic Planning Bill and the Humphrey–Hawkins Full Employment Bill, were brought by him before Senate. The latter bill alone, if enacted in its original form (it was in fact emasculated), would have placed 'strong multiyear planning requirements on the President' (Hartman, 1978, p.309). In 1976 planning was the chosen platform in Jimmy Carter's presidential election campaign. Although it is claimed (Graham, 1979, p.83) that President Carter withdrew some of this support once the Democrats came to office, sensing the reversal of mood which was to take many, leftist, liberals into the non-interventionist camp, Carter's administration was 'deliberately setting long-term spending targets' (Hartman, 1978, p.308).

From the outset the CBO made economic projections for its own budget exercise; its provisions require it to make five-year forecasts of the cost of every bill reported out of Committee. But the Congressional budget 'does not explicitly incorporate a multiyear framework' (Hartman, 1978, pp.312–13)—long-term effects are not included in the spending proposals.

However, in early 1978 the President directed all agencies to prepare their budgets in a 'multiyear framework', i.e. for the budget year and the three years to follow (four years in all). The aim was to identify 'the long-term effects of the proposal'. According to Pechman, the President's 1979 Budget proposal provided 'considerably more detail on prospective developments than any budget in the past' (1978, p.276). As part of the exercise, the Office of Management and Budget provided a standardized 'planning base' for the three fiscal years 1980–2—including outlay targets; and also a standardized projection of economic growth and other economic conditions.

For its part, the CBO was now led to propose 'advance targeting', with budget targets set for five years ahead. It would also 'keep score' and draw attention to the probability of overspending in aggregate if a particular bill goes through, thus forcing Congress to choose and plan ahead. A 'Congressional

Scorekeeping Report' is issued periodically as a guide to what scope there is for additional spending.

There are other examples of the changed approach to the problems of economic planning. In Britain the change came in 1975–6; the new so-called 'Industrial Strategy' (a conscious change of nomenclature from the ambitious National Economic Plan issued with great fanfare, and negligible subsequent results, in 1965) aimed to identify a number of selected targets for priority industrial investment which were intended to serve the purposes of accelerated economic growth over a stated period of years. The Labour government's strategy was then to work out with each industrial sector a means of financial leverage and the adaptation of individual enterprises to secure the resources required for the selective expansion of output. This was a far cry from the comprehensive five-year plan of the Labour government of the mid-1960s.

The general point which emerges from these various initiatives is that the changed circumstances of the economic environment have made part at least of the old-style rhetoric of the struggle between business and government something of an anachronism. Of course, the relationship continues to have large elements of conflict. But the picture of government constantly pushing out the confines of its power at the expense of private business, which is longing to make its own decisions but is not allowed to do so, is a diverting rather than an illuminating one. The instrument of economic planning in its most modern manifestation is not a way of transferring comprehensive responsibility from the market to the government. It is rather a device for supplementing, by decisions made centrally on the basis of a careful analysis of the best data available, the signals coming from the market place (which will generally do sufficiently well by themselves as a guide to short-term decisions). This is needed because the signals from the market are often either too weak or positively misleading for longer-term purposes. They may be misleading simply because the market's rate of discount of the return on certain long-term investments is too high to permit them to be embarked upon in time. The state then has to intervene, to alter the terms of the bargain in such a way as to provide the incentive for the realization of the investment which it judges to be necessary.

This has become a commonplace activity in such fields as

energy, the environment and in the provision of social needs. Why has it proliferated in this way? The answer in its most general sense is, clearly, that our situation has become more crowded, and is likely to become much more so. There is a simple sense in which resources like air and space and water have to be deliberately protected by collective decisions and public power, if private demands on them are to be met. Things previously regarded as available in practically unlimited quantities now have to be deliberately conserved. In economic jargon the 'externalities', i.e. the costs incurred by those who are not involved in a given economic transaction, have been greatly enlarged. Once a collective decision has been made to protect a resource from the depredations of untrammelled private consumption—by direct rationing, by price manipulation, by fiscal means, or by whatever other system appears most acceptable—its allocation is, in the logic of democratic politics, expected to become a public function too. The state is the guardian of 'externalities'.

But there is a deeper sense in which life grows more crowded and the scope for independent entrepreneurial decision becomes more constricted. It is not only the physical reach—our capacity to fill space and to eat up natural resources—of the average person which has grown with mass affluence. At the same time our requirements for personal ease and for a greater measure of predictability in our own lives have also increased; we object to being grossly disturbed by innovations and expect that these will be introduced in organized ways which minimize the discomfort to ourselves. There is altogether a more exacting standard of what constitutes socially tolerable adjustment to abrupt change. In this sense the would-be innovator finds the place crowded, because people are sticky— slow at changing habits, slow at displacing themselves.

These are more of the 'externalities' which the businessman has to bear closely in mind; and the terms on which he has to meet their cost are set by public decisions rather than by private bargains. Part of the planning activity of government is to anticipate them in such a way as to reduce the strains and personal discomforts caused by changes in jobs and the lifestyles that go with them. In sum we have the seeming paradox that the modern state, which has been discovering the limitations of its capacity for short-term management of the economy, is called upon increasingly to take charge of its long-term management. The two things are, however, entirely different functions and, as the examples we have considered clearly indicate, involve quite different administrative techniques.

Notes to Chapter 3

1. This is true of such countries as the US, in spite of the prevalent rhetoric. 'While the spread of government regulation is decried, more and more decisions about land use, mineral exploitation, and plant location are being subjected to governmental scrutiny and influence with apparent popular support' (Owen and Schultze, 1976, p.8).
2. The definition belongs to Michel Albert of the French Commissariat du Plan. He used it in presenting the VIIth Plan in an article in *Le Figaro*, 24 April 1976.
3. See successive Annual Reports of the German Council of Economic Experts (*Sachverständigenrat*) during the 1970s.
4. The '*Modèle Dynamique Multisectoriel*', developed from 1974 to 1976 by the Service des Programmes of the Institut National de la Statistique et des Etudes Economiques (INSEE).
5. The *Grandes Entreprises Nationales* (GENs) include the French postal services (PTT) and also the following public corporations:
   Energy: Charbonnages de France (coal); EDF (electricity); GDF (gas).
   Transport: SNCF (railways); RATP (Paris transport); Air-France; Air-Inter.
6. See the detailed analysis of individual country trends in *European Economy*, Special Issue 1979, ch.V.
7. Ibid., p.65. Taking the figures for industrial productivity alone, the change in the relative performance of France and Germany post-1973 is striking. Germany, whose industrial productivity had grown more slowly than that of France during the years of economic expansion, actually achieved an acceleration of its rate of growth in the four years after 1973, while the French rate of growth showed a significant decline. Preliminary evidence for the later part of the 1970s does not change the impression of an apparent reversal in the relative performance of the two countries.

4

THE INTERNATIONAL SYSTEM
AND THE MIXED ECONOMY

Is there, then, evidence of the emergence of a stable equilibrium between public and private power in Western capitalist society, with the prospect that the balance between the two, arrived at before the pressures of the 1970s business fluctuations asserted themselves, is unlikely to be significantly changed in the period immediately ahead? Perhaps the most notable shift that has occurred is towards a recognition of the considerable limitations on the capacity of governments to determine the level of economic activity in the short term. In this sense we have moved away decisively from what may be termed the cult of arrogant Keynesianism of the immediate post-war period. At the crucial time of the post-1973 recession, the earlier confidence gave way in the face of deep uncertainties about the varying time lags in the operation of measures designed to induce economic expansion or contraction (p. 19 above). The result was disastrous hesitation—and government abstention from remedial action.

Other factors, to do with price expectations, added their force to the process of making governments hesitant about pump-priming. The new pessimism about the limits of government intervention-ism was given expression by Franco Modigliani, a main-line Keynesian, in his 1976 Presidential address to the American Economic Association. Once a 'price shock' has been absorbed by the economy, 'there is no macro policy', he said, 'by which domestic prices can be made to fall except by creating enough slack, reducing vacancies and thus putting downward pressure on wages.' In these circumstances governments could not, by the application of well-tried Keynesian formulas learned in the miseries of the 1930s, avoid 'a period of both above equilibrium unemployment and inflation' (Modigliani, 1976; see p. 15 in 1977 version).

Once again the particular phenomena which make present-day public intervention a more difficult and hazardous task than it would have been in the 1950s and 60s assert themselves. One has been identified (p.20) as the reduced responsiveness of the economy both to downward pressures and to demand stimuli. But even more important is the dominant feature of our economies— their dependence on an ever-obtrusive international environment.

We have observed (p.5 above) in the context of the 1979 Tokyo economic summit, that these constraints, however real and relevant, are not necessarily taken into account in policy-making. This is in spite of the fact that the advance of the national state into a wider range of economic activities within the domestic sphere has coincided with a massive increase in the volume of transactions between nations. The most obvious and familiar case is that of international trade in industrial products, which has, in most years during the past quarter of a century, grown at an annual rate which is two or three times as fast as the increase in industrial production. This is a more extraordinary aspect of the world in which we live than is generally recognized, and the reasons for it are not sufficiently understood to make us confident that it will necessarily continue for the rest of the century as it has done ever since the war.

However, it is not the object here to predict the future; it is sufficient for our purposes to point to the effect of what has happened to date on the attitudes of those responsible for policy in both the public and the private sectors in the advanced industrial countries.

The necessary consequence of the fact that trade has increased much faster than production is that the proportion of industrial output which is now directed to foreign markets has become very much larger. And as so much of the demand for the goods comes from abroad, it is essential to maintain an international system in which goods and services move more or less freely. It cannot be repeated too often that the one thing we cannot afford is trade wars.

Yet, in the context of the mixed economy, the governments whose activities have been described here find themselves under pressure to do a variety of things—in the promotion of the social welfare of disadvantaged groups, in regional policy, in creating fresh opportunities for employment in a period of slower economic growth—that impinge on the interests of other states which depend on free access for their trade to the market that is being interfered with. Intervention at the national level constantly grows at the same time as the international consequences of interfering in the operation of market forces become an increasingly sensitive issue. Evidently there are dangerous risks ahead of a clash between the welfare-state ideal—of which the mixed economy is one expression—and the international order among advanced industrial countries, whose benefits we have enjoyed in such a large measure during the period since the Second World War. The cause for wonder is, perhaps, that it has taken so long for the potential conflict between these two forces which have moved the economic policies of Western countries in the second half of the twentieth century to emerge as an actual threat. So far, we have been strikingly successful in keeping this source of conflict under control. That conclusion applies, it should be added, only to economic relations among the advanced industrial countries; it is regarded by many of the developing countries as being merely the expression of a conspiracy among the affluent. If so, it is a remarkably effective conspiracy which has endured a remarkably long time.

It is worth noting that, as a broad generalization, international economic policies have been pushed forward with comparative success in precisely those areas which are affected by state action in pursuit of the social objectives of the mixed economy. This point can probably be most readily made by means of concrete examples. Take the efforts of the state in a mixed economy to ensure that employment opportunities do not suddenly collapse in a particular region or industry. The textile and clothing industry is a familiar example of the way in which governments try to preserve jobs in an occupation which still provides more employment than any other single manufacturing industry in most of the advanced industrial countries. The impulse to be protectionist is very strong. On the other hand there is a well-established fear, among governments and industrialists alike, of the cumulative process of trade restriction which could well be set in motion by the arbitrary use of import controls by each country at its own will.

Out of this combination of anxieties has come the series of agreements, painfully negotiated under the aegis of the GATT (General Agreement on Tariffs and Trade), on the collective limitation of trade in textiles coming from low-wage, developing countries.[1] The sense of the agreements—which express what must be regarded as a characteristic compromise of the mixed economy when faced with some awkward pressure deriving from the international system—runs as follows:—Yes, we recognize the right of foreign countries to sell in our markets things which they make more cheaply. But we also insist that the rate at which they increase their exports shall not be so high as to cause sudden major disturbances, social and economic, in our countries.

Once the limits have been set, the next step is a highly complicated and hotly contended series of negotiations with individual exporting countries about what in detail they will be permitted to export to whom. Without holding the system up as an ideal means of conducting international business, the important point is that it works, more or less; if only in the sense that the importing countries have been strong enough to enforce it and to persuade exporters that the alternatives are worse. The developing countries increase their textile exports and the welfare states of the Western world engage in the style of market intervention to which they have become accustomed, in support of the interests of groups of their citizens who are vociferous and feel menaced. The connection with the regional policies which have become a standard feature of public policy in the mixed economies of the West is that textile employment is often concentrated in certain traditional centres and that, in some of these, alternative jobs are not readily available.

What is so interesting about developments in the 1970s is that this kind of effort, which tries to accommodate the interventionist activities of the state in a mixed economy to the need for a predictable and orderly set of rules governing transactions with the international community, has become the everyday business of international politics. A notable example of the genre is the agreement made in the GATT, again laboriously negotiated point by point over the five years of the so-called 'Tokyo Round', 1974–8, on a new code of rules on public procurement—setting limits to the freedom of governments to place orders for goods for public programmes with suppliers whom they have chosen hitherto, naturally among their favourites at home, in total disregard of possible foreign interests. The new code of conduct does not bind the hands of governments for all procurements; but it is more effective than earlier, voluntary, codes in that it places some constraints on blatant local favouritism.

The picture, then, is one of a slowly creeping tide of international intervention, at the same time as the territory influenced by national government action in the modern mixed economy is steadily extended. This is not to suggest that the speed of the encroaching tide matches the rate at which these islands of national government activity extend their borders. But there is at least a visible movement in both directions.

Contrast this with the policy-makers' preference for inertia in the day-to-day management of demand and employment which asserted itself in the 1970s. To use the jargon of economists, the micro-economic intervention by the state is growing and is increasingly the subject of international negotiation, while macro-economic policy-making is increasingly in doubt and decreasingly subject to international co-ordination. It is as if governments, having built up a vast arsenal of extremely powerful weapons on the macro-economic front over the past thirty years, and having also made a point of consulting closely with their allies abroad about the way in which this weaponry should be employed, have now decided that their armoury is after all too dangerous to be used. Nobody knows precisely the range of the guns and there is some doubt about the direction the missiles which are fired off may eventually take: some of the strategic experts even suggest that most of them are boomerangs.

With short-term demand management so much out of fashion in so many countries, it is hardly surprising that the Western world failed totally to arrive at any joint policy for tackling the severe business cycles of the 1970s, the worst that had hit them for forty years. There is a tendency for governments to say: we have each sinned individually, usually by failing to control our own money supply, and now we must each make individual amends. Indeed, the extremists among them take the view that control of the national money supply is a complete and better substitute for any amount of international co-ordination of policy. It is a slightly surprising doctrine to find being adopted at a time when national frontiers are being simultaneously opened ever wider to international transactions. Britain's abolition of all exchange control in the autumn of 1979 was a striking example in a series of such moves. In fact international interdependence grows, while the notion of international management of the world economy moves into disrepute.

If anyone feels that that is an exaggerated statement, let him consider the way in which the great nations of the Western world have approached the major economic problems of the 1970s.[2] They started off with the most extreme kind of inflationary boom in 1973. This was all too well co-ordinated; indeed it was the simultaneous timing of that violent upswing in so many countries which made it so dangerous. Next, they ran involuntarily into a thoroughly co-ordinated slump in 1975; and then failed entirely to engage in any joint endeavour to exploit the opportunities for economic recovery which emerged in 1976. The years 1977 and 1978 were spent mainly in wrangling between the strong and the weak economies about who should do what first; and when that had finally been sorted out, there was the second big oil shock (from Iran) in 1979. The Western economies reacted to the price increase by agreeing that this time all of them would deflate their economies simultaneously—a decision which, ironically, might be counted as a piece of common macro-economic policy. The truth is that each of the major countries decided to give a deflationary bias to its economic policy for its own *national reasons*; the underlying thinking was that Germany and Japan had been so successful after the first oil shock because they were quicker off the mark in deflating their economies, and that it would be worth trying to follow a similar tactic the second time round. In short, this was not a case of co-ordination, but rather the accident that everyone happened to have read the same (German) drill book.

A particular trouble about this old drill book was that it made no concession whatever to the facts of international interdependence. It laid its faith in the principle that when each nation independently does the right thing, via the control of the money supply, to hold inflation down, the other good things automatically follow. Now this is a slightly paradoxical outcome of the new mood of distrust of the conventional post-war practice of demand management in the Keynesian manner, since one of the causes of the loss of confidence in macro-policy is precisely that the international forces beyond the control of national governments have increasingly asserted themselves and frustrated the policy-makers. Great nations have spent a great deal of time during the past few years in trying to regain their economic autonomy and control, which they believe they have temporarily mislaid, rather than lost, through inadvertence.

The obstacles to international co-ordination of national monetary policies are spelled out in an essay by Niels Thygesen (1979). He emphasizes that until the beginning of the 1970s at least there was no real effort to co-ordinate the different methods of monetary demand on the part of the leading actors on the international finance scene. Nor did these countries—the USA, Germany, Japan—have any discernible intention to surrender nationally designed monetary policies. Indeed the highly divergent effects of such short-term monetary policies as US interest rates manipulation and Japanese credit rationing resulted in very sharp responses from the sensitive system of interdependent economies. Fine tuning by individual governments was in fact having a short-term effect on their own national economies but with unpredictable international shock waves.

In the early 1970s fashions in monetary theory moved decisively towards two main objectives: firstly, the stable growth of monetary aggregates (although no agreement emerged about the nature of these aggregates); secondly, the introduction of floating exchange rates. In fact the first part of the years 1972 to 1975 was a time when 'exaggerated notions of policy autonomy under flexible exchange rates' prevailed (Thygesen, p.220); the floating rate was supposed to obviate the need of policy co-ordination, and the logic for jointly agreed exchange rate targets was totally rejected. However, the same period saw 'a major new development' (Thygesen, p.220): the start of a limited but significant consensus about the need for explicitly stated monetary targets. By 1978 only three of the members of the Group of Ten[3]—Belgium, Italy and Sweden—did not have precise targets for their 'monetary stock'.

The role of central banks in inhibiting the process of international co-ordination needs to be taken on board in this connection (it is of course also true that they can perform a most important function of international co-operation—see Shonfield, 1982, p.109). They were bastions of national sovereignty and did not want to spell out in detail, let alone attempt to co-ordinate with others, the varied devices which they use to manage their own domestic situations.

Under these circumstances the question whether it was generally desirable to subordinate national economic policy objectives to an internationally agreed consensus remained unanswered; in particular, the belief that the long-term effect of pockets of instability may be beneficent was not seriously challenged.[4]

Milton Friedman was one of the chief propounders of the philosophy of national economic autonomy. In advising the Joint Economic Committee of the United States Congress on this subject in 1963 he wrote: 'Foreign payments amount to only some 5 per cent of our total national income. Yet they have become a major factor in nearly every national policy.' This he plainly regarded as silly, and he went on to recommend the United States to adopt a system of floating exchange rates as a means of overcoming the trouble. After a characteristically self-confident piece of argument about the way in which market forces, once brought to bear on the determination of the value of the dollar, would automatically solve the problem of the balance of payments, which had been unnecessarily created by an incompetent lot of busybodies, he concluded: 'It is not the least of the virtues of floating exchange rates that we would again become masters in our own house. We could decide important issues on the proper ground . . .' Three years later, again in evidence for the Joint Economic Committee, he repeated his earlier words verbatim and reaffirmed his standpoint in the strongest possible terms, having 'nothing new to add to that [1963] statement' (Friedman, 1966, pp.30–6).

As a remedy for the loss of national autonomy, Friedman's formula of a floating exchange rate must be judged a resounding failure. The dollar was, and is, much more exposed to the decisions taken by people outside the United States than he so confidently believed; in fact his purported measure of the low international dependence of the United States is a largely irrelevant number, and most especially so for a country running an international currency which is often in trouble. Still, Friedman's statement is worth recalling because it so well illustrates an underlying mood of Americans and of others—a mood which expresses the conviction that there must be some remediable defect in a system which makes 'us', whoever we are, quite so dependent on the views and actions of foreigners.

There is almost certainly no such remediable defect. There is either a way forward towards greater international co-ordination of the day-to-day management of our economic affairs, that is of macro-economic policy, or a decisive move backwards towards the dismantling of the welfare state and of its concomitant in Western society, the mixed economy. The latter was in fact the choice that was being proposed, by people who were looking for ways of regaining the lost satisfactions of national autonomy. Arthur Burns, as we have seen (p.3 above), traces the trouble in the United States, whose condition he tends to equate rather too readily with that of all other advanced industrial countries, back to President Roosevelt's New Deal. It is, Burns believes, simply the advance of government regulation and government-supplied welfare benefits, a process that took a further huge leap forward during the 1960s with President Johnson's 'Great Society Program', which makes rational management of society impossible. The consequence is American inflation, 'which has become a major threat to the well-being of much of the world' (Burns, 1979). And he concludes sadly that there is no remedy which central bankers can provide: what is required is a major reversal of those forces which built the interventionist state into the monster which he believes it has become. That will require, he says, a deep change in the 'political environment'. Burns of course reflected an important current of thought in the United States today. This is incidentally far more radical in its rejection of the *charitable* and supervisory role of the state than that of the contemporary British Tory party.

There are also other forces, less extreme than this, which express a spirit of frustration in the United States that will make their effect felt on the rest of the world for some time to come. We in Europe tend to underestimate the elements of the tragic in the American experience of the late 1970s. Starting from President Carter's election, the government acted as if it could by its own will manage to generate a great economic expansion in the United States, regardless of what was done in the rest of the world. From 1976 onwards it embarked on a programme which vastly increased the number of people employed, gave a powerful and sustained lift to international trade, raised the level of welfare and of business profits—and then, in 1979, it had to bring the whole operation to a dead halt, essentially because the other key countries in the world economy had refused to join the game, or to do so soon enough. Of course there are other reasons—for which the Americans must in part at least blame themselves—which have contributed to this failure. But it is essential to register the key fact: the inability of the

United States to run its economy in its own way without the accord of the rest of the world.

An important factor in all this is that the old style of United States leadership, with the world-wide dollar system as its base, which made the international context of the mixed economy rather comfortable and comparatively easy to manage, has now probably gone. This coincides with a need to increase the range of international co-operation in economic policy beyond the bounds at which it got stuck in the 1970s. We thought that we could deal with the international repercussions of our changed domestic economic system on a piecemeal basis, without calling for any major change in the day-to-day management of the world economy. International action was on the whole directed to questions which can be labelled 'micro-economic'—including some very important matters, but *not* touching those critical questions about the different responsibilities of individual countries to run their internal affairs in such a way as to maintain the prosperity of the international system as a whole.

Back in the 1960s it all seemed so much easier. International economic policy consisted in agreeing to the OECD's target of 50 per cent growth in the decade—all of us expanding together. It is quite another matter to reach agreement on collective action which involves allotting different roles to individual countries, some going forward faster while others deliberately stand still or retreat. They collaborate by a process of de-synchronization. There is nothing bizarre about that; but it will mean getting rid of a lot of old habits of thought before nations get used to it.

Notes to Chapter 4

1. The fruit of these negotiations was the Multifibre Arrangement (MFA) which first came into effect on 1 January 1974, and has since been extended every four years after long and heated parleys. The MFA, which also established a permanent Textile Surveillance Body and a Textiles Committee within the GATT, covers most wool, cotton and man-made fibres, as well as fabrics and made-up articles of which these fibres constitute an important part.
2. This subject is analysed at some length in the author's *The Use of Public Power*, 1982, ch.3.
3. The Group of Ten consists of the United States, Japan, Canada and

Sweden outside the EEC, and of France, Germany, Italy, Belgium, the Netherlands and the UK inside the EEC.

4. It should incidentally be noted that, in working towards an international consensus, the organizations such as the European Commission, which are explicitly designed to foster co-ordination but depend on exchanges of nationally collected and *interpreted* information, are noticeably less influential than those international bodies like the OECD and the IMF which may be regarded as a forum for discussion and have their own secretariat staff.

PART TWO

Japan:
A Corporatist Phenomenon

5

BIG IS MALLEABLE

THE Italian journalist, Arrigo Levi, an astute observer of economic convergences and differences, summed up the impressions of an extended tour of Japan in 1979 with a dismissive shrug: 'There's no mystery about the Japanese. They feel they're different and like to think they're unique.'

One can only sympathize with his desire to demystify and to point to parallels in the Japanese and Western experience. A number of features which the Japanese themselves, and also their Western appraisers, regard as special to their nation are present elsewhere, though in lesser measure. Even a modified form of Japanese lifetime employment principle exists widely in the West, under the label 'first in—last out'. In most of Western Europe and in the United States we have job security by law; dismissal just because a younger (or better trained) person might be thought to do the job better would be a very costly business. 'Voluntary retirement', with a golden handshake, is also well known outside Japan. In fact, quite apart from the encouragement of early retirement of employees in their late forties and early fifties, the Japanese policy of reducing wages by fixing the general retirement age at fifty-five (until the 1970s this was the widely accepted limit to lifetime employment cover) was more ruthless than anything tolerated in the West.

However, when it comes to economic performance, Japan is different—extraordinarily so, by any standards. This became clear in the 1960s and 1970s when the country's economy grew at an extremely rapid rate; much faster—up to the first oil shock—than the other Western-style economies, and subsequently more slowly, but still at a rate well in advance of theirs.

Speaking to Japanese economists about the gap between the Japanese and the Western performances one encounters broadly two views. The first emphasizes the cohesiveness of Japanese society—though it does not take into account the fact that the underprivileged, including the small ethnic minorities and people of mixed parentage, speak in very subdued voices. It dwells on the peculiarities of the Japanese work culture, on the flexibility of labour, on the sensitive adaptability of both business management and government intervention. All this contributes, it is said, to a state of discipline in the economy which ensures orderly high growth.

The other viewpoint does not rate the inherent, culture-based characteristics of Japanese labour and management quite so high. It attributes the undoubted advantages of Japan in the growth race to more transient features, such as Japan's relatively low dependence on its export trade. While not underplaying the importance of typically 'Japanese' features such as national homogeneity, the high degree of loyalty to one's place of employment, the peculiar combination of authoritarianism and consensus-producing consultation, this second view augurs an increasingly convergent future for Japan and the West.

Despite the low proportion of exports in GNP (at 15 per cent in 1980, for example, it was not much more than half the UK figure) Japan has been becoming more dependent on what it sells abroad. On the assumption that growth in world trade is going to remain much slower than in the past, growth in the Japanese economy will also be slower and unemployment may well rise. In such circumstances, government will have to do more to strengthen the social security rights of the weaker groups of society, especially those not benefiting from lifetime employment: the old, women. This implies costly extensions of public expenditure paid out of increased taxation. Will Japan then be able to avoid the economic rigidities which have accompanied the growth of the welfare state in the West? Will the Japanese style of social relations—inside the firm, between organized labour and management, between public authority and the business community—succeed in making the next phase of economic development, characterized by reduced growth rates, less turbulent than our Western experience?

Much will depend on whether Japanese economic planning will remain as effective as in the past. This in turn will be determined by how far the planning process, depending as it does on obtaining consensus in the private sector for decisions involving public policy, continues to enjoy the support of the small number of conglomerates which are responsible for the bulk of industrial capacity. This concentration of power in the hands of a few conglomerates makes their role crucial in the planning process, and should therefore be examined to understand how the planning works. And it also impinges on another characteristic of the Japanese system—the extraordinary adaptability of its workforce, in both the privileged big enterprise sector in which about one-third of the manufacturing labour force work, full-time, and among the remaining two-thirds who work casually or are employed by the smaller firms. In the top sector there is labour mobility within the conglomerate itself and its constituent firms. The inconveniences of such mobility to the individual are compensated by the advantages of lifetime employment; the employees of the large groups see themselves as belonging to a highly privileged élite. Equally important is the high turnover of companies—bankrupts and new business entrants—and also of workers, in the unprivileged sector of the economy, which gives employment to rather more than half of the manufacturing workforce.

The civil servants in charge of the Economic Planning Agency argue that Japanese planning requires such a concentration of power, with a relatively small number of people responsible for making key industrial decisions. The problems of planning in the tertiary sector of the economy, where enterprises are typically of small or medium size, are viewed with considerable trepidation.

While this 'small business' sector is highly competitive, so that casualties abound, the big company sector is less so. Here the fact that company finances interlock (63 per cent of big company shares is held by other financial and industrial concerns) will prevent any member of a conglomerate 'family' from going under. At times of strain the group shareholders step in fast to help (or tamper with) management, and meanwhile provide medium-term financial support to give the firm a second chance.

Such tutelage and face-saving impedes the conventional competitive process, besides giving an advance signal to other large companies that they need not fear the ailing firm. And this sense of security makes Japanese big business more responsive to administrative guidance on the restructuring of industry as a whole.

Public policy in Japan views with favour this type of loose

integration. The policy-makers' dominant motive has changed in the post-war period. First it was to secure orderly and non-wasteful reconstruction and industrial development; next, to foster effective export strategies by eliminating unproductive competition; and what is foremost in the minds of the present generation of officials who decide on the detail of administrative guidance is the restructuring of Japanese industry, the redeployment of economic effort, and the circumvention of the pitfalls which the recession has dug in the path of Japanese growth (Magaziner and Hout, 1980).

Industry for its part tolerates government intervention partly because of the direct influence which the leaders of the conglomerates exert on public policy. This influence is a longstanding feature of the Japanese system. In the decades immediately preceding World War Two, two of the *zaibatsu*,[1] Mitsui and Mitsubishi, not only controlled the bulk of the economic life of the country but also financed and ran its two leading (and equally conservative) political parties. The penetration of the modern *keiretsu*[2] is less narrow, but it is still alleged that individual members of the *keiretsu* clans exercise a particularly strong hold on political circles. It is their executives who supply the *zaikai*[3] who represent the capitalist point of view, in trade associations and on ministerial advisory committees, as well as more informally.

How big are the conglomerates?

There is some debate about the exact weight of the conglomerates in Japanese economic life, but there is no doubt that the *keiretsu* are a key feature. The very scale of their thinking makes a first-class instrument of long-term strategy. Conglomerates, whether of the old *zaibatsu* style like Mitsubishi, or the more modern Fuyo, held together essentially by the presence of a strong bank at its centre and by special relationships among its members, act in many respects in an integrated way. While the parts are independent, the group as a whole can take responsibility for decisions, sharing risks as well as hopes and ambitions. Within such a group the firm which makes a point of asserting its independence is the exception: the bulk speak with one voice.

Three of the pre-1945 *zaibatsu*, Mitsui, Mitsubishi and Sumitomo, continue under their original names in the front ranks of the new *keiretsu*. The fourth, originally controlled by the Yasuda family, which had historically concentrated on banking, has taken the name of Fuyo and revolves round the financial interests of its leader, the Fuji Bank. Fuyo, Dai-Ichi Kangyo and Sanwa come nearest to a type more familiar in the West, notably in Germany. Dai-Ichi and Sanwa, also with banks at their centre, are groups of post-war creation, although not entirely new: Dai-Ichi was one of the oldest banking houses, with a special position as a non-*zaibatsu* bank. As is the case with Fuyo, the ties linking individual members of these two groups are predominantly financial; this makes them less 'Japanese'—less family-like, and benefiting rather more evidently from clear short-term advantages which can be expressed in terms of measurable return on capital.

By contrast, Mitsubishi, as well as the smaller Sumitomo and to a lesser extent the Mitsui group, are imbued with many characteristics which cannot be so measured. In each of them, the group bank, backed by other 'family' financial institutions, is the pivot round which the life of the group revolves; but the character of all three is also determined by their chief productive units and above all by their several trading companies.

Yet even here there are important differences of emphasis. Mitsui has acquired many of the characteristics of the newer 'financial' groupings. This may in part result from its emancipation from Mitsui family domination in the management of everyday business at the time of the Meiji restoration, and from the non-assertiveness of the latter-day Mitsui; there was to be a new wave of family withdrawals from running the group's affairs in the 1930s when Mitsui was especially hit by violent labour unrest. Moreover, the fact that the Mitsui conglomerate has absorbed very large industrial groups with strong individualities of their own gives it a rather heterogeneous character when compared with the more unified Mitsubishi and Sumitomo.

Sumitomo has a character all of its own. This solitary, Osaka-based *zaibatsu* has probably kept alive its original style more than any other conglomerate. It has a consistently independent stance, with its emphasis on the local interests of the Osaka prefecture, and its stand-alone character is symbolized by the group's practice of retaining the name of Sumitomo in the names of most individual companies. It also has a reputation of being openly contemptuous of government. Part of this has been put down to the unorthodox character of its chief spokesman, Hosai Hyuga, the seemingly everlasting boss of Sumitomo Metal Industries whose first managerial job in the enterprise dates back to 1949. But the defiance which has manifested itself over the past ten or twenty years cannot be entirely attributed to Hyuga alone; there is no evidence that the other members of the group ever seriously tried to restrain his individuality. The most important manifestation of this Sumitomo assertiveness was the refusal to go along with the generally agreed cut in steel output in 1965 (see below, pp.95–8), an event notable because it is one of the very few documented rebellions against administrative guidance.

An enquiry as to the size—in terms of numbers employed—of one of the top Japanese conglomerates would meet a puzzled, even embarrassed, response. The numbers employed by the chief components are there for all to see, but do not convey the relative importance of the champion industrial/commercial combines. Apart from the specific problem of the segmented labour market (generally speaking the company tabulations represent only permanent full-time employees, excluding a significant section of the workforce) only the core of the most important firms of each group is included. The ramifications of each of the combines are such that no chart can contain them or even fully clarify their nature.

The original clear structure of the *zaibatsu* with a holding company as leader, and under it a pyramid of main producers, subsidiaries and more or less fully controlled affiliates, flanked by commercial houses, banks and shipping lines, has been lost, as a result of the deliberate effort of the American occupiers. What has emerged is of a different nature. The *keiretsu* that have replaced the *zaibatsu* are much looser, more amorphous networks, with the company bank usually in a leading position alongside the trading company and the strongest producer unit or units. Then, at a slightly lower level, the *keiretsu* also includes a great number of larger and smaller fully- or partly-owned industrial concerns, transport enterprises, finance houses, insurance companies—all that goes to the making of a complex industrial and commercial system; chemicals and heavy engineering are invariably in this mix, and also such growth industries as motor vehicles and electronics. The phenomenon of this heterogeneous assortment within individual conglomerates which have at least one enterprise in each main industrial sector is known as 'one-setism'. Some of the giants are also associated with several of the largest 'single-industry' groups, themselves complex industrial structures.

These single-industry groups (or, as in the case of Toyota, 'solar-system' groups) concentrate on a relatively narrow line of production, tending to conventional vertical or horizontal structure. The 'Japanese' element of strong identification with the parent company, which makes Toyota or Nissan employees loyal above all to Toyota or Nissan, and hardly aware of the *keiretsu* giant with which their parent company is loosely linked, is not really all that different from an identification with Volkswagen, IBM or Philips. The identification is perhaps especially marked in Toyota, which is 'untypical' of Japanese companies in several respects. It has almost complete financial self-sufficiency: interlocking shareholdings are dominant in Toyota companies and the parent has developed a particular financial interchange relationship with its own main bank, Tokai. Tokai Bank's holding of Toyota shares is on much the same scale as Toyota's financial interest in Tokai.[4]

Toyota is also 'special' in the pre-eminence of the original owners—the Toyoda family—on the boards and in day-to-day management. The company has a particularly cohesive *keiretsu*-like structure of its own, with a large retinue of firms, some of them creatures of Toyota with heavy capital participation, some of them nominally independent subcontractors. This is a really powerful decision-making structure, with the power very clearly concentrated in the parent firm, in a way which is markedly different from the looser arrangements of the giant conglomerates. Toyota's particularly 'authoritarian' structure is, however, something regarded as peculiar to the firm, even by the executives of its major motor industry competitor, Nissan (which incidentally also has many *keiretsu* attributes).

The bond between the elements which compose each of the *keiretsu* groups can be purely financial; they may share the same bank or have directly interlocking shareholdings. They may depend on one another for supplies, for custom. The sales of their products may be channelled through the parent concern's trading company which also perhaps imports, in ships built and run by the group, the raw materials they need in their industrial processes.[5] However, the trade name of the parent firm is not of necessity borne by the affiliate's products nor incorporated in their own name. Indeed the only obvious sign of their common genealogy may well be the presence of the parent company's name in their list of major shareholdings.

The closeness of financial ties is reflected in turn in the practice of exchanging executive officers between the companies of any one group. Two in three of the companies which form part of the main six conglomerates have at least one officer from another company in the group on their staff, and nearly one-third have board members who have served or are serving elsewhere in the group (Industrial Review of Japan, 1980, p.50).

To Western observers such mobility—the ease with which the Japanese are prepared to transfer from one unit to another—in business and industry is one of the most striking features of the economic scene. White-collar as well as blue-collar workers will at short notice or even without notice accept a posting to a new department or location, generally in the same enterprise, but likely to be in a completely different capacity. Moreover, if company policy dictates, executives and operatives alike will go to distant places where climate, housing and educational and social facilities may be quite dissimilar from those they have experienced before.

This surprising acquiescence to frequently inconvenient moves is not just part of an inbred respect for authority, but results rather from the recognition of inexorable career patterns. Where a Western employee might resist being sent from pillar to post and having to face unfamiliar work surroundings which could impede his progress to a better position, the Japanese employee knows that every rung up the ladder will be ready for him at predetermined intervals. For the chosen candidate for the absolute heights of company presidency, the last few hoists will be slow in coming. In Japan you rarely meet a company president who on appointment is not over sixty. While this reflects the awe in which geriarchs are held, more important perhaps are the practical problems posed by the intake of retired high civil servants in late middle age into senior executive positions in industry and finance. The foremost talent in this new intake belongs to individuals in late middle age. On taking up their new positions these must not be contemporaries or older than the presidents and chairmen of the concerns they are joining, for if they were, the new recruits would themselves lose face or even possibly embarrass their new colleagues by asserting age status. As it is, even without seniority in years, the ex-civil servants command very considerable respect in the companies they join.

We shall say more about the particular flexibility of the labour force when discussing the structure and characteristics of Japanese industrial relations. Within the top sector of the economy, the mobility of labour in combination with 'one-setism' are certain keys to easy adjustment in times of adversity as well as to controlled competition when markets are buoyant. They allow the Ministry of International Trade and Industry to promote concentration and to stimulate growth industries without too much fear of encouraging monopolies. Above all they enable a conglomerate to absorb a considerable loss in one sector of the group's 'economy' without great upheaval, because some other sectors are almost certain to be flourishing. The Japanese experience exemplifies the benefits that can be derived from a policy which starts from the proposition that 'big is malleable' (Shonfield, 1981, p.12).

Bailing out; the Ataka incident

Though the typically Japanese sequence of preparatory consultation, opinion shaping and consensus building (see Chapter 7, p.91, *nemawashi*) which precedes policy decisions in business as in public affairs may appear mysterious, even mystical, in reality it makes a most efficient practical use of the diversified structure of the conglomerate. Among other advantages, it has the virtue of allowing the firms in each group to help one another in a way that has been almost entirely absent in other Western-style economies. Some of this process takes place through the institution of the Presidents' Club, a regular and relatively frequent meeting of the heads of the chief component companies in the conglomerate. The size of the clubs varies, from the twenty-one participants of the integrated Sumitomo to the forty or more of the looser *keiretsu* like Dai-Ichi Kangyo, and the extent to which details of policy are laid down in these meetings is almost certainly in reverse correlation to their size. But though the meetings may be too large to perform an executive role in sorting out the problems of constituent firms, they provide a forum where common strategy can be proclaimed, difficulties aired and the basis for subsequent negotiations established.

The workings of the process remain elusive, but the sequence of preliminaries, meetings and decision-taking would help to explain how such delicate operations are performed as the shedding of some three thousand redundant workers from Mitsubishi's shipyards at Nagasaki and the temporary absorption of all or most of them into Mitsubishi Motors (an 85 per cent-owned subsidiary) and other vigorous Mitsubishi plants. The reabsorption of these men back into shipbuilding (the move was on a three-year basis ending in 1982) sets an even more ticklish problem. Mitsubishi Motors was not booming, and the shipyard operations, though much healthier after restructuring, had been bearing the brunt of the world recession. Of the three thousand workers, some four hundred will have retired or dropped out over the period of three years, but the rest may have to move on once again, perhaps into copper smelting or specialized steels sectors. There is in any case talk about re-engaging shipbuilding workers on less favourable terms, giving them only contingent contracts of employment, and thus removing them from the secure lifetime employment sector.

Moves such as the transfer of labour within Mitsubishi have helped to rescue the vastly overgrown Japanese shipbuilding industry and to reorientate the new slimmed-down shipyards towards the construction of the much smaller ships now required. The Japanese shipbuilding industry could have perished in the years following the first oil shock, had it not been for the fact that most of the shipbuilding capacity was in the hands of the robust giant conglomerates; these were amenable to administrative guidance by the Ministry of Transportation (the ministry responsible for shipyards) and well able to withstand temporary financial shocks—and moreover organized, through their industrial association, into an effective recession cartel.[6] As it was, 85,000 workers were shed—the equivalent of the total labour force in British shipyards—though in spite of the Japanese propensity for consensus, major disagreements arose within the industry about who should bear the brunt of retrenchment. The history of this shipbuilding industry's recession cartel is in fact a healthy reminder that even in Japan consensus building does not always work smoothly. A case in point is the volte-face of ministries and banks in relation to Sasebo Heavy Industries Shipyards in 1978, when the employees of a relatively localized firm, which ran the eighth largest shipyard in the country, successfully petitioned members of the Diet against the ministerial decision to allow their enterprise to fail (Magaziner and Hout, 1980, pp.70–1).

The intricacies of Japanese rescue operations are well illustrated by the history of the salvaging of Ataka in the mid-1970s. When this important trading company was on the point of coming to grief, the usual reluctance of Japanese officialdom and the business community to let a business in the top sector of the economy flounder helped one of Ataka's main financing banks, Sumitomo (the other was Kyowa), to persuade the dynamic trading company C. Itoh to come to Ataka's rescue. But the rescue was slow and painful. The Japanese recognize that international trading companies need particularly stable management and financial support. Ataka had been respectable and successful, but had got into a critical mess over some Canadian operations. Though largely financed by Sumitomo, it was not a member of the group; it is said that Sumitomo Bank let the crisis develop to breaking point in order to force a change of management (which could have been effected more smoothly had Ataka been a Sumitomo company). And C. Itoh was closer to Dai-Ichi Kangyo than to Sumitomo. This may explain the un-Japanese lack of initial detailed preparation, with the deal nearly falling through because C. Itoh objected to the word 'merger' in Sumitomo Bank's press release about the rescue operation; they eventually compromised on the phrase 'business tie-up with the intent to merge'![7]

Even under the favourable economic circumstances of most of the 1970s there have been several similar rescue operations, which have attracted a great deal of comment. The truth is that no company of any size is allowed to deteriorate to the point of bankruptcy; if it did, the very ramifications of the structure of Japanese business might endanger its good name and make large parts of it collapse like a house of cards.

Notes to Chapter 5

1. The *zaibatsu* were the large family-controlled industrial, finance and general business groups which dominated Japanese economic life from the mid-nineteenth century until their dissolution under the American occupation after World War Two. The chief ones were Mitsui, Mitsubishi, Sumitomo and Yasuda.
2. The *keiretsu*—readily identifiable conglomerates of interlocking

firms—usually have a bank (their 'main bank') and a trading company as their core and include a set of companies, often from a variety of key industries, as well as other business interests. The degree of integration (including in most instances the cross-holding of shares by the conglomerate's companies) distinguishes the *keiretsu* from most Western combines.

3. The *zaikai* are business elders who set the tone of Japanese economic management. Some say, ironically, that the *zaikai* system makes the practice of 'business statesmanship' possible; once people reach the pinnacles of the various mountains in their business structure, they leave the younger men to look after the profit-making side of the business. They, the seniors, do not by any means always aim to maximize profits (they have no need to do so in the short term since their shares are predominantly held by other business enterprises which depend on them for benefits other than dividends). Of course, in the long run the companies concerned cannot drop too far out of line with what is regarded as a reasonable rate of return on capital assets; but this leaves the *zaikai* with plenty of room for manoeuvre.

It is also asserted that this consensual élite leadership is breaking down, because of the demise of the first generation of post-war *zaikai*, the increasing formalization of business–government relations, and the growing internationalization of the Japanese economy. But the *zaikai* themselves continue to be confident of their own capacity to remind government about the longer-term effects of economic decisions. (On the *zaikai*, see Curtis, 1975, and Tanaka, 1979.)

4. For Toyota's financial independence see Elston, 1981, p.517.

5. The completeness of the integration of the conglomerates can be exaggerated. In Ronald Dore's view the companies within a group may have preferential bilateral relations with one another, but these networks are not necessarily part of a centrally directed strategy. [*Private communication to the Editor, 1982.*]

6. The role of recession groupings is usefully summarized in Magaziner and Hout (1980, pp.33–7), who make the point that these 'cartels', unlike the 'industry associations' of which they form part, are limited in duration and serve specific restructuring purposes. The term 'industry association' is used here in inverted commas to distinguish the Japanese style from the Western, open to all-comers, type. In Japan, the 'industry association' or 'trade association' may consist of only the leading firms of the main conglomerates, being in effect a cartel. [*Ed.*]

7. For the details of the Ataka case, see Zushi, 1979, pp.204ff.

6

HOW INDUSTRY IS FINANCED

AN important factor that facilitates long-range strategic thinking in economic policy is the comparative freedom of private management from capital market forces. It is even said that the special position of Japan's economic policy-makers is due not to the special relationship between government and businesses, but to the relationship between businesses themselves. The predominant stock ownership in corporations is held by other corporations, and these in turn influence policy, most especially in the banks, towards objectives which may have little to do with the maximization of short-term profits. Their approach is quite different from that of an ordinary private shareholder who has no long-term attachment to the company in which he has invested.

In practice, pressures from the Ministry of Finance have helped to keep dividends low. Whether accruing from an investment in a bank or other financial institution, or coming from industry, a 10 per cent return has been regarded as the maximum. An individual investor with a preference for steady year-by-year income stood to gain from keeping his money in a postal savings account with preferential tax treatment.

Those individual investors who chose to go for capital gains benefited handsomely. The Brookings study, *Asia's New Giant* (Patrick and Rosovsky, 1976, p.306), estimates that there were in the mid-1970s some six million individual shareholders in Japan. But the typical individual shareholding is very small and the aggregate share of private shareholdings has been progressively reduced as owners of these shares have taken very large capital gains, which have come their way as a result of the thirtyfold increase in the value of the stocks quoted on the Tokyo stock exchange during the high growth period prior to 1973. During the last ten years of this period (to be exact from December 1962 to

December 1972) the average yearly return on shares was 20.1 per cent, consisting of perhaps one-third of the total in dividends and the remaining two-thirds in capital gains.[1] All this simply emphasizes the point that in the period of extraordinarily high growth of capital assets (though not of distributed profits) there was a big incentive for the individual shareholder who wanted to make some cash to sell his shares and realize his capital gain. The buyers of these shares have been other corporate enterprises, which by 1979 owned nearly 70 per cent of all the quoted stock of the 1,700 companies listed on the Tokyo stock exchange.

The dramatic reversal in the positions of individual and corporate shareholders is brought out by figures derived from a study by the Nomura Research Institute,[2] and contained in its 1978 annual report, which show the trend over a long period. According to Nomura, individual shareholdings, which stood at 61.3 per cent at their high point in 1950, fell to just under 21 per cent by 1979. The corporate stockholdings included a large proportion of financial companies (nearly 39 per cent in 1979) but this was not just a disguised growth of mutual funds providing a new vehicle for individual investors. In fact, mutual funds had been a favourite form of investment in the early 1950s but then lost their popularity as a result of large losses made by a few of them. By 1972 the proportion of total shareholdings in mutual funds was down to 1.3 per cent, and it has only made a modest increase since then.

There is no real competition among those who run the mutual funds (including Nomura, the finance house which controls the Nomura Research Institute) on the level of declared dividends. Nor do the managers of these funds change their composition very much. According to Nomura executives, their idea is to demonstrate that they are 'stable shareholders' of certain stocks. They would expect to develop a durable relationship with companies in which they have an investment—and also to obtain some of their other financial business. When it is remembered that the four leading securities houses, which hold the mutual funds, have a number of subsidiaries, and together control close to 90 per cent of the whole market for shares, the effect of this set of institutional practices will be seen as decisive.[3]

Interlocking shareholdings

The striking feature of interlocking shareholdings of non-financial companies was referred to above. These non-financial companies increased their shareholdings from 16.6 per cent in 1954 to nearly 34 per cent in 1972, just about doubling their relative importance. It is of the nature of the system of interlocking shareholdings—and in line with the characteristic competitiveness of Japanese industry—that the corporate shareholders are by and large not other corporations in the same line of business. They are rather, more often than not, related companies which have an interest in the stability and success of the company in which they invest, not only because they want a high financial return from it but because they do a trading business with it. This is most clearly expressed in the three biggest conglomerates—Mitsubishi, Mitsui and Sumitomo. But the principle applies, although on a smaller scale, to the other *keiretsu*. And the big securities houses see themselves above all as intermediaries whose business it is to help to introduce stable and reliable shareholders into the share ownership of the companies which are their clients. This is where their real effective power lies.

The amount by which this intra-conglomerate cross-financing diverges from the figure of 23 per cent—the average in 1977 for the six giant conglomerates—is a first-rate measure of the degree of their integration.[4] Mitsubishi claims that 30 per cent of its share capital is held by members of the group itself. The 1977 average for Mitsui, Mitsubishi and Sumitomo was 28 per cent, and this contrasted sharply with the average of 18 per cent for the looser Fuyo, Dai-Ichi Kangyo and Sanwa groups. All these proportions are much higher than those that prevailed in the 1950s, after the American attempt to abolish the *zaibatsu*. There has been a tightening of intra-group financial reins in recent years, and within the top sector, Japanese industry finds it much easier to finance its investment needs from its own resources than in the past.[5]

The Nomura view is that the trend in operations since the late 1950s, giving companies and institutions a steadily increasing proportion of the total shareholding in industrial and commercial quoted companies, will continue in the period ahead. Industrial companies try to make sure in any case that a substantial packet of any new share issues—at least some 20 per cent—is allocated to certain favoured groups of shareholders; these are invariably companies with which they have a special relationship.

In Mitsubishi's case, the conglomerate includes not only the Mitsubishi Bank but also two of the biggest insurance companies in Japan, and they are in turn very large shareholders in the group's main bank. In common with other banks and financial institutions,[6] the Mitsubishi Bank was in 1977 ordered by the Fair Trade Commission to reduce *its* holdings in the other companies to a maximum of 5 per cent of their capital. They have been given ten years in which to do this, and there is no suggestion of panic about following the directive. The excess holdings are in any case never large since they have been kept down by the Anti-Trust Law after the post-1945 shake-up. The maximum permitted stake up to 1954 had also been 5 per cent (Miyazaki, 1980, p.323) and in the years 1954 to 1977 was limited to 10 per cent of the equity of any one company. In the late 1970s, Mitsubishi Bank's holding of the conglomerate's own equity amounted to around 8 per cent. Like the other main banks of the *keiretsu*, it is proceeding very gradually in the placing of its excess holdings, looking around for 'stable' shareholders of the stocks which it has to sell.

The idea is simply that a company needs the freedom for its management which is provided by having a large number of corporate shareholders who are durable investors in its stocks. It is evident that a shareholding of one-third or so held by other members of a group who concert their policy through the group's own collective machinery means that no one is likely to challenge their effective control. In fact it is the custom for companies before their annual meeting to have a series of special meetings with the big shareholders. These are invariably other corporations. The result is that annual 'general' meetings pass off with only a very rare intervention from the side of the individual shareholders questioning any management decisions.

The other effects of the degree of intra-conglomerate cross-financing have been referred to when discussing the various types of group structure. Toyota, we saw, was an extreme example, and complaints have been voiced in the Ministry of Trade and Industry (MITI) that the all but complete financial independence of this company has made it impervious to the pressures of governmental intervention, whether by administrative guidance or by the control of credit.

A number of other groups, predominantly in the high-growth industries, remain relatively independent simply because of successful trading and also by reason of their centralized structure. In these groups—concerns such as Hitachi, Toshiba, Matsushita—the parent company almost invariably owns 50 per cent plus of the share capital of other subsidiary enterprises in the group, on a pattern familiar in Western experience.

There is no likely escape from this interlocking structure— indeed it is highly convenient to the managers of companies who no longer have to take any notice of individual owners of anything— *unless* the authorities in the Ministry of Finance and MITI decide to liberalize their attitude to dividend rates. But there is no sign of any change towards a high dividend policy. When in the past some of the steel companies and the electric power companies decided to raise their dividends, MITI intervened to dissuade them. And, after all, why should companies raise their dividends when their main stockholders are happy enough with the existing arrangements? A natural consequence of this lack of competition for new shareholders and of the non-assertiveness of existing private shareholders is the general reinforcement of technocratic power throughout Japanese big industry and commerce.

Changes in the financial power structure

All in all, the private sector is highly sceptical of the degree of change which the Ministry of Finance will willingly permit in the present system despite everyone's lip-service to the freeing of market forces. One factor is the obvious self-interest of officials of the Finance Ministry in the present system. If market forces were really allowed to rule, then the post-retirement careers of officials would be much less attractive. Nor is it at all clear that the people in the four main securities and finance corporations (i.e. the underwriters and dealers in securities) would like to see a change in the system.

It is occasionally a nuisance for a firm such as Nomura to be accused by the government, as it was in late 1978, of rigging the bond market and forcing up the rate of interest on government bonds. The accusation could not easily be rebutted, because Nomura does control some 30 per cent plus of all government bond transactions in the secondary market. They were, according to their own account of the case, engaged in a heated controversy on this matter with the Ministry of Finance. They argued that their case was after all no different from that of the German financial market, where the three big banks very largely determine current interest rates and therefore the price of bonds. This at least was the argument the Japanese themselves propounded; it is in reality a considerable exaggeration of the degree of control exercised by the *Grossbanken* on the German money market. Nevertheless, since the German banks do conduct the great bulk of the stock market transactions on behalf of their customers, there is a certain similarity between their position and that of the Japanese securities houses.

The power of these Japanese securities houses in fact goes much further, since as we have seen, the apparently independent smaller institutions which amount altogether to less than a hundred companies are to an overwhelming extent controlled by the Big Four. Permission to engage in different types of securities business has to be obtained by licence from the Ministry of Finance. It is only the biggest of the securities houses, including some seven houses in the layer below the Big Four, which have the right to engage in all forms of transactions, including underwriting. The satellite companies find it convenient to live under the shadow of one of the Big Four, since the parent will in case of need provide them with temporary finance to cope with the rather sharp fluctuations in share prices which occur in the Tokyo stock exchange, and they accept managing directors and other senior officials who are sent out to govern them from the middle ranks of the officials of the Big Four. The actual shareholding in the smaller companies is generally rather small, between 3–5 per cent. However, on occasion it may become larger when the smaller house becomes indebted to the bigger as a result of the financing of share transactions (on behalf of its customers) which leaves it in a position where it has to turn to the big company for finance; but it is no part of the aim of the big to obtain larger shareholdings in the smaller companies—effective control can be secured by more personal means. The net effect, so far as the Ministry of Finance is concerned, is that through its contacts with the Big Four and their responsiveness to its behests, it effectively exercises control over companies conducting the great bulk of transactions in the market.

All this explains why the Finance Ministry is likely to resist proposals for reform which might create an effective secondary market, although such a market would have considerable, recognized advantages for the management of public finance.[7] With the budget in huge deficit, the government finds it difficult to mobilize the large volume of long-term savings by individuals. These savings should be readily available because the big industrial companies are not coming forward with heavy demands for finance; their own liquid resources have been built up to the point where they are able to take care of their own investment needs to a far greater extent than in the past. They also have access to international sources of finance. So there is no question of 'crowding out' by the government in the capital market.

One major dilemma remains. The government has been considering how it might turn over some of the public corporations to the private sector, in order to take the weight of financing them off its back. Unfortunately, however, the bulk of these corporations, at any rate those which are profitable, are included in FILP[8] and so do not affect the general budget deficit, running at the end of the 1970s at an annual average of around 35 per cent of total government expenditure. But the fact that this kind of device is being discussed indicates how seriously the budget deficit is regarded. It is in fact a constraint on the major increase in the public financing of social infrastructure which forward-looking Japanese officials see as one of the main sources of growth in the period ahead. They are not looking for an increase in the scale of direct public sector involvement, but an expansion of the sources of finance available to public authorities for the financing of the new generation of investments in the private sector.

Notes to Chapter 6

1. This is necessarily an uncertain calculation, and is based on the rate of return on different kinds of deposits and bonds: one-year bonds yielded 6 per cent and longer-term deposits something more than this. Life insurance, which might be regarded as an alternative form of investment for the individual shareholder, yielded 8.3 per cent.
2. The Nomura Research Institute is associated with the largest finance house and is a 'problem-solving' consultancy and research institute in the fields of industrial economics, business planning, environmental studies and biology.

3. The main securities houses are—besides Nomura—Nikko, Daiwa and Yamaichi. The implication is that only those parts of *new* issues which issuing companies reserve for their own associates (see pp.81–2) are outside the control (whether direct or indirect) of these four houses.

4. See *Industrial Review of Japan*, 1980, p.50. For a fuller study of intra-group cohesion as measured by interlocking shareholdings, see the essays by Kiyonari and Nakamura (1980) and by Futatsugi (1980).

5. This has two results: one is that the break-even point for industrial activity of the big corporations has been lowered—they no longer need to press to the limits of capacity in order to meet the high fixed costs which were characteristic of the operations of Japanese companies during the period of very high growth until 1973; the other is that the control exercised by creditor banks, and through them by the central bank, over the economic activities of companies has been weakened. By the same token, the big companies are no longer queuing to obtain the concessionary finance which has been made available to them in the past, and is still available for certain purposes, from MITI. The net effect is that the old-style system of the guidance of Japanese investment from the centre is breaking down, because the companies have managed to break loose from the financial constraints which have hitherto tied them.

[*Editor's note*]:
According to Uekusa (1982), while there was generally a slight increase in intra-group cross-holding of shares between 1975 and 1978, the proportion of loan finance drawn from the groups' main banks declined.

In this connection the article by C. D. Elston (1981) argues that the financial involvement of Japanese banks in industrial finance has been exaggerated by Japanese accounting practice: 'Contrary to received doctrine, between the periods 1954–63 and 1964–73 companies' dependence on borrowing declined and internal sources of funding increased in importance' (p.517). At the same time many successful firms have been turning to foreign sources of finance. The indigenous bank funds have been going to the less well-situated companies.

6. Trusts, insurance and securities companies and mutual bonds.

7. Proposals for the reform of the money market and of the financial system were in the air at the end of the 1970s. It was being stressed that one of the first things which had to be done was to establish a secondary market in government bonds; otherwise the banks which are more or less compelled to subscribe to these bonds would get stuck with them as their price diminished (with the rise in interest rates), and at the same time government itself, because of its commitment to the big thirteen

'city banks', would not be able to go to a wider public for direct subscription to such bonds.

That such changes were still some distance away was apparent from the fact that a number of extremely powerful institutions, including the Industrial Bank of Japan, were strenuously against the development of a free market in bonds. They themselves had too much at stake in the business of issuing their own bonds to the public at large, and wanted to leave the government bonds in their existing state, confined to the 'primary market'. This had proved extremely inconvenient to the government during a period of falling bond prices when it was compelled to buy back bonds held by the banks at higher market prices in order to avoid the dangerous effects on confidence of the large losses which the banks would otherwise have had to show on their bond holdings. However, the fact that the Industrial Bank's holding of government paper is low-powered money, in the sense that it cannot be used as collateral for any further credit transactions, means that the official control over the system, a non-inflationary type of control, is reinforced (Wallich, 1976). There is therefore a reluctance to give up this additional instrument for putting pressure on the system.

8. The Fiscal Investment and Loan Programme (FILP) provides financing for public (central and local government) enterprises, such as railways, roads and public housing. It also supplies the funds which public lending agencies such as the Japan Development Bank lend to selected private companies. The funds distributed via FILP are not part of the government's regular budget, though they are subject to control by the Diet. In the late 1970s and in 1980 they amounted to more than 40 per cent of the budget (or around 8 per cent of GNP) and were an important means by which the public authorities exercised discretionary short-term fiscal pressures. [*Ed.*]

7

STYLES OF INTERVENTION

THE Japanese are expert at integrating short-term pressures into long-term structures. The authorities, to a degree unusual in the West, have manged to combine the Japanese style of fine tuning—a system in which government got individual firms to respond rapidly to short-term policy changes while maintaining the long-term strategy intact—with a high rate of growth. This is because the Japanese economy has in the past been exceptionally responsive to short-term shifts in credit policy. At the same time Japanese business remained confident that as soon as the central bank was satisfied that balance of payments *and* relatively stable prices had been attained, it would allow credit to accommodate long-term expansion needs.

But even though short-term advantage has not been bought at the cost of long-term rigidity, fine tuning has been losing credibility, in Japan as elsewhere. The declared preference now is for an effective market system, though this has not stopped the authorities from exercising their very special style of nudging the economic system in the chosen direction.

If Japan is a mixed economy, it is in the American and German sense of having a government which systematically intervenes at various levels of the economic structure—not in the British, French and Italian sense of taking over entire or partial responsibility for certain sectors of the economy, be it the most successful or those which limp in the most pronounced fashion. However, compared with the US and German and, for that matter, most European planning, the Japanese variety is considerably wider in scope. The intervention is more thorough and its effect also more thoroughgoing. It relies, like so many other aspects of Japanese life, on the preparatory process of consensus building.

Planners' brushwork

These nuances are reflected in recent Japanese notions on planning. The voice of the administration in the discussion on the new seven-year plan during the summer of 1979 was perhaps not hectoring but also by no means halting. The new plan relied heavily on the use of public expenditures, especially in the first phase of the plan up to about 1983, to stimulate investment and increase the level of employment. The second instrument for boosting employment was seen to be in the continuing growth of the tertiary sector of the economy. The official view, as expressed by the Economic Planning Agency (EPA) vice-minister, Isamu Miyazaki, held that no special measures would be required to secure the second; it would just be a continuation of a process which has been strongly in train during the 1970s. The problem might be to secure sufficient investment in this sector, in view of the fact that the big businesses with the strongest finances were somewhat disinclined to invest in it. This has been clearly borne out by the attitudes of the executives in the big industrial groups like Mitsubishi, who claim that they have no expertise in this kind of activity and that it raises problems of the management of employment which they would find difficult to surmount.

The trouble could however be precisely the other way about. The planners were relying on the relative inefficiency of the tertiary sector and the high labour intensity to deal with the unemployment problem. Achieving full employment was one of the stated aims of the plan. If by some awkward chance efficiency in the tertiary sector were to rise very sharply, then the employment plans of the EPA would be jeopardized.

The plan stated as one of its objectives the general extension of the five-day week to a much larger proportion of the working population, using government offices as a model for the reduction in the hours of work. It would of course be open to the policy-makers, if employment in the tertiary sector did not rise as rapidly as had been planned, to raise demand, or accelerate the process of reducing working hours and increasing paid holidays, or to postpone further the achievement of another objective which was to increase the levels of employment of older workers, between sixty and sixty-five, towards which some progress had been made before it was held up during the recession which followed the second oil shock. The conclusion, as Japanese commentators were quick to point out, was that a great deal of fine tuning would be required to make the plan work. The government would among other things have to increase its share of the national product taken in taxes by around 0.5 per cent each year up to 1985, partly in order to get rid of the very large deficit (which had grown to 40 per cent of total expenditure in the 1979[1] budget), and partly to raise the level of social security payments and investment. This is the exact opposite of the trend in the rest of the OECD. But the Japanese do not seem to be ready tax-payers and their high level of business investment in recent years has been at least in part due to the relatively very low rate of personal income taxation. Certainly, the Finance Ministry was, at the time of the 1979 debate about the new plan, feeling very constrained about any proposed increase in taxation beyond that required to eliminate the budget deficit. Social welfare plans were being stretched out over very long periods. In education, for example, the original plan foresaw a— plainly overdue—reduction in the average size of classes from forty-five to forty over a period of five years. This was subsequently increased to nine years, and it looks as though other economies too had watered down the original plan.

In the sphere of social security, there was in the 1979 plan considerable fluidity—not to say uncertainty—about the total amounts to be paid over annually in pensions.[2] The sole reason for the sharp rise in transfer payments in the period to 1985 is the changing demographic structure of the Japanese population. The EPA's calculations suggest that, because of the ageing of the population, the Japanese welfare requirements would, on the trends prevailing at the end of the 1970s, reach something like the current Swedish level by the end of the century. During the early 1980s Japan would continue to have exceptional advantages over the other OECD countries. Although the demographic trend would begin to deteriorate at this stage, the structure of the population would remain for a while highly favourable, with a large proportion of young people in the labour force. The rate of decline thereafter will be very steep indeed. This eventual big increase in the proportion of aged causes a number of people to regard the years up to the mid-1980s as the last opportunity in which very high levels of investment will be feasible. Some of the EPA planners consider that the rate of growth of the economy is bound to decline quite sharply from the middle 1980s onwards, so that very high levels of investment in social infrastructure as well as in productive equipment will be required until then in order to secure the very high rates of productivity necessary to support a much older population.

There is, besides, the whole issue of moving much more social welfare activity over from its present sources of funding, by private firms in the top sector of the economy, to the public sector. The big private firms, whose finances are in any case strained by the new economic circumstances, are in favour of such a move. They want to maintain their capacity for self-financing, their relative independence from banks; their current slogans are high profits and the maintenance of liquidity, and not all of them remain enthusiastic about maintaining the full advantages of the lifetime employment system for a very large proportion of their employees.

Administrative guidance

There is no doubt that administrative guidance is used in Japan on a much larger scale than anything we know in Europe, let alone in the United States. It is seen to work and its effectiveness expresses, most of the time, a consensus in which the will of the industrialists is at least as much involved as that of the officials. Above all, acts of government intervention are designed to promote market forces, not to inhibit them. Before guidance takes place many hundreds of people will often have been involved in reaching a consensual decision. Much has been written about this process of consensus preparation. It has been likened to an operation which the Japanese call *nemawashi*—the methodical preparation of a tree or shrub for transplantation. Anyone who has stood by while a patient team of gardeners lowers by crane a full-grown evergreen, its huge bole of earth-surrounded roots carefully bound with straw and sacking, into a hole prepared in a minuscule Tokyo garden will appreciate the sense of the metaphor. The Japanese talk of *nemawashi* first when they try to explain their record of successful government relations, or of harmonious labour relations.

There is no evidence that the formal institutions for achieving consensus at high administrative level, the advisory councils which exist in Japanese ministries and other government agencies, are particularly effective. This inheritance from the American occupation is 'little more than window-dressing for the public'.[3] But the informal network of former civil servants who have become absorbed into big industry is much more important. Most Japanese senior officials retire early—no later than fifty-four or fifty-five. In particular there is a convention which makes the contemporaries of a newly-appointed vice-minister (the ministry's senior official) resign in order to avoid the embarrassment of orders passing from him to those who are his equal in seniority. As vice-ministers are appointed for two years only, every second year sees the retirement of, say, four or five directors-general from MITI and a similar number from the Ministry of Finance (which, incidentally, has been the training ground of several recent prime ministers). Quite a few of the senior administrators will moreover have left the civil service much earlier, probably in their late forties as soon as it became evident that they could not aspire to vice-ministerial heights.

After a decent interval of apparent retirement each of these former civil servants (or at least every one who does not choose to enter politics) will be absorbed into big industry, a process known as the 'descent from heaven' (*amakudari*). The regard in which these late entrants are held by business concerns and the competition for securing the best of them has become well known in the West. There is, however, also evidence that the key jobs in the prestige firms are very much sought after, so that the more far-sighted senior civil servants will during the run-up period seek to get on especially good terms with the leaders of the industries they regulate. Thus the industrialist may try to please the civil servant in order to secure his future services, and conversely, the civil servant puts a great deal into the effort to be on good terms with the leader of a concern in which he hopes to work after his first 'retirement'. Most important, the two groups, senior civil servants and top executives, know each other and each other's aspirations, and may, indeed, have been exact contemporaries at the same university. Those of the retiring civil servants who have preferred a late political career will also have nursed their connections with chosen big firms, depending on contributions from industry for the astronomical costs of conducting a Japanese electoral contest.

MITI's light touch

At the end of the 1970s the Ministry of Finance was obsessed by the idea of cutting down the budget deficit. It was accordingly seen as the villain of the piece which made planning impossible. The frustration of the old-style planners, for example in the Japan Development Bank, has been evident. They look back on the heroic period of the middle-60s onwards when they chose 'trigger industries' like steel, petrochemicals and most especially tanker shipbuilding (which was given preferential rates of interest at a rate as low as 3.5 per cent—well under half of the market rate)[4], with undisguised nostalgia. In the late 1970s they were talking about the possible trigger industries for the 1980s, which were going to be especially needed now that the rate of investment had fallen so much, adding resignedly that the Finance Ministry was bound to frustrate them—much as the French planners complained in the middle 1960s when de Gaulle's government reduced the significance of the plan in the allocation of public finance and largely ignored it when making the budget.

The view in the Japan Development Bank was that unless they were given a freer hand in providing low-interest loans—they in fact had plenty of cash but were restricted on the rates of interest they were allowed to charge—it would be the end of indicative planning in the private sector. They saw their new mission as promoting housing, the aircraft industry and advanced technology generally (as well as investing abroad), but the tight money policy of the Ministry of Finance hampered the process. What was needed—and there were a few senior officials at the Ministry of Finance who also recognized it—was a return to the 1960s' form of planning, aimed at raising the level of private investment well above what it would reach if it depended entirely on market forces, in effect an argument for high subsidies to increase the marginal efficiency of capital during a period of structural change.

While the Ministry of Finance was hanging back at the end of the 1970s, MITI, like the Japan Development Bank, continued to be eager to boost selected industries. MITI is by far the most important channel of administrative guidance, although several other ministries perform parallel roles: the Ministry of Health and Welfare in the case of pharmaceuticals, the Ministry of

Transportation for shipbuilding, the Ministry of Posts and Tele-communications for telecommunications equipment.[5]

In the thirty or so years of its existence, not all MITI's methods have been the relatively gentle ones of administrative guidance. Until the mid-60s it kept a tight rein on the allocation of foreign exchange for purchases of essential materials abroad. More recently it continued to make use of import licensing to encourage the purchase of promising foreign technology. However, its chief tool has been, and continues to be, the power to regulate the allocation of new investment, whether to secure orderly expansion, or more recently, to prevent a net increase in capacity while improving the value-added in chosen industries.

By late 1979 the prevailing view was, however, that the old power which MITI derived from its authority over distribution of import licences and export aids had diminished. But another tool, MITI's influence in determining favourable ('two-digit') rates of depreciation for tax purposes, remains. In a period of industrial restructuring, with the need to write off, for example, new plant in the shipbuilding industry, the power of determining depreciation allowances may be an important means of leverage.

Although the increased profits and liquidity of the big companies, as well as the rationalization of their investment policies, may have made them less responsive to MITI's pressures, people with specific experience of applying administrative guidance claim the Ministry continues to exercise a major influence, and to be the chief instrument for deciding economic priorities.

Despite the earlier shift towards a market economy, in the current period of industrial restructuring, with public policy stressing the need for growth in the service sector, the areas of private enterprise in which government intervenes to determine priorities are once again becoming more numerous. Equally important is the more active role of government in managing international transactions, not only in the allocation of export quotas in restricted products such as cars, steel, ships, which are restricted by Orderly Marketing Agreements, but also in financial operations such as guiding the flow of Japanese investment abroad, for example through differential investment guarantees according to country and type of industrial enterprise.

Challenging guidance: the Hyuga case

In the process of administrative guidance, the corporatist forces in Japanese society come into full play. However, there are particular matters on which a ministry official may take the initiative on his own. Certain Nissan executives for instance are convinced that delay in obtaining official acquiescence to their proposal to introduce a 2.8 litre engine into a sports car model was the result of the resentment of a middle-grade official at the Ministry of Transportation, who considered that on a previous occasion Nissan had bypassed the proper channels and made contact over some matter of company business at 'too high a level' in the ministerial hierarchy. No wonder that managers, at least at the middle operating level, believe it could be highly inconvenient to ignore the wishes (if this is how one can refer to quite powerful pressures) of the people in MITI or the other departments in charge of administrative guidance.

Textiles provide an illustration of some special difficulties which the government administrators encounter when the industry they are trying to guide comprises, in addition to several major units, a large number of unintegrated small producers. At the time of the great controversy over textile exports to the United States, in 1969–71, both Prime Minister Sato, and the minister responsible for foreign affairs, Fukuda, badly wanted agreement with the US government over the limitation of the trade in Japanese textiles shipped to America; they had moreover persuaded the MITI minister to go along with them. But the case proved peculiarly recalcitrant: the MITI minister was defied by his own subordinate officials, who worked with the various textile constituencies to resist the high-level political decision to restrict textile shipments. A particular problem was that Sato was believed to have given President Nixon a promise about the matter before the necessary *nemawashi* had been completed. In the end the American promise to return Okinawa to their sovereignty counted for less as persuasion to the Japanese than the very generous provision of subsidies in the form of 'adjustment assistance' by the Japanese government to the small textile manufacturers.

On the other hand, there are few examples of overt resistance to the direction by public authority. The sequence of events most commonly cited—perhaps because it appears to be the earliest and the only major instance of sustained defiance of MITI ordinances—is generally known as the Hyuga case, the surname being that of the chief actor, Hosai Hyuga, chairman of Sumitomo Metals. The case is worth examining in detail, for its very existence underlines the more common success of guidance by Japan's administrators.

Back in the early 1960s, MITI, impatient about the slow response of the steel industry, decided to promote the construction of new blast furnaces by some of the steel giants. Sumitomo's policy at this stage was to follow its own planned rhythm of growth, in the belief that problems of financing and technology do not in any case allow firms to pursue indiscriminate expansion.

In the mid-1960s Sumitomo once again fell out of step. A new vice-minister, Sahashi, had recently been appointed to MITI, who was regarded as something of a maverick. On his own admission, he was certainly not the most conciliatory of civil servants: he later wrote a book describing his struggle within the ministry with another official who eventually replaced him. As for Hyuga, he was in the mid-1960s chief executive of Sumitomo Metal Industries, Osaka-centred and, as noted earlier (p.72), traditionally assertive of its independence—the third or fourth largest steel producer in Japan, with around one-tenth of total output. Both Hyuga and Sahashi seemed in some measure to enjoy the open conflict. Sumitomo, incidentally, had an advantage over the ministry in that it possessed a public relations section of which it made good use, whereas MITI at that time had no public relations office at the ministry.

When, during a period of relatively difficult trading, MITI tried to arrange for the orderly cutting of output until business improved, Sumitomo protested. The dispute came to a head over the allocation of the production quota of crude steel for the third quarter of 1965. MITI subjected Sumitomo to a 10 per cent cut which Hyuga said was excessive. He refused to adhere to the allocation of reduced output between the big companies, which was accompanied by an imposition of a higher price on sales for domestic consumption (aimed at meeting foreign complaints about the dumping of Japanese steel on their markets). MITI, on its side, as part of a general programme of deceleration of investment, postponed the granting of an application by Sumitomo for the construction of additional blast furnace capacity.

Moreover, at this stage Sumitomo also found itself in conflict with the other major steel companies which, along with the rest of the industry, had accepted the proposal for this deceleration of investment. As seen from the point of view of Hyuga's firm, the market shares of the biggest companies, notably Yawata and Fuji (the latter soon to merge with Nippon Steel), were being protected by former colleagues of their executives, in the Ministry of International Trade and Industry. (As it happened, Sumitomo was at that time the only big steel producer which did not have a former MITI official on its board of directors. In several of the other companies the ex-MITI man was the president.)

Hyuga argued that even though the ministry was right in its fear that the new investment would lead to over-capacity, Sumitomo, as a capitalist enterprise, had the 'right to lose money' through following its own judgment. Sahashi's reaction was to threaten to cut the allocation of imported coking coal for Sumitomo Metal, in spite of the accepted rule that such allocations were made by licences issued by the ministry on the basis of proven need, and that no one had expressed any doubt about the need of Sumitomo for the raw materials to keep production going.

At the early stages of the argument a first compromise was arranged which allowed Sumitomo to go ahead with its investment (presumably at the cost of some other steel company cutting back *its* investment plan) while Sumitomo agreed to accept a 10 per cent reduction in its output quota for the second quarter of the year. However, it refused to cut back again to the same extent in the third quarter, arguing that its exports should be excluded from the allocation calculation. MITI offered a second compromise with a somewhat smaller cut than 10 per cent for the third quarter, but this too was turned down by Sumitomo.

In November 1965 Hosai Hyuga publicly announced his disagreement with the MITI allocations, but the ministry stood firm and refused the request for a review of its arrangements for the reduction of output. At the same time it again threatened to cut the import allocation of coking coal for Sumitomo. The MITI minister, Takeo Miki (who later became prime minister), next stepped in and offered a compromise designed to meet Sumitomo's special needs. However, this offer, which was made in private conversation, was withdrawn on Sahashi's insistence, and the next day Sumitomo announced that it refused to accept the new allocation for the period January–March 1966, despite a repetition of the MITI threat about raw material cuts. A number of other organizations now intervened. From Osaka the Kansai Business Federation protested on Hyuga's side; in Tokyo the Keidanren (the powerful federation of business organizations) tried to settle the business by agreement between the industrialists involved. With the conflict out in the open, there was the additional problem of avoiding loss of face by anybody.

Finally, at the end of December 1965, 'after forty days of fighting', Sumitomo agreed to cut its output on condition that MITI engaged in a 'fundamental review' of the allocation system, which was to be initiated in the first quarter of 1966. The minister agreed to this, and Sumitomo did reduce its output, though by a smaller amount than the 10 per cent originally proposed.[6]

Toeing the line

People in the know say that the Hyuga case was wholly exceptional, especially since the parties concerned did not try very hard to arrive at a consensus before the disagreement came out into the open. There have been other cases in the past when a particular ministry disagreed with some corporate decision—notably the Ministry of Finance and the Bank of Japan during the early stages of the very high growth of Japanese industrial production (which they thought excessive)—but MITI was always expected to argue matters out in advance with the industrialists, and it usually won out in any conflict. It did so in the accelerated growth of the automobile industry in the 1950s and also in some of the early big steel investment decisions to which the Finance Ministry objected at that time. Open conflict is regarded as extraordinary. That is not to say that there are not disagreements on particular matters with individual officials. They seem to happen not infrequently, and they are bound to occur when an official is given discretion in decisions over so many matters of important industrial concern. In spite of all the consensus-seeking routines, there are also, as we have seen, particular matters on which the official himself will have the initiative. But the art of consensus building, aided by the movement of former officials into big industry, almost invariably prevents administrative guidance from becoming an issue of public controversy.

And so the conclusion must be that though some Japanese companies like the rhetoric of contempt for government and for bureaucracy in general, they take administrative guidance very seriously indeed. In this respect they are much more like French business than any other Western one. Even a high-up company manager in an important group such as Nissan finds that a middle-grade official in the bureaucracy will simply summon him to his office to discuss some point of company policy; and the company executive, although annoyed, feels it necessary to send some people over—slightly less senior than himself—in order to placate the civil servant. Managers are taught that it does not do to lift the level of controversy with a ministry official to the top, if this can possibly be avoided. It tends to have secondary effects when other issues come up and the offended official mobilizes his colleagues to make life difficult for the company concerned. The Japanese themselves comment that, in this respect, their practice is totally different from the American one—the US idea being that you take things 'right to the top'. So although it is feasible for Japanese company managers to use the political channel, via committees of the Diet, to exercise pressure on officials—the politicians being rather sensitive to company objectives in view of the large sums spent on political party contributions—there is a certain reluctance to do so. It may be that managers will gradually learn that they have more freedom of manoeuvre than they at present think. But the view of middle-grade officials at operating level seems to be that not very much has yet changed.

One of the incidental effects of the awareness of government intervention is to make it more attractive for some companies to take their business investment abroad and expand rapidly there, in order to liberate themselves from some of the domestic pressures. This applies particularly to the newer companies which do not see themselves as being on the 'inside track' (i.e. belonging to one of the established industrial groups with whom the ministry officials like to do business).

Certain companies—once again Nissan is an example—have set up importing organizations which aim to internationalize the sources of their products. By the late 1970s, Nissan (through its importing organization established in 1974 as part of the firm's

Procurement Department) was importing foreign components at the rate of 17 billion yen or more a year. Handling such an enormous volume of import business involves the company in all sorts of foreign relationships which government officials know they can interfere with only at some risk. This is a clear example of Japanese business learning to use international pressures in order to influence the decision over some domestic matter in its own favour. Nissan's more recently established general company— DAT Export—which was first set up with the aim of helping the British improve their trade balance and thus afford the import of more Nissan vehicles—appears to be diversifying part of its purchases. What has been essentially a Japanese manufacturing organization is beginning to turn into a *general* trading business.

This internationalization, which enables the big Japanese companies to mobilize resources for investment in foreign capital markets—and also to invest much more freely abroad, possibly at the cost of home investment—almost certainly does more to free the big firms from official influence than their greater financial independence.

A weakening of control

Everyone agrees that *some* of the instruments of government planning used so effectively in the past have been weakened; but there is considerable disagreement about how significant the effects of the change are likely to be. Those who aver that the old system has gone forever believe that already the greatly increased liquidity of big companies, having made them very independent of the banks, has also lifted many of the pressures exercised through the banks by the Bank of Japan on behalf of the government. Moreover, because of the process of 'polarization', which is recognized to exist between the performance of the leaders in a large number of industries and the other big firms with a lower level of efficiency, this spirit of financial independence among the firms which set the pace in the Japanese economy is likely to increase. There is statistical evidence based on a sample of Japanese manufacturers to show that in a number of industries the 'leaders' are increasing the gap between themselves and the 'followers' (although the latter include some very large and hitherto quite successful Japanese firms). The leaders typically generate much more profit and are far more independent of outside financing than the followers. At the same time the return on their shares is higher, while the followers have to distribute a larger proportion of their profits in dividends and so have less left over for the self-financing of company investment.

What will happen in the long run as these industries tend to become more and more concentrated in the hands of the leaders, who will grow very much faster than the followers? Will it be possible for Japanese policy-makers, who in spite of their marked attraction to oligopolistic solutions may wish to curb any excesses, to use regulation as a means of avoiding the consequences of a highly monopolistic type of structure? The followers will tend if anything to grow increasingly dependent on the good will of the officials in MITI (another example of dualism in the economy in the making). But in the ordinary way the planners really want to exercise their influence chiefly on the leaders, who are seen as growing less dependent on the good will of the powerful regulators sitting in government offices.

There is the prevailing impression that MITI and the other administrative guidance bodies have lost some of their original leverage, but that the *capacity* for public intervention may not have been eroded. In fact, besides the obvious direct power afforded by anti-depression measures, new means of asserting influence (such as regulation of the relocation of industry) are being added to the armoury. Officials of the Economic Planning Agency seem to assume that it will be possible to reach out and influence those concerned because there will continue to be the necessary concentrations of power, and it is true that administrative guidance in one form or another is still very much a factor in the thinking of the big firms, though whether it would be treated by them as a source of *precise* guidance on future investment policies is more doubtful.

Was it in fact consistently influential in the past? The guidance was important for certain selected industrial sectors, which had been chosen for attention by MITI. But plans were much less significant as a source of guidance for entrepreneurs over the economy as a whole. That much is shown by the fact that during the 1960s and early 1970s actual performance in investment and production consistently exceeded the planned amounts.

Those who hold that there is still a great deal of mileage in the

Japanese style of public control can perhaps stand this argument about planning on its head—as some of the most sophisticated Japanese observers have been doing—and argue that it was at the end of the 1970s, when entrepreneurs became aware of the probable limits to be set on the rate of expansion by factors beyond their control, that the views of the EPA began to be taken more seriously. In the 1960s, when expansion had been a free-for-all, the issue of guidance for particular sectors had been of much less importance. This is not to say that the EPA has retained all its earlier reputation. But the notion that it has lost credibility altogether and has simply been seen as a rather weak rival of MITI seems to be mistaken: some of its planning documents have been treated very seriously, as indeed has been the more recent development of long-term forecasting, the Long-term Fiscal Plan of the Ministry of Finance.

Notes to Chapter 7

1. April 1979–March 1980.
2. The standard cash benefit for a retired fully-entitled married couple was in 1977 comparable with those of Germany, Sweden and USA. However, the state comprehensive social pension system is of relatively recent date and covers only a small proportion of the retired population (see Japan, EPA, August 1979, p.35, and OECD, *Japan*, 1976, pp.39–40).
3. This is the view of Toshio Shishido, a former MITI official (quoted from Allen Taylor, 1973, p.200, in Patrick and Rosovsky, 1976, p.785, n.56).
4. This boost to shipbuilding operated from 1953 to 1974. It was resumed in 1979 in an attempt to tide shipyards over a critical period and to improve the competitiveness of the Japanese shippers. Government covered between 3 and 3.5 per cent of interest charges; these subsidies, which were intended to last until the end of the fiscal year 1982, were, like the earlier ones, funded by the Japan Development Bank.
5. Not all the organs of administrative guidance are contained in ministries. The Industrial Bank of Japan has a quasi-public function: it is treated by the authorities as retaining part of its historic role, from the time when it was a public sector corporation. In the period of reconstruction after the end of World War Two, the Americans took a highly ideological position in the matter of the Industrial Bank of Japan: it was felt to be an agent of Japan's imperial–commercial complex, a dangerously effective instrument for the intrusion of

government policy into what, in the eyes of the occupying forces, ought to be the purely private sector. It was therefore privatized. But in the event everyone recognized that IBJ's function was still very much the same as prior to privatization. All that was asked of it was that it make sufficient profit to keep up with the dividend payments which were normally made by successful banks in the market. But it is seen by the informed as an instrument of long-term public policy. It does not obtain its funds from the ordinary investor but from FILP (see p.87, n.5) and by the sale of bonds to other banks, and its staff is recruited from people who are not predominantly profit-oriented.

6. A vice-minister of MITI who was appointed later on, after the Hyuga débâcle, became the president of Sumitomo Metals in the 1970s. But the contentious vice-minister Sahashi never got a big appointment in a large industrial corporation on his retirement.

8

LABOUR AND THE DUAL ECONOMY

ONE is inclined to point to a particular feature of the Japanese economic system as being the one that makes for health. The truth is less simple. These special 'Japanese' features apply in combination; moreover, they interact in subtle ways. Administrative guidance would not work if receptive business was not organized into large constellations with a degree of cohesion and a large measure of co-operation. The system would break down if individual component firms of these conglomerates were not capable of forming 'anti-recession cartels' which link the main competitors in a single industry in the pursuit of common objectives; these 'cartels' are formally under the tutelage of their 'industry association' (see n.6, p.78), but are stimulated and shaped by MITI.

Business would neither adapt nor innovate but for the flexible labour market—depending on the dual structure of the economy, which in turn depends to a large extent on the weight of the conglomerates. (It is incidentally a curious example of prevailing moods in economic thought that the concept of the dual economy, to the fore in the late 1960s and early 1970s, has more recently gone out of fashion.)

The belief that the key to the high growth rates of the Japanese lies in the operation of special labour market mechanisms, and that this is the prerequisite for success in the 1980s, is a widespread one. The workforce's outstandingly flexible responses to changes in the economic structure (for example, its acceptance of mobility and also, on early retirement, of re-employment without seniority) appear crucial. It is a combination of the high productive performance and the response to innovation of the big company sector, coupled with the rapid labour turnover and the unprotected position of workers in the small companies, that allows Japan to contemplate the big structural changes necessary for the maintenance of high employment in the 1980s.

Essentially it is a matter of adapting to the increased emphasis on the growth of activity in the tertiary sector with its relatively low productivity. The high-wage/high-productivity manufacturing sector is diminishing in importance and the 'dual economy' system makes it easier for workers to adjust to this. The determining factor is that the sector called upon to make the big adjustment—the small company sector, in which individual enterprises typically employ less than a hundred workers—is comparatively unprotected, often hungry for labour, and very competitive. It is also little influenced by the much higher wage and fringe benefits standards set in the big company sector.

There is remarkably little definition of the dual structure: the size of the top sector of the economy is uncertain in terms of gross production (let alone value-added) and even in terms of the number of firms in it. The economists at the Keidanren, for example, think of it as representing from as little as 20 per cent to as high as 40 per cent of Japanese industry—rather a wide span. All that they can say with any certainty is that without exception (or only with such exceptions as go to prove the rule) the eight hundred or so companies affiliated to the Keidanren are in the privileged sector.

Most of these, of course, belong to the conglomerates or to the leading single-industry groups, and we know a great deal about their operation. It is in the bottom sector of the economy that commentators easily lose their way. Some of the obscurity stems from the heterogeneous nature of this part of the economy. It contains borderline enterprises, with sizeable labour forces, but deprived of the vaunted advantages of lifetime employment, regarded by many as the key to success in the Japanese economy. It also contains many tens of thousands of tiny ventures of the 'mom and pop' cornershop variety, hiring no one and relying on family labour. In between there is a vast number of small producers, in manufacturing and in service industries, of casual birth and even easier demise. They find it difficult to raise credit and no one bails them out when they founder. They have little choice but to engage their employees from the rejects of the top sector firms and find it difficult to keep those they themselves have trained. If they are subcontractors to big firms they may in times of recession be under pressure to employ the surplus labour from their stronger associates, only to find that these same workers move back into the top of the dual economy when conditions improve. On the other hand their employees are seldom unionized: the hirer of non-unionized labour can get away with less 'benevolent' employment behaviour, has less burden to bear in the way of fringe benefits such as bonuses and retirement allowances, and generally pays lower wages.

Although this may be narrowing, there is in fact clear evidence of a very sharp division in the treatment (and in the welfare prospects) of people employed in the two different parts of the economy. Even without taking non-wage costs into account, the basic wages in small firms[1] were in the late 1960s and early 1970s just under 70 per cent of those paid in large firms. A more recent analysis estimates that the wages in the lower sector have risen to 75 per cent of the rates prevailing in the top sector firms.[2] One union estimate is that in the big corporation lifetime employment sector, incomes are on average 40 per cent higher than in the rest of the economy. These two different approaches in fact amount to a rather similar perception of the gap between the two sectors: the difference may lie in the size of biannual bonuses, which lead to a relatively larger gap between basic wages and earnings in the top sector.[3] There is evidence that some of these differences are accounted for by the fact that smaller firms employ cheaper labour: women, the semi-retired, the less educated, the less skilled, and those who are less trainable, and therefore have been left behind after the big firms have had their pick.

The gap between employment conditions and earnings at the very top of the economy and at its lower ranges is of course not peculiarly Japanese. But in the Western industrialized countries the underprivileged sectors of the labour market are seldom as big as in Japan.

The top sector of the dual economy and the lifetime employment sector overlap to a very large measure, but do not entirely coincide. For one thing by no means all those employed at any one time in the larger firms in the privileged sector are permanent full-time workers. The proportion of seasonal workers, or workers taken on without employment guarantees after they have retired early, can be considerable: at the height of seasonal pressure Nissan, for instance, takes on some 3,000 temporary workers (over 5 per cent of its permanent labour force) drawn in large part from young agricultural workers underemployed during the early spring slack on the farm.

The lifetime employment sector

There is again some uncertainty about the precise size of the labour force on the privileged side of the dual economy. The most frequently quoted estimates, near-guesses in reality, put the proportion of lifetime employment workers at around one-third of those employed (after the exclusion of family businesses)—some 12.5 million out of 37.5 million employees (Galenson and Odaka, 1976, p.614). In addition, members of the public services appear to have the benefit of permanent employment, with the possible exception of manual workers in public corporations. This may account for another 2 million or so workers, bringing the total in lifetime employment to not much less than 15 million or some 27 per cent of all people working at the end of the 1970s (38 per cent, excluding the self-employed and family businesses).

Writing in the mid-1970s, Galenson singled out Matsushita as an exceptional concern which extended to women (on whom it chiefly relies for its workforce) the privileges of return after a gap for marriage and maternity at lifetime employment conditions, and concluded that the great majority of women workers do not enjoy the benefits of permanent employment (Galenson and Odaka, 1976, pp.615–16). The participation of Japanese women in the labour force is high. In 1980 they accounted for 37 per cent of all those employed, self-employed or working in family enterprises. Nearly one in two (45 per cent) of women aged fifteen and over was gainfully employed in some way—though not all of them by any means full-time, especially in manufacturing, where the proportion of women is of course much smaller.

Despite the obscurities of the dual economy, much has been said about the differences between the sectors, from the point of view of both the employer and the employee. Those recruiting for the top sector certainly have it easy as far as selection of entrants is concerned. The care with which a big Japanese employer chooses his young intake and the involvement of the entire management, from principal downwards, in the choice is the direct response to the competition of candidates for top-firm jobs.

The smaller underprivileged firm spends less on training of the new intake, attracts less loyalty and, commensurately, must be prepared to lose a far larger proportion of its young entry in the early years of employment. And the employees will, for their part, have much less security of continuity of employment when the company falls on bad times. However, there was apparently, in the boom full-employment years in the 1970s, a widening area of medium and small firms which at least tried to maintain a near-permanent labour force and where the workers, in turn, recognizing the effort made by the employers, were willing to help their firms by agreeing to redundancies, with the assistance of generous retirement allowances.

In the latter part of the 1970s a new feature has come into evidence: the young well-qualified trained worker who during the early stages of his work career tries to improve his prospects, without waiting for the slow-motion progress of seniority promotion, by moving to a job in a new firm. On the face of it, if he no longer sticks like a limpet to the company which gave him his first job, the much vaunted loyalty of the Japanese worker appears to be waning. Job changing appears to be associated with the assertion of new demands for people with special technical skills and may in fact be characteristic of the input bottlenecks which arise in high-growth technological industries during periods of maximum expansion. A more permanent feature is the relegation and perhaps gradual disappearance of the seniority promotion rules in some of the most dynamic firms. Whereas the working careers of their fathers, providing they were employed in the top sector of the economy, were to a degree predictable (though it is debatable how predictable) new employees face a far more complicated system. In many large firms, both promotion and salary increments are increasingly subject to a dual scale which combines age with merit.

There are also a few instances of companies which overcome the rigidities of the seniority system without sacrificing the traditional emphasis on age promotion. Management in these concerns maintains a secondary 'internal' ladder of promotion, in addition to the formal seniority ladder: 'internal', because although it counts inside the company—and is given formal recognition in a ceremony conducted by a director with the employee—he may not put his acquired rank on his visiting card and advertise it to the outside world. His official status, grade, title and salary correspond to those for his age group, but his true responsibilities may be considerably higher—probably rewarded by fringe benefits which are not necessarily part of the official scale. Conventions are maintained, jealousies apparently circumvented, yet the ambitious employee gets his reward without delay and is spurred to further effort—and management has another powerful instrument of control over its staff.

Flexibility and the retirement age

During the success years of the 1960s and 1970s many employees in the top sector of the economy kept their lifetime employment jobs until fifty-five, the most usual retirement age. And, after they officially retired, management saw itself as having a recognized (though not contractual) duty to find remunerative employment for lifetime employees up to the age of sixty, when state pensions begin.

Mid-1970s Ministry of Labour estimates suggest that 80 per cent of all the retired worked on as employees and another 4 per cent changed their status to self-employed, in small enterprises often financed out of the lump-sum retirement allowance. Generally the participation of older workers (up to the age of sixty-five) is high compared to other industrialized countries. This is where the company has maximum discretionary authority. Even senior executives are sent off to occupy 'window seat' jobs with seniority but little importance, or to a genuine managerial post in a smaller affiliate company. The company may alternatively do the bare minimum and re-engage the retired person at a lower level, on basic pay only, with no security and no benefits.

Towards the end of the 1970s, the government declared itself in favour of raising the retirement age to sixty, in an effort to close the gap between the retirement age and the pensionable age. This did not prevent employers with surplus workers, or those wishing to 'rejuvenate' their wage structure and cut their pay bill, from trying to persuade employees to accept early retirement at their peak income level, around the age of fifty. These employees are entitled to an advantageous retirement allowance, with in some cases the added sweetener of a special early-retirement bonus. A proportion, usually in their late forties, are re-engaged by their original company, but on conditions similar to those of the provisional worker: employed part-time or seasonally (with no job protection), as market conditions dictate. From the employer's point of view this middle-aged labour force has many advantages, in addition to bringing down payroll costs. It has the same training and experience as the peak age-group, as well as apparently undiminished loyalty to the company and its products.

That the loyalty, once established, is remarkably persistent is noted by all observers of the Japanese scene. By preference, employees and their families shop in company outlets and buy company products. And the loyalty can even pass from parents to children. 'I always drink Kirin beer,' confided a Tokyo friend (somewhat shamefacedly). 'Of course, Kirin is in the Mitsubishi set and father was a Mitsubishi man.' One might argue that it would be hard not to drink Kirin products since the company has nearly two-thirds of the beer market in Japan, but the emphasis on company/brand loyalty is nevertheless a real one.

After the first oil shock, when industry embarked on a programme of rationalization and cost reduction, employment in manufacturing took a sizeable dip. There was a significant cut in numbers employed by the thirty or so top corporations quoted on the stock exchange and there is evidence of a fall of some 10 per cent in employment in manufacturing between 1975 and 1979. Most of this reduction was achieved by shifting employees from manufacturing to the labour-intensive service industries, sometimes within the same conglomerate, in valiant attempts at diversification. Mitsubishi, for instance, added chains of laundries and snackbars to its empire, though on the whole there is, on the part of the conglomerates, little enthusiasm for such excursions into uncharted waters.

The simultaneous pressure from the government to bring the male retirement age up to sixty ran counter to the tendency to trim down the manufacturing labour force. But the large companies continued to prove pretty co-operative, and in many the retirement age went up from 57/58 to 59/60. Although evidence is not yet available for the medium and smaller firms it seems more than likely that they as usual followed the lead from the top firms and held on to their older employees for rather longer.

Are the unions ineffectual?

It would be a great mistake to see Japanese unions either as weak or, in the private lifetime employment sector, as simply 'company unions' in the Western sense. Nevertheless Japanese unions have some features which make them quite distinct from those of other advanced industrial countries.

One is simply the vast number of unions—over 72,000 in 1980—at establishment level. The number of unions has actually been growing (more or less in line with a slow increase in membership) while the level of unionization has declined since the mid-1970s, to an estimated 30.8 per cent in 1980.[4] Further, Japan's unions are virtually all in the lifetime employment sector. Corresponding to the sharp segmentation of the labour market between the privileged and unprivileged sectors, there is therefore an institutional separation: union activity concentrates overwhelmingly on the public sector and the big company sector. And within the latter, the members and leaders of the unions respond with great sensitivity to the ups and downs of their firms; this makes it much easier to achieve trade-offs between employment and wages than in other countries.

It is said that Ichiro Shioji, the Nissan union leader, encountered opposition when he became chairman of Jidosharoren (the Japan Federation of Automobile Industry Workers' Unions). He had created a 'general union' of 35,000 members employed by the smaller, often subcontracting, ring of companies which were Nissan suppliers—upholstery, textiles, small components and so on—but was opposed by the unions from Toyota and other companies when he proposed the development of a systematic relationship with 'outside' workers employed by the smaller companies. The others were afraid of dilution; nor were they prepared to spend union funds on the underprivileged, who were admittedly hard to organize.

Nor do the unions in the established big federations interest themselves in the 'temporary' labour force (which does not legally qualify for membership in enterprise unions). They are also not in the main concerned with women, who are just beginning to demand things that go with lifetime employment, such as the right to continued seniority wages after an absence of three years for childbearing. These are crucial sectors of the labour force. We have already noted the importance of women's employment. The proportion of temporary workers was at the beginning of the 1960s according to some calculations (e.g. Taira, 1970, quoted in Patrick and Rosovsky, 1976, p.619) not far below 20 per cent of manufacturing employment. After decreasing for some years in the 1970s, temporary work appeared to be once again growing at the end of the decade, prior to the recession.

It would be useful to have some precise figures on the overlap of union membership with the lifetime employment sector of the economy. The data do not exist, but given that unionization has been around one-third for some time, the overlap may be pretty well total. Unlike in most other industrial countries (with the exception of the Scandinavian ones) white-collar membership of enterprise unions is high—a particular contrast to the United States and France for example. This only serves to emphasize how unorganized the majority of employees are. The field has been left open to such forces as the Communist Party and to unconventional influences such as the Buddhists. But these groups have had little impact so far.

All the same, union officials speak of their target as being to raise the level of wages, or improve conditions of employment, for workers in the second part of the system—at least that sector of medium-sized firms where unions wield a certain influence—to match that of the large corporations. Their method is clearly to lift the standard in some big and visible large corporation and then to draw the medium-sized firms allied with it up to the same level. This is the technique being employed in the motor industry, for example, where Nissan conceded the right to a retirement pension at sixty (as against the standard fifty-five years in the past) and other firms connected with the company have been pressed, fairly successfully, to raise the age of retirement towards that target level. Nevertheless, as the proportion of employees benefiting from lifetime employment continues to decrease, if only because of the structural change away from manufacturing to service industries, the percentage of workers gaining from these advances is also falling.

The concentrated effort of the unions in the area of the big corporations means that the dual economic structure is reflected in a kind of dual social structure. The failure of the unions so far to secure from the government a reasonable level of retirement pension for *all* workers is a striking fact. They are a powerful body and the fact that they are disunited, or at any rate divided into two main blocs under the banners of Sohyo (the General Council of Trade Unions of Japan) and Domei (the Confederation of Japanese Labour), hardly provides an adequate explanation for this lack of success. In fact the Italian case, with three large trade union groupings, suggests the opposite. The more plausible explanation is that their main effort has been directed towards improving the already considerable welfare benefits secured by their own members, who are overwhelmingly in the big company sector.

The history of post-war Japanese trade unionism is admittedly complex. There are no doubt reasons connected with the meteoric union growth encouraged by the occupying power and the subsequent major political conflict inside the union movement, superimposed on a tradition of enterprise-based unions, which explain why Japan's unions continue to concentrate on the privileged sector. However, there is little evidence to suggest any different pattern of behaviour at any time since 1945. True, there was some attempt to move towards inter-enterprise unions and industry-wide bargaining in the immediate post-war period. But this movement was largely confined to the union federation which contained a majority of government and public sector employees, and the public sector, with a relatively high level of unionization, continues to be the area of greatest union militancy in Japan.

A further factor influencing the peaceful conduct of much of Japan's industrial relations is the prevalence of biannual bonuses. This is a twice-yearly additional payment, amounting to three or four months' salary (in good years).[5] The actual amount is at the discretion of company management—in agreement with the union, for the system is very much part of the lifetime employment sector, serving to tie a significant portion of the employee's income to the company's welfare. The biannual bonus can be seen, along with the retirement lump-sum payment, as a short-term loan by the employee to the firm (Ballon, 1969).

The pension, as Ballon sees it, is a way of withholding a month's salary (or a little more) per year, and then repaying it later, after the firm has had the use of it for up to thirty years of an individual's working life. With the biannual bonus, it is an inducement to stay with the firm; it provides the firm with yet another means of ensuring that the core of the labour force is stable as well as a useful source of finance. In addition to adjusting the amount of the percentage increment to pay in the light of the commercial results of the individual business, the actual cost of the bonus to the company may be reduced by an agreement to deposit part of it in the savings account with the company (company savings by employees are common) or by distributing part in goods rather than money. Moreover a portion of the bonus sum set aside is pooled and distributed by the company on merit, either individual or group, at management's assessment. While this is a relatively small proportion of the total bonus sum, it is significant for the selected individuals receiving it.[6]

Ronald Dore sees Japanese labour relations as expressing a superior form of living together that relies on a 'fairness principle' and achieves conflict resolution by institutionalized yet informal means. This is not a uniformly held view. Walter Galenson, voicing a more tangible explanation, emphasizes the docility of unions and the high degree of discretionary authority retained by managers. While admitting the achievements of the Japanese in 'grievance resolution' without resort to tribunals or courts, he argues that it is not the special character of Japanese people that is responsible, but the weakness of trade unions. Because of the political events of the 1950s, Japan's unions are even weaker than the fragmented labour organizations of Italy or France (Galenson, 1976, p.63). Even more forthrightly, Galenson and Odaka, in their contribution to the earlier Brookings study, say that 'if the desires of Japanese wage-earners had been given more effective organized expression during the past two decades, the nation's economy would look quite different than it does today' (Galenson and Odaka, 1976, p.668). They identify five main areas of difference. While the rate of industrial investment would have been lower, the share of collective consumption would have been higher; there would be better housing; probably a more adequate pension system; and probably Japanese workers would have the five-day week and take their holiday entitlement in full. All this would have been the outcome of stronger unions, though at the almost certain cost of a slower pace of economic growth, with the concomitant—again hardly to be avoided—of a slower improvement in living standards.

This raises the question of why the Japanese unions are less effectual than their Western counterparts. Is it not because they have ridden on the prosperity of the large-corporation sector and ignored the underprivileged? The latter have also enjoyed, though in a more modest way, the fruits of growth and they have therefore tended not to become obvious objects of pity, to be fraternally supported by their more fortunate fellow workers. If prosperity fails, these employees of the less privileged part of the economy will be the ones to feel the pinch; will the unions then remain weak—or non-militant? Some evidence of potential militancy came in the extraordinary wage movements of the early 1970s. It was these claims (eventually conceded) that were probably the main influence on the government's decision to squeeze the economy and engineer the drastic curb of the second quarter of 1973 (*before* the oil crisis). After the oil price had risen, at the end of the year, the government continued stubbornly on its deflationary course, chiefly out of a fear of a possible resurgence of inflationary wage claims. Company profits had to be sharply cut in 1974/5, chiefly by a substantial increase in corporate tax rates, before the rise in wages could be brought under control.

Hideaki Okamoto of Hosei University detects a movement of international convergence, tending towards something closer to the Japanese pattern. He takes the view that there is, abroad as in Japan, an endemic weakness of unions in the face of employers with so much influence over enterprise-based organizations. Japanese company-centred unions have, however, been moving very gradually to novel industry-wide arrangements in cars, steel and so on. Okamoto's main contention is that in all countries the locus of decision is moving downwards, from industrial and national level to the level of the enterprise or the plant. Generally decisions and activities which previously involved outsiders are being internalized. Promotion to the board of directors is increasingly from inside; there is less reliance on outside finance (the relative independence having been hitherto a purely Japanese phenomenon).

Japan's extraordinary union fragmentation is surely special, but perhaps there is a tendency elsewhere towards something akin to the Japanese 'pacesetting union' (recently the steel union) setting the standards for the rest in the annual spring offensive. Something of the sort has become more familiar even in the uniquely fragmented world of British industrial relations in recent years, and the United Automobile Workers union in the US has for a long time undertaken 'key bargaining' with the car companies. This, however, has undergone some modifications since the crisis which hit the Chrysler Corporation in 1979.

Perhaps the most instructive similarity is between Japan and Germany. Although in principle German unions do not negotiate at plant levels, but at industry or regional level, in practice local bargaining has been on the increase. However, in the larger companies the main channel of influence is the works council, in which union representatives have no formal place, but are in fact very active. Council members have the formal right to call in trade union officials to advise them. Moreover, the 1976 co-determination law makes it obligatory for management to engage in *prior* consultation with workers' representatives (at plant level or elsewhere) whenever changes in operating conditions are introduced. This is also the effective working practice in big Japanese firms, though it is not legally enforceable. It occurs in the 'workshop consultative meeting' including all the members of a small production team, usually twice a month. It is a continuous dialogue at workshop level, whereas in Germany the equivalent dialogue is at the monthly *plant* level meetings of the works council. For Okamoto, the German sense of common interest and 'partnership' is stronger at plant level. In Japan it is both a workshop and an enterprise attachment.

Notes to Chapter 8

1. In this calculation, taken from table 9–8 in Walter Galenson's and Konosuke Odaka's 'The Japanese Labor Market' (1976, p.603), small firms with from 30 to 99 employees are compared with large ones, employing 500 or more employees.
2. See *White Papers of Japan 1978–79* (p.196), where it is claimed that the 'double wage structure', the gap between high wages in the top sector and the lower wages in medium and small businesses, is rapidly disappearing. The figures, without being directly comparable with Galenson's and Odaka's, certainly point in that direction.
3. Recent Ministry of Labour figures (Japan, *Year Book of Labour Statistics*, 1980, table 88, pp.120–1), show that the annual special earnings in small firms (10–99 employees) were only 48 per cent of those in large firms of 1,000 employees or more. [*Ed.*]
4. Ministry of Labour figures for June 1980. The decline reflects, at least in part, the shift of emphasis to the tertiary sector, where workers are

more difficult to organize. It must be recognized that the terms in which the Japanese describe their own unions may be different from Western concepts. There appear to be, for instance, some 17,000 public sector 'unions', of which over 4,000 are in Jichiro, the National Council of Local Municipal Government Workers' Unions. The image of a plethora of completely independent enterprise or establishment unions may therefore be rather misleading.

5. According to Ronald Dore, Japanese bonuses are in fact almost as sticky downwards as wages. There was for instance very little sign of bonuses being reduced in the mid-1970s recession. [*Personal communication to Editor, 1982.*]

6. More recently some companies have begun to incorporate far more merit-related and skill-related factors into their payment systems. See for example 'The Japanese Wage System', Nan Weiner, 1982. [*Ed.*]

9

CONFIDENCE AND LIMITS
TO GROWTH

Is Japan in the process of becoming another ordinary mixed economy in which market forces become decreasingly amenable to the control of public and quasi-public authorities? Though it may take some time before the process is complete, there are a number of strong arguments to support this school of thought; the following four are regarded as most relevant:

In the first place, corporate enterprise is breaking loose from central control: the newly-found independence has come with the greater liquidity accompanying the decline in investment needs and also the noticeable erosion of the lifetime employment system since the recession of the mid-1970s. Japanese industry in the big company sector is now (as we have stressed above, pp.73, 81) much better able to finance its investment needs from its own resources than in the past.

Secondly, there is a positive desire, in some of the central institutions at least, to create a more effectively functioning market system. This is noticeable for example in the central bank itself, where the attenuation of the earlier controls limiting bank lending, which operated with a multiplier effect through the economy, is positively welcomed.

The third factor is the internationalization of the sources of finance available to Japanese industry, which reduces the capacity of the purely domestic organs to exercise effective control. The initial response to this, during the period of the very rapid appreciation of the yen in 1978, was to introduce new controls curbing the inward movement of foreign funds; but this tends now to be regarded as a regrettable incident, not as a permanent feature of central banking in the new era.

The shift in the structure of domestic demand, with the

progressive rise of the share of the service sector, and the consequent difficulties in controlling a multitude of small units, is the fourth element which emphasizes the impression that Japan is becoming a Western-style mixed economy. Unless it is absorbed by the large conglomerates, which on the showing of unsuccessful diversification attempts in the 1970s seems unlikely, a growth sector consisting of masses of small enterprises will be that much more difficult to control than the big groupings have proved in the past.

The traditional sector of big industry—the six giant conglomerates, the other big groups and the foremost single-industry firms—is likely to continue to dominate. Signs of their dynamism are clearly discernible in the growing importance of exports within their total sales, in the multiplication of foreign ventures and also in the increased counter-cyclical employment figures of quite a few of the individual companies within the groups.

At the close of the 1970s there were good reasons to believe that the rhetoric of worry about the future uncertainties and dangers to 'vulnerable Japan' on the part of sections of academics and officialdom was grossly overdone. This rhetoric ran counter to a notable mood of popular confidence in Japan's ability to cope.

Though many recognized that the rate of growth could, in the early 1980s, fall well below the target set in 1979 for the Seven-Year Plan at 5.7 per cent, it was also recognized that it would still be above that of the other OECD members. Unions were expected to acknowledge this relatively favourable circumstance and to accept adaptations of work conditions in order to maintain it.

However, it is difficult to reconcile the forecast of a relatively high growth rate for Japan with the depressed predictions for the OECD as a whole. The Japanese forecast implied a low rate of 2 per cent approximately for the rest of the OECD, and such a low average was bound to affect the potential market for Japanese exports. This in turn implied that Japanese growth in the 1980s would have to be led by booming domestic demand. In the optimistic mood of 1979 even usually cautious British embassy officials were heard to declare, in response to the euphoria of some of the business community, that nothing could stop the current Japanese boom. But interest rates rose in the middle of the year, savings continued to be very high indeed and the level of real unemployment showed little sign of declining. The more cautious—for instance at the Industrial Bank of Japan—were talking of continuing hesitant demand for investment finance and of determination on the part of business to stay liquid. Nor was there any evidence that the Ministry of Finance was contemplating financial innovations which would give it more room to manoeuvre in helping to fund the next phase of Japanese economic expansion.

Thus by 1980, a less favourable scenario was already emerging. Moreover, if the general decline in growth rate was heavily concentrated in the industries and other activities of the leading conglomerate groups, and if, in consequence, their finances got into trouble, the loss of confidence would have incalculable results. It could lead to even higher savings which would not be channelled into investment capital for the medium and smaller companies and effectively prevent them from taking advantage of the opportunities implied by the difficulties in the top sector.

Public spending dilemmas

Other chances of sharply increasing domestic demand might have offered if the personal savings ratio had shown signs of a sizeable drop—leading to higher consumption—but there were no such signs; or if the mainstream top sector of the economy had been greedy for investment for replacement or innovation—but its demands for investment funds were moderate (and increasingly met from abroad).

There is also, it seems, little potential for growth in public sector investment plans. Social infrastructure, including housing, would require the liberation of public finance from its current constraints (reduction of budget deficit) and better mobilization of funds for borrowing. But Japanese government does not want to give up the chance of getting money on the cheap—in the easy, traditional way, through the banks.

Increased injections of public funds could be combined with the belated construction of the Japanese welfare state. If for example pensions (and other benefits) were made larger and more secure, people might save less, and the economy would receive a stimulus from consumer demand.

It was to be expected that, when the slowdown in economic growth ultimately hit Japan and the big companies were no longer willing to strain their liquidity by carrying the burden of welfare (see p.91 above), social security for the weaker groups in society and the right to social benefits would emerge as very important issues. This would matter particularly for the most vulnerable to the effects of slow growth: older workers and women workers. (The competition between older persons and women for jobs in the tertiary sector was in any case almost certainly going to be quite fierce, and further unemployment inevitable.)

If Japan attempts to follow the same path as Europe and, to a lesser degree, the USA, protection of the weak will eventually consist of rights guaranteed by law, in addition to or as a substitute for services rendered through the good will of private corporations. This will push the tax cost extremely high, and necessitate drastic changes in finance, in both private and public sectors.

If Japan moves in this direction, will it not introduce into Japanese society the very economic inflexibilities from which Western countries are now suffering? The increased tax take will necessarily bring about a certain amount of rigidity. But, at least in the short term, because Japan has its own particular style of social relationships, especially among individuals in the working environment, it may be able to avoid other types of rigidity, such as stalemates in industrial relations. It is reasonable at least to hope so.

Constraints of interdependence

While domestic demand looks like being sticky and the growth of exports is halted by low growth overseas, a growing impulse to invest abroad is manifesting itself in economic comment and in the views expressed in such bodies as the Industrial Bank of Japan. However, it is not clear how Japan could become a capital exporting country, with a big net service income from abroad and less dependence on exports of manufactured goods.

The concept that every aspect of domestic policy must be considered in terms of both its domestic and international impact continues to be unfamiliar and uncomfortable to many Japanese. Even the Economic Planning Agency did not think it imperative to take the reality of mutual dependence into account in formulating its Economic and Social Seven-Year Plan in 1979. It could even be said that this was devised according to the planning methods of the

Tokugawa period, based on the illusion of Japan's continued isolation from the rest of the world. And in principle the planners ought to have been right: it should be possible for Japan to exploit its unusually low dependence on foreign trade (see above, p.68) to secure a balanced expansion of domestic demand, at a faster pace than elsewhere—so long as import elasticity for manufactured goods and imported services remains low enough to avoid major balance of payments problems.

The alternative scenario is one in which people working away from the export sector will jib at the high prices resulting from the protection of Japan's high-cost industries, and turn increasingly to imported low-cost manufactures. Japan's overall trade surplus will therefore gradually disappear and only the services sector will be a growing net exporter.

Since the burst of co-operative effort immediately following the 1978 Bonn Summit (see Shonfield 1982, p.52) the rate of change in attitudes to interdependence has progressed very slowly, with a truly Japanese graduality. However, assuming that the pressures from Japan's foreign trading partners combined with considerations of self-interest become irresistible, attitudes and actions must adjust. But when the exchange rate of the yen is no longer maintained at an artificially low level and the domestic market accepts imports somewhat more readily, there is certain to be a dilemma: How to fine tune international transactions, so as to avoid the usual effect on an expanding country of an unsynchronized business cycle (see the US in the years 1976–9)? Japan will have to be more competitive in its vulnerable, relatively low productivity, activities. (Fortunately many of these are not internationally tradeable.)

Nearly all—optimists and sceptics alike—agree that any Japanese process of change is bound to continue to be very gradual. This leaves us with the unanswered question whether it is possible after all to achieve structural change over the whole system if each of the lines of change is to be governed by the principle of minimum overt disturbance. One cannot help feeling that major structural change of the kind foreseen for Japan will almost inevitably be associated with *discontinuities* in the performance of particular sectors. These discontinuities may well affect the power structure itself and they therefore imply some loss of control—albeit perhaps only temporary—by the established institutions of Japanese society. That seems to be something which no one is seriously willing to contemplate, and it also goes against the underlying thrust of the whole of modern Japanese history.

PART THREE

*On Corporatism,
Intervention and Choice*

10

CORPORATIST APPROACHES
IN THE NEW SOCIETY

WE have not fully understood the causes for the discrepancies in national economic performance during the past decade. The successes—Japan, Germany, to some extent France, and a number of smaller 'northern' social democracies ('northern' in inverted commas, as Austria is an outstanding example)—all have different formulas for dealing with economic crises. But, while the whole sequence is not clear, there are many pointers to the relative success of those societies whose institutions rest on some sort of corporatism—societies either deliberately making room for corporatist processes or which, like Japan, have slowly evolved into a type of corporatism. This corporatism is not the authoritarian system of management familiar from the experience of fascism. It is, by contrast, a systematic dialogue between interest groups both private and public; at its best, it succeeds in putting order and a priority ranking based on recognized standards of social justice into the expression of divergent voices which characterizes the pluralist democracies. This form of government is usually benign—though not, unfortunately, invariably so. Its effectiveness and its acceptability both depend on the adaptation of existing institutions, adjustments which are political as well as economic. Behind these adaptations is the ultimate aim of moderating and mediating conflicts between the needs, aspirations and claims of the various competing interest groups.

From the experience of the past twenty years we have inferred some signal lessons: about the need, in the immediate future, to buy extended industrial peace at the cost of a viable incomes policy (see Shonfield, 1982, pp.58–66 and here, pp.139–44) and, in the longer term, to plan—and to secure assent to the plans—for the fundamental restructuring of our economies so that they may remain open and continue to grow (see above, Chapter 3 *passim*).

The securing of these aims (about which more is to come later in this text) must be the outstanding use to which we put the corporatist tools at our disposal.

In addition to the primary function of government—that of promoting the general interest—the corporatist state has a role both as broker and as guarantor of bargains between pressure groups. None of this necessarily requires a large interventionist apparatus. It can nevertheless add to the perception of the state as a top-heavy, expensive burden on our pockets, especially as it coincides with the rise of marked impatience with the state as 'universal nanny', an impatience which began to simmer in the mid-1960s and boiled up in the 1970s.

There is, as well, the deeper, all-pervasive fear of having passed a certain threshold in the general expansion of *all* aspects of public activity, power and regulation, which then stultify the mixed economy and the society which sustains it.[1] Manifestations of this fear, motivated by a revulsion against the collective welfare provision and the public regulation of matters which people prefer to be conducted by private action, made themselves felt in the Californian Proposition 13 (see pp.30–1 above), and the non-interventionist policies of France under the Barre prime-ministership and of the UK under Thatcher. What strengthened the non-interventionists' case was that existing public institutions were shown to be incompetent for their enlarged tasks.[2]

Many countries have suddenly become aware of the practical anomalies that programmes whose objectives are worthy but insufficiently thought through have generated, such as, for instance, the 'poverty trap' in the UK and elsewhere which, through a combination of high marginal tax rates on quite low earned incomes and high welfare payments to those who do not earn, or earn little, makes it positively disadvantageous for certain classes of poor people to try to better themselves by earning some more money. The example serves to illustrate the way in which low-level welfare decisions become deeply entangled with major policy questions on progressive taxation and on minimum wage levels. Social welfare transactions in Western societies have in quite a short period of time—little more than a couple of decades—become so pervasive in their effects on the economy as a whole that it is hardly surprising that the ramifications of each decision, often hastily taken, have not been understood or even properly explored.

Reinforcing the persuasive motivation imposed by the decline in growth rates and the depth of the recession which started with the second oil shock, and with inflation rates in double figures, all this provides the occasion for a pause in the advance of recent years. And as was to be expected, simultaneously with the levelling out in the advance of public spending there has been some change in the nature of the welfare services which the state was dispensing. One of the symptoms of this change is a growing intolerance, among the planners and distributors of welfare services, of the indolent and those with low initiative. Weak members of society—children, the old, the otherwise disadvantaged—continue to be protected by direct means but whenever practicable adults endowed with reasonable mental capacity are now being helped materially to fend for themselves while how they do it is left to their individual decision.

There has also been—and this too was to be expected—a slight decline in the driving force which sustained many welfare programmes in the 1960s. The evidence of a certain loss of fervour in the United States for policies of 'affirmative action' in support of civil rights (again reflected in the spirit of the Supreme Court of the 1970s) pointed in that direction. Comparable indications are not wanting in other countries; above all those muddles and inefficiencies, which can be ascribed to a pace of advance in the formulation and fulfilment of the objectives of social welfare well beyond the concomitant pace of the administrative apparatus, are being severely questioned, reduced or abolished.

As with the discovery of the limitations of short-term management of the economy, the first impression is of a Friedmanite reaction, leading to a longer-term reversion to the economies of strict non-intervention, relying on the 'hidden hand'. Despite the evidence of the Thatcher and Reagan policies, this is a misleading impression. Governments have sobered up; they tinker less; they try to spend less; but they have not been able to retire from the business of intervention.

Given the conjunction of the growing socio-political objections against high growth in public spending and the perceived need to slow the momentum derived from a combination of errors in economic management, it is clear that a temporary reaction was bound to follow. The late 1970s and 1980 saw a political movement of this kind. And, paradoxically, the power of governments had to be strengthened to make possible the withdrawal from public overcommitment to the pursuit of 1960s ideals.

The experience of some of the smaller democracies which clung to old-style demand management *plus* highly interventionist methods is relevant here; this worked for a time—but with the onset of the second slump at the tail-end of the 1970s the small countries, too, started to wilt.

The fact of the backlash is not to be denied. Its salient aspects have been discussed earlier in this book (pp.30–3). It is evident that to make the 1980s less uncomfortable, the rate of growth of public spending relative to the national product needs to be reduced. We must also make sure that the public intervention in our societies is fully effective. The first slowing-down of the growth of public expenditure has been considered earlier, in Chapter 2. The second requirement—that of making public intervention fully effective—has two aspects. Intervention must be effective to produce useful short-term demand management at a time of slow growth, and also to help the restructuring of the economy when the marginal efficiency of capital is reduced and private investment is hesitant; at such a time the efficient application of public capital becomes crucial.

The best mechanism of all, it is becoming clear even to those who started with a strong ideological preference against the recognition of the fact, is one which approximates to the market process. 'Market mechanisms have a capacity for fine-tuned adjustment and innovation that is irreplaceable, and their defects can be reduced by means of suitable corrective signals' (OECD 1979, p.188). In the market, consumers signal their needs directly to suppliers, who are in turn motivated to respond to them by the pursuit of their own interests. Yet in modern conditions, where there is a built-in tendency towards oligopoly, this process of market signalling and response cannot reliably be left to the spontaneous forces of competition (see p.51 above). There must be regulation to secure the public interest. The argument applies more obviously and more powerfully to the provision of public goods, which will almost certainly absorb a rising proportion of economic effort in Western society—and also attract a great deal of attention from single-interest groups arguing on corporatist platforms.

In these circumstances, the advance of the corporatist style of policy-making is probably irreversible. The 1970s, with the growing fear of ever-increasing power of the state and of the oligopolistic firm, saw a number of assertions—attempts to cut down regulation, reduce the amounts that the public authorities could pass on to disadvantaged groups in the form of transfer payments on the one hand; attempts to reinforce consumer countervailing forces on the other; and from all sides, a growing insistence on more transparency and accountability on the part of government and quasi-governmental agencies.

If the growth of consumer power, in its various, often contradictory manifestations, is inevitable, so is corporatism by contagion. Those who might have been ready to use market forces (partly because they hold 'market power' and can therefore manipulate the market to good effect) will feel compelled to organize and establish a place in the hierarchy of decision-making. This will be helped along by the increasing efficiency of communication and the relative ease of organizing small pressure groups (as well as large ones). Affluence itself of course also leads to the greater articulation of particular group interests, and can make the participants in the exchanges more prepared to take risks in the pursuit of these interests.

Once we have absorbed the major lesson of the primacy of institutions over any purely economic formula for resolving the problems of our economies, corporatism—with its hopes for securing the active assent of labour to incomes policies and technological innovation—appears, particularly in a period of slow growth, as the key to effective management.

Aspects of current corporatism

In the years of growing Western economic prosperity following World War Two there has developed—even in those countries which, like West Germany, resisted the language of economic planning—a marked degree of communication and concertation of objectives, involving government (and quasi-governmental agencies), organized labour and large-scale business enterprise (or associations representing groups of business enterprises of whatever size). The chief object of such concertation and co-operation has been to control and reduce business fluctuations and, more generally, to secure a more predictable economic environment. To these ends, the broad interests of big business could be made to coincide with those of the state and also with those of trade unions; but the means of achieving the ends almost always diverge, and call for compromises on the part of all interests concerned. Further, the growing assertions of other interest groups, when they pursue a single interest (which may be essentially economic, or political—or neither clearly political nor clearly economic), require a voice in decision-making, and in most cases some allocation of public resources.

The situation is complicated by the fact that most of the actors in the decision-making process now have international dimensions: big business is often multinational; labour and single interest groups have international affiliations. The state itself almost invariably forms part of wider political or economic (or political/economic) organisms which to some degree curtail its sovereignty and at the same time confer on it the reinsurance which comes from group access to financial resources (e.g. IMF) or from group defence arrangements (e.g. NATO). These advantageous tie-ups of course also bring responsibilities. Negotiations about both advantages and responsibilities in turn affect the interests inside the national system—and more give and take has to take place, more freedom of action be surrendered.

In the corporatist set-up the interventionist activities of government are subjected to veto pressures; to gain consensus, the state enters into coalitions with the various agents of pressure groups—labour leaders, big-business organizations. Other interests, and public interest in general, demand control over these coalitions, in the shape of more effective surveillance by, primarily, new judicial instruments; parliament is not so effective and therefore secondary in the process.

The processes of concertation, of consensus-seeking, have generated a new vocabulary round the core concept of 'corporatism'. The word itself, we remember, has unfortunate associations dating back to Mussolini's fascist experiments of the 1920s and 30s. Modern political scientists, wishing to accentuate the essential divergence of the new forms of corporatism from the totalitarian ones, have produced qualifying prefixes or adjectives, each of which, if nothing else, reflects the more or less positive attitude of the name-giver to the phenomenon of corporatism. Thus we have new corporatism, neo-corporatism, the societal corporatism of Schmitter, the liberal corporatism of Lehmbruch, social democratic corporatism.

What are the features of the brand of corporatism which is the subject of this chapter?

—It is seen as an inevitable concomitant of government in a modern Western democracy.

—It is a means of preserving pluralism when the state has to become increasingly interventionist.

—Its mode of making public policy is commonly, though not invariably, benign.

'Benign' is a term which without being completely neutral—it suggests the beneficence which can often accompany modern corporatism—has the virtue of not pre-empting any particular political road to the desired aim. The state, in our type of corporatism, does not dominate: it acts in the main as a 'decision broker' who occasionally persuades. The state's own agencies are penetrated and deeply influenced (if not controlled) by representatives of the interest groups. In general a wide variety of quangos and other institutions with independent authority, such as central banks, also act as guardians of the public interest.

The guiding principles of this type of corporatist government are legitimacy, hierarchic control by the 'corporatist' group over its members, and specific features of leadership.

Legitimacy is about the relationship with formal government. The corporatist body must have official recognition; it need not, however, necessarily have a monopoly of representation of an entire interest group. It can with advantage be involved with political parties; some elements in the corporatist bargain are at times the subject of parliamentary debate and eventually secured by law (see for instance German procedures which give legal status to collective agreements, pp. 143–4 below).

The hierarchy principle expresses the recognized pecking order which should operate at any given moment.[3] As relations between interest groups in a corporatist situation do at times involve conflict, the rules of the game have to be transparent; the German employers' lockout power goes with more orderly and transparent industrial relations than those which prevail in the UK. Here lies the advantage of nations with a corporatist tradition—such as Germany or Japan—over the Anglo-American type of political culture. But even in the UK the summit organizations, such as the CBI (and its predecessor, the FBI) and the TUC, which now are typically weak, were not always so, especially not in the second and third decades of this century.

Leadership factors are difficult to pin-point: e.g. in the maintaining of 'grass roots' relations, leadership is to do with the performance of an efficient information function, and with a regular dialogue with constituents, and also with representation (legal and other) *vis-à-vis* outsiders; it also involves organizing effective voting procedures. It might be defined as that group of features which British trade unions—and also, traditionally, British trade associations—have in weakest degree.

Streeck points out that while the relationship must be voluntary—*freiwillig*—and can be interrupted, it involves some (equally voluntary) surrender of autonomous power in order to arrive at consensus (Streeck, pp.15–18). The question of how far the corporatist institution has to be in a monopoly situation and exercise some degree of compulsion over its members or affiliates is clearly very important.

A fourth category—overriding, perhaps, the three earlier ones—is a measure of self-regulation, recognized by the authorities. This connects up with all the problems of transparency and the accountability to public authority on which the UK is particularly weak.

A characteristic of modern corporatism is the way in which powers are, in practice, delegated by the state to business enterprises. They acquire the right to employ, export, etc. by belonging to a recognized association. As this still leaves scope for the entry of new and competing recognized undertakings, the situation does not necessarily encourage monopolies.

Is it possible to construct a scale of degree of corporatist power, pure and simple, and—a different question, this—is it possible to construct a scale of the effectiveness of the corporatist elements in any one government?[4] We have pointed out that effective corporatist organization has been at the root of successful economic and social performance in several of the countries we survey. We have also seen that in the uneven economic experience of the 1970s,

Japan was the outstanding success. It is no accident that it has the most advanced *large* corporatist system (Austria is a candidate for having the most elaborate corporatism, regardless of size).[5] Among the successes of Japanese corporatism was the holding-down of prices at the expense of profits by the big industrial concerns and trade associations in collusion with MITI to keep within tight limits the inflation which elsewhere rose by leaps and bounds after the oil shock of 1973. Intra-conglomerate exchanges of labour helped to maintain a high level of employment—and consensus between company trade unions—while the orderly process of the spring wage offensive kept wage rises down. The Japanese-type recession cartels for long-term restructuring are, one must suppose, another area in which corporatist behaviour is important.

Corporatist institutions have been part of the secret of the success of small countries under the pressures of the 1970s cycles—the Austrian *Proporz* (Shonfield, 1965, p.193) with its hierarchy of interest groups being an outstanding example. In such countries the 'corporations' *are* the government. But parliamentary institutions are not thereby rendered ineffectual: it is false to see parliament and corporatist entities as rivals. It is easy to fall into this error as the British and American definitions suffer from too sharp a distinction between 'public' bodies which are seen as accountable and 'private' ones which are not.

In Europe, Germany is the outstanding example of a major economy where corporatist procedures have been successful. Among the examples of the success has been the *Konzertierte Aktion*. This never was the bargaining exercise that foreigners tended to see, but the mere process of looking at the figures together, and agreeing on the economic effects of alternative fiscal, wage and investment decisions set, for a time at least, a narrow framework for the real bargaining which followed in other meeting places. The state acts as a provider of 'neutral' forecasts; as an agent which can sweeten deals by fiscal side-payments or which can threaten to punish deviant behaviour through fiscal and monetary policies. In many narrower areas of economic policy, i.e. the introduction of better energy technologies, or the stockpiling of commodities, or the creation of jobs for the young, the state tends to announce its wishes to private agents—national associations— using the threat of direct legal action in case of non-compliance. Equally, in cases of industrial rescues, it allows private banks to have a first go to defend the national interest, with direct action a threat of last resort (see pp.160, 173, n.5).

What made German (and Austrian) trade unions, which had been so conflict-prone earlier, so collaborative with the state in the post-war period was, according to Mancur Olson, the phenomenon which he calls 'encompassingness' and involvement in government.[6] This is the subject of comment by Colin Crouch who has enlightening things to say about the history of socio-political relations in these countries (Crouch, 1981). There is nothing here of Olson's theory of wiping out guilds, which make for 'institutional sclerosis', through wars.[7] Guilds were built into the Continental union system and were of the essence of the political system—the opposite of the UK. But in the 1920s and 1930s a great effort was made to keep unions away from the high levels of political power. The post-war social-democratic style of decision-making changed all that.

Lehmbruch (1977) sees two distinct flows in policy-making. One is *Ordnungspolitik* which covers such matters as the maintenance of competition, anti-cartel legislation, the management of the business cycle; it also lays down general rules for the conduct of society (e.g. about property rights and responsibilities). In most countries, all that tends to remain in the sphere of parliament and political parties. The other flow includes bargaining about income shares and other zero-sum game decision-making which go naturally to the corporative decision-making system; there it is easier to arrive at a discreet bargain. He notes, however, in his interesting comparison of Germany and Austria that, while the Germans stick to this view of *Ordnungspolitik* (e.g. in legislative decisions about the new industrial co-determination law), Austrians have accepted the 'spillover' of corporatism into all forms of political life. The habit was formed in the two decades of post-war coalition of the two main parties; built into the management of a wide range of institutions; and is now unshakeably established in all spheres.

In Lehmbruch's eyes, Germany is by comparison with Austria only a hesitant practitioner of corporatism. Typically, *Konzertierte Aktion*—the characteristic product of corporatist thinking—'has mainly served as an instrument of crisis management, not of continuous economic guidance' (Lehmbruch, p.107). This is because of the hesitations of the participants (with too many people—as many as fifty at a time—attending meetings); the unwillingness of government to give a clear lead; and above all because it has not allowed the concern with wage restraint (its chief preoccupation) to develop, as the unions wished, towards a fully fledged incomes policy, involving control of profits, prices, etc. Here, Lehmbruch says, Austria is very different.

Lehmbruch's chief examples of 'liberal corporatist' countries— the Netherlands, Scandinavia, Switzerland, Austria, Germany— are all distinguished by a 'co-operative' variety of incomes policy (characterized by the participation of trade unions and business in the process of governmental policy-making). There, the straight power of legislation does not suffice; statutory power does not work; political parties are the wrong instrument for bargaining. Lehmbruch sees incomes policies as the key issue, a test of effective corporatism which the French (whose concertation of labour markets is government-organized) and the British fail.

A necessary element of Lehmbruch's liberal corporatism is an élitist leadership by technicians, crossing party lines formed around popularly accepted doctrines of economics. If the experts advising the political consensus-makers were to be Marxists or Chicago monetarists, the system would break down. For liberal corporatism to work, organized labour must both have a high degree of centralized power, and be involved integrally in the processes of government—either directly through the socialist party inside the government (as in the Scandinavian case) or by being integrated into an élite cartel of the 'consociational' type (of which Austria is the extreme case).

Lehmbruch's emphasis on incomes policies as the main criterion of effective corporatism may be something of an over-simplification. For instance, he omits the difficulties attendant on the introduction of new technologies and the resultant restructuring; also special problems attendant on the enhanced strength of small groups occupying a strategic place in the system, who have to be persuaded not to use their power of blackmail. They can be bought off only on terms which encourage others in turn to use *their* veto power.[8]

Olson argues that the UK, in contrast, suffers from institutional sclerosis (see p.152, n.7 below), which is the chief reason for its economic failure. He holds that once interest group organizations develop a dominant oligopolistic character this creates rigidities

(Olson, 1978, p.34) which makes them very slow to change: they are behaving like characteristic oligopolists—slowing down, resisting market forces. In Sweden, by contrast, Olson believes that the interest groups take a positive view of the economic interests and growth of society as a whole, because they encompass so large a share of the nation's economic activity (1978, p.38).[9] He also argues that while lost wars and upheavals help economic growth, growth rates are negatively correlated with the range and established power of *small* interest group organizations. His prime examples are the UK and the long-settled parts of the US outside the South. This leads to the argument that the deleterious effect of established interest group power on innovation is effectively countered by a high degree of 'encompassingness', as in Sweden. This is nearer the bone. Small is conservative. Olson's logic of 'collective action' shows that the bigger the interest group, the less the private gains appropriated by members of the collective body tend to outweigh the general loss of welfare through inefficiency.

If the argument concerns the political devices required to bargain with group interests so that they promote public interests, then the character of Olson's thesis is profoundly changed. The problem may be met by an energetic government, which responds to the wishes of major interest groups and at the same time imposes some constraint on them (this was what the social democrats did in Scandinavia, and also in Germany after the late-1960s). Japan's MITI and big business (in a setting of highly fragmented trade unions) are also effective; the Keidanren and the other major business organizations are *not* defied. France has secured concertation, through the Plan: it is the Plan's main utility.

In the UK, as was observed by the author in earlier writings, corporatist bodies found 'a congenial soil in which to flourish' (Shonfield, 1965, p.162); they were encouraged by 'the peculiar style of British democratic processes which accommodated parliament rather too easily to the bargaining, conducted, very largely out of sight, between interest groups' (Shonfield, 1974). What resulted was a modified variety of corporatism which did not fulfil the transparency conditions. Nor did it bring the public interest to bear adequately on the corporatist bodies. This described the UK in the 1960s. In the subsequent period, from Heath's initial principle of 'no talk', through the Labour government's social contract in the mid-1970s, to the apotheosis of anti-corporatism under the Thatcher government, the UK made little progress in establishing a regular system of corporatist collaboration between government and the representatives of business and labour. It is precisely because the UK, and also the US, have not developed methods for such collaboration sufficiently that they are markedly disadvantaged under present economic pressures and at times appear ungovernable.

Incomes policies: successes and failures

'. . . keeping a lamb in a cage with a lion requires a large reserve supply of lambs. Similarly, society may need a reserve supply of incomes policies.' (Okun, 1979, p.5)

A key prerequisite for the governability of our Western societies is that labour should be persuaded to recognize its 'public interest' function. There are of course some instances when organized labour does just that, as there are a few laudable exceptions of companies which take their public role seriously. But even if on occasion both labour and management are motivated by reasons other than self-interest, what we generally have to rely on is a straight trade-off. This is why—and we have made the point elsewhere (Shonfield, 1982, pp.59–66)—incomes policies are bound to increasingly determine the texture of our economies.

How was it that in the mid-1970s organized labour, which was said to be alienated to a high degree from national policy-making by the big business–government alliance, gave governmental policies of wage restraint (in conditions of relatively high unemployment) such a high degree of co-operation, not only in Britain and Sweden but in several other North European countries? Indeed, looking around the Western world in the second half of the 1970s one found in one country after another—almost as if they had communicated the same impulse to each other—a systematic effort to reduce the *share* taken by wage incomes and by publicly-financed social services from the national product. It seemed, moreover, to elicit widespread electoral support. It was a matter of indifference whether a government of the Right or the Left or the Centre was in charge, although it was notable that the job was done most prominently under the impulse of two social-democrat governments—in the UK and in Germany.

This was a special moment, when one could say that in 1975–6 'productivity in several countries with powerful trade unions will have gone up significantly faster than wages—and the chief beneficiary, with the assent of the trade unions, will be profits' (Shonfield, January 1977, pp.17–18). Is it possible to make such consensus a regular component of the management of our economies?

The straight power of legislation is not sufficient to produce a workable incomes policy. Political parties are an inadequate instrument for the bargaining which can only be done successfully by a coalition of government and its corporatist partners.

Nor is the tripartite solution, of getting the consensus of government, business and labour, enough, when incomes policies are apt to collapse if inflation is not contained. Without securing a political climate in which other claimants on shares of the national product (including single-interest groups) know how to contain their demands, no incomes policy will work.

In *The Use of Public Power* (pp.59–66) and also in the second chapter of this book (pp.15–16) we examined what use had been made of incomes policies in the attempt to dampen inflation, and reflected on some of the issues which had turned Western policy-makers against such tools. We came to the conclusion that as it is becoming less effective and more expensive than in the past 'to tackle the problem of rising prices by the traditional instruments of deflation' it would become necessary to strengthen and adapt the 'network of implicit contracts, on which a large part of the substructure of the economy has come to depend . . .'; it was also pointed out that modern-style incomes policies did not necessarily have to be committed to a fixed figure, and that it had been the German and Japanese 'insistence on the flexibility of the response by the workers to business conditions and profit opportunities', that had been at the core of those countries' successes (Shonfield, 1982, pp.65–6 and 107).

Some of the most useful things said about articulated and flexible approaches to the subject of incomes policies have come from Arthur Okun. Characteristically, in view of his analysis of price formation by convention and habit,[10] he argued for a systematic incomes policy, using all the instruments of publicity, moral pressure plus tactical legal measures (like the threat of anti-trust suits when prices were raised by more than increased costs in the face of sluggish demand), but not using price controls. Informal 'semi-voluntary' policies of wage and price restraint could, Okun held, help over relatively short limits of time, but such policies had been proved vulnerable to fast-changing economic conditions. He favoured offering wage-earners real income guarantees, in the form of tax relief if prices rise by more than 5 per cent.

This is not yet the great reserve of incomes policies for which Okun foresaw the need, but a good beginning to flexibility. Taxes are an explicit part of the bargain. His aim was to avoid the prospective loss of output through deflation (which he put at 250–500 billion dollars in the mid-1970s) by collective action; in his view the use of market forces to change expectations enough to bring down inflation decisively was too expensive.

It is illuminating to see how certain attitudes firmed, towards the end of the 1970s, in favour of incomes policies. Not that they were suddenly seen as a sovereign remedy for all the ills of Western capitalism. But the 1979/80 Annual Report of the Bank for International Settlements concluded that '. . . monetary policy will have to be complemented not only by fiscal policy but also by some form of incomes policy appropriate to the country's institutions and circumstances' (p.178). A careful 'Occasional Study' by the OECD (OECD *Economic Outlook*, July 1980) also regards incomes policies as a useful part of the apparatus of short-term demand management, so long as they are employed in a sustained fashion and *not* as an emergency expedient as was the wont in the UK and the US in the 1960s and early 1970s.

The study raised questions about the relationship of other— fiscal, monetary—policies to incomes policies: it is now generally accepted that these policies must operate in harness, and not allow high demand to pull in an opposite direction. But Austrian policies in the 1975–8 period were an 'important exception to this general prescription of combining incomes policy with restrictive macroeconomic policies' (p.43). In that instance the incomes policy worked because of a bargain guaranteeing 'expansionary demand management' and full employment combined with a 'hard currency policy'. Wage settlements went down from 15 per cent in 1975 to 5 per cent in 1978.

Austria's incomes policy has indeed been the centrepiece of successful management with an impressive growth performance of an average annual 5 per cent; inside the OECD only Japan performed better. The incomes policy is supported by selective government intervention holding down prices, high employment (only 2 per cent unemployed in the late 1970s) and increasingly generous social welfare. On the debit side have been big budget deficits, high, and rising, taxation and growing foreign indebtedness; together, these are thought to make the currency highly vulnerable. The OECD study noted that such difficulties might undermine the Austrian policy. Will Austria's low inflation rate and strong currency give in the 1980s?

In Germany too, the containment of pay push has depended on effective corporatist practices. Wolfgang Streeck performed a valuable service in his analysis of the functioning of the powerful *IG Metall* union (which, with over 2 million members, covers a wide variety of industries) when he showed how the 'solidaristic' wage policy of the German unions—in effect, the 'long established practice that . . . all unions settle at about the same rate of increase—the rate got by the union settling first, usually the *IG Metall*' (Streeck, typescript, ch.3, p.10)—has profound consequences for the whole German economy. Even so, in line with the underlying German preference for discretion (which in the instance of the search for consensus on wages takes the form of allowing the individual unions to go on with collective bargaining and to explore employers' ability in different industries to give more), there is an agreed aggregate figure as an unadmitted, though sometimes all but overt, target.

Perhaps the crucial feature of these large-scale solidaristic wage negotiations is that through them organized labour becomes unavoidably involved in economic policy choices. No leap-frogging of wage claims is allowable under this system. Trade unions are therefore in practice forced to take a view of what in general the economy can afford. 'Unions in a centralized, comprehensive bargaining system generally act on behalf of a significant fraction of the national workforce'; their decisions 'have direct and predictable consequences for the state of the economy as a whole' (Streeck, typescript, ch.3, p.11). The 'macro-economic side effects' of union decisions on productivity, investment and inflation are all taken into account by these sophisticated German trade union officials, figuring much more in their discussions than in the deliberations of work-place negotiators in Britain. For the typical British trade union negotiator the logical policy is to exploit to the full the bargaining advantage offered by the particular circumstances; he must always consider the risk that others will behave irresponsibly and, if they cause inflation, leave the members whom he represents even more disadvantaged. Macro-economic rationality can only be achieved by large-scale collective decision. In the UK the large unions are too weak to do this; here initiative devolves to the work-place representatives. Paradoxically, though, Streeck asserts that the *Deutscher Gewerkschaftsbund* (DGB) has less power than its British equivalent, the TUC; co-ordination in Germany proceeds by a different route.

The most significant economic consequences of solidaristic union behaviour are, first, to intensify competition and, with it, the threat of extinction for weak firms, which are forced to pay the same wage rates as the strong; and second, to give a financial bonus in earnings to strong firms—assuming that unions demand wage increases close to the average of what can be readily conceded while assuring the going rate of profit (as they must do if excessive wages are not to lead to large-scale bankruptcies). This is like the system pursued by Swedish unions.

In Germany the prime condition of all this is a very high degree of power centralization, with effective, very extensive and highly professional grass-roots consultation. The union provides services and is actively involved in everything, through the works councils (the overwhelming majority of whose members are supported by the union) and the *Vertrauensleute* (the German version of shop stewards).

The increasing professionalisation of the unions in the 1960s and especially the 1970s is striking, especially by contrast with British circumstances. Thus in a number of German companies the chief *Vertrauensmann* has a professional assistant or two, as well as secretarial help, and offices, all provided by the company. The assistant is often an economist. At the same time the senior *Vertrauensleute* are in effect also running the works councils and have a quasi-managerial status.

Finally, it is of the essence of the German situation that unofficial strikes are very awkward to run, with no funds available and in view of the highly legalized system of industrial relations. If employers can demonstrate that the union encouraged and supported the wild-cat strikers who broke the collective agreement, it is brought to court. The legal sanctions in themselves are not decisive, but they are an additional factor—along with centralization of power and 'democratic centralism' (the phrase is Streeck's)—in making for orderly conflict.

In Britain, the two biggest unions, transport and engineering, led by Jack Jones and Hugh Scanlon, played a similar solidaristic role in 1975–6, with a dominant concern for the macro-economic effects (on prices, on employment) of the policies of the individual unions. But there it ended. Why was there no follow-up? Was it due to the reassertion of a temporarily suppressed state of civil war? Or to political mishandling?[11]

Skilful political handling can be critical as was demonstrated in the first half of the 1970s by the successes of the social democrat parties in Scandinavia. The *savoir faire* of the policy-makers is thought to have been decisive in both Denmark and Sweden. The Swedes under Olof Palme's first social democrat prime-ministership went to the length of holding daily lunch meetings between the leaders of the LO (Sweden's confederation of trade unions) and the ministers concerned with labour affairs. When in 1976 a coalition government succeeded the social democrats, it found bargaining with the trade unions on broad social policy issues more difficult, and therefore the path to incomes policy agreements much more thorny.

Asserting consumer rights

Looking back on the years since the end of World War Two one is apt to see the new consumer movements as a popular groundswell of mounting dissatisfaction on the part of citizens of Western societies with what they buy, whether with cash or taxes. This is not so; the movements are by no means always spontaneously generated: in a number of countries and under a variety of circumstances the original impetus which gives rise to them depends on government intervention.

The overt reasons for this intervention are invariably connected with the pursuit of public interest. Here we are not concerned with the rationale for state-sponsored consumer action, but with two aspects of its history: first, the recognition by policy-makers that where consumers do not speak up, they—the government—have to stimulate vocal interest groups; secondly, some options on approaches to the problems of supportive legislation.

Consumer protection by statute and inspection is not new. In Britain it dates back to the medieval assizes—the regulations which from the twelfth century onwards controlled the weights, measures and prices (and often also the quality) of bread, ale and other articles in general consumption. In modern times the US government has been in the forefront of protection by regulation, pioneering elaborate anti-trust and food and drug laws. America has also been the forerunner in the development of popular consumer movements, which did not spread elsewhere until after World War Two. From the late 1940s increasingly affluent consumers (especially in the United States, the UK and the smaller North European democracies) trooped under the protective umbrella of the consumer associations initiated and run by independent groups of citizens. It could even be said that their efforts embraced informing and advising the consumer as well as political action which seeks legal or other official remedies. The underlying momentum was powerful: US membership soon topped the 2 million mark; UK subscribers to the Consumers' Association passed the half million mark in 1968.

An international office of consumer unions, the IOCU, was set up in 1960 by the consumer associations of USA, UK, Australia, Belgium and the Netherlands, and grew to cover a hundred or so member organizations. But the formal attempts to set international standards of protection, including those of the EEC,[12] are beset by difficulties arising out of traditionally different national practice. Spontaneous action by the new radical environmentalist interest groups has been much more effective in exercising parallel pressures in various national situations.

The second phase in the history of the national consumer movements started in the 1960s and had two contradictory currents. The first was part of the more general backlash against regulation and public expenditure. The slogans it chose were mainly about the cost-effectiveness of consumer protection. For some ten or twelve years the terminology of cost-benefit analysis became part of current parlance, until at some point in the late 1970s we made the dual discovery, that we had in any case habitually taken the cost of regulation into account, and that to calculate cost-effectiveness accurately was a complex, time-consuming and often expensive venture.

The other manifestation originating in the 1960s—the one which concerns especially our main topic here—was the rapid increase in the pace of active intrusion of public authority in consumer protection. Two main arguments were behind this extension of public intervention: first, that competition does not necessarily happen spontaneously, but has to be actively ensured by public intervention (the old approach of the US Federal Trade Commission); and second (less certainly), that competition by itself does not guarantee the result: thus stiffer laws on labelling and generally on information, control on use of advertisement claims, and on artificial product differentiation are needed. Particular difficulties arise in the field of services, especially where the service is attached to a product sold or worse still, leased (such as IBM equipment).

Most of the French consumer movement and a great part of the German were and continue to be wholly or in large part publicly financed—an expression of the public concern to control the growing oligopolistic tendencies in the economy. But in the UK the backlash mood has prevailed and had the opposite effect: two public initiatives—the 1963 Consumer Council and the local consumer advice centres—have fallen victim to it. The Office of Fair Trading set up in 1973 (under the same Conservative government which had abolished the Consumer Council on attaining office three years previously) took over some of the function of the latter, and also substantial powers over monopoly and merger policy and restrictive practices. The OFT has the status of an independent body; its creation marks an important stage in the grudging and gradual transfer of interventionist powers (with a great deal of political content) from ministries to autonomous agencies with judicial authority.

The great inflation which followed on the shocks of 1973–4 has given an additional boost to that part of the consumer protection movement which is concerned with 'fair prices'—in particular, with preventing the exploitation of the weakness which arises from lack of information. In the UK, as in most other West European countries, governments already concerned with monopolistic practices and the exploitation of market power greatly reinforced their efforts. Price control by mobilizing consumer interests became the favoured technique, but it never made much difference. It chose the wrong instrument—active reporting of infringements of price controls and other violations of regulation, such as quantities stated on packages—to get quick but patchy results. Spontaneous consumer pressure typically makes its effect felt more slowly, systematically, and inexorably.

Some countries, those with government-initiated consumer protection movements, such as Germany and France, continued to rely on market forces while strengthening (at least in the former) anti-trust measures and the supply of useful market information. Others—with the USA, UK, Sweden and the Netherlands in the lead—developed a widespread sense that after all most of the new forms of protection, with the emphasis on information and lobbying, did not in fact protect the weak, easily intimidated, risk-avoiding consumer. The authorities had to go further if consumers were to develop the force necessary to control sellers, providing easy access to procedures which would ensure quick and adequate redress of abuses, in a conscious reversal of the principle of *caveat emptor*. In most countries the existing judicial systems were too ponderous and expensive to perform this role adequately, and once again the state (or state financing) intervened to provide alternative machinery for redress procedures. In the UK the Office of Fair Trading is a manifestation of this impulse to give legal and compulsory forms to arrangements which had previously depended on self-regulation and publicity. In a more experimental mood, Small Claims Courts were set up in several areas to help the consumer to invoke the protection of judicial or quasi-judicial authority; before the combination of anti-welfare backlash with stringent economies of public funds arrested their progress, Legal Advice Centres were beginning to tell him of his legal rights.

As so often, the Swedish system provided a complex and articulated model of a resource for ensuring that wronged consumers got adequate redress. Its history, the subject of an essay by Martin Eisenstein (1979), is worth noting, because it is an example of the underlying trend away from regulatory agencies to institutions whose powers are judicial.

The year 1968 saw the establishment in Sweden of the Public Complaints Board, specifically for the investigation of complaints affecting consumer products and services. Its origins are corporatist: it was originally conceived as an amalgamation and reinforcement of private complaints boards set up by individual trade associations. The latter continue to be part of the structure of the

Public Complaints Board, participating in the *travaux préparatoires* on individual cases.

The Board does not adjudicate individual claims; all the same its 'recommendations' (which are biased towards consumer protection and against *caveat emptor*) have an extremely powerful effect. Several associations guarantee to accept the Board's recommendations as if they were judgments and compensate injured consumers accordingly. While on occasion a few non-members of trade associations have defied the Board's recommendations, such firms are a tiny minority of the total. It should be added that the prevailing respect for the expertise of the Board's secretariat (which consists of specialists on individual products and services) is a significant element in making its recommendations acceptable.

Nevertheless, even in a disciplined setting such as this Swedish one, in practice reliance on non-binding procedures and self-regulation on the part of trade associations soon proved inadequate. Consumers continued not to pursue claims because of the cost and the risk of having to meet defendant's costs in the case of adverse judgment. To remedy this, several measures were introduced from 1972 on, granting complainants entitlement to legal aid (on top of the Swedish practice of insurance against legal costs—that ultimate in *embourgeoisement*) and establishing small claims procedures. Moreover, by the latter part of the 1970s the whole non-binding principle of the Public Complaints Board was subjected to a thorough re-examination; the main grounds for retaining it were the concern to preserve maximum flexibility and to keep within the spirit of corporatism. In spite of the frustration of the main effort to make people *feel* protected, all this represents an impressive sustained effort at ensuring justice for the consumer.

If ever there were lessons to be learnt about the advantages of gradual, stage-by-stage institution-building, this example of the widening and strengthening of Swedish consumer protection provides them in profusion. Further lessons can be learnt from the US where such legal tools intended to help the previously inadequately protected consumer have developed in the past two decades, helped by a similar spirit of gradual melioration.[13]

The British mode of institution-building suffers from being staccato: a thorough examination of the need by a Royal Commission precedes the making of detailed and articulated laws; these are then allowed to become slowly and deeply rooted over many years, with little concern about shortcomings revealed by practice, before Parliament eventually disinters, re-examines, and amends them. What attempts there have been to make the process of this type of reform more in the nature of an initial pilot experiment with a succession of quick adjustments[14] have been bedevilled by the contingencies of miserly budgeting.

Is corporatism compatible with planning?

Faced with a proliferation of interest groups—often set against one another in seeking conflicting objectives—one is led to ask 'Can a society which is devoted to this riot of pluralism in public as well as business affairs plan itself?' When this question was formulated, in the mid-1960s, '*anti-planning* deliberately elevated to a way of life' was the most obvious challenge to the orderly pursuit of the capitalist system in the countries—such as UK and USA—which made a virtue of spontaneous government.[15]

It will be evident to the reader by this time that the author is committed to planning—certainly, not the command planning with fixed goals to be reached by narrowly defined channels (this, even in the relatively innocuous form it took during the early French plans, has been found to be full of holes), but the indicative planning on which the French government based its VIIIth Plan. Earlier chapters have shown in what ways the Germans and the Japanese and the British have come to terms with it, and that the American resistance to it has to some extent been broken down.

It was Hugh Heclo who, in writing about the difficulties of inter-sectoral management of welfare policies which involved big, often indivisible investments, asserted that the demand for longer-term planning would come in the US only when the costs of uncoordinated government action are recognized to be too high, and there is a 'customer' for planning in the executive branch of government (Heclo, 1975).

Indeed, in addition to the school of American academic economists such as Leontief, who never doubted that a complex modern economy must be directed from the centre not just by short-term demand management but according to medium and longer-term guidelines, there are now many political practitioners whose implicit belief in planning comes from the very experience of trying to run the complicated system on the basis of *ad hoc* decisions—and finding the method wanting. In a plea for institutional reform which, he claims, would ensure effective government for the USA, Lloyd Cutler[16] writes of conflicting interests which make the Administration's task of reconciling needs and allocating resources increasingly arduous. Some of the most powerful pressures come from abroad, from the effects of the domestic policies of other countries at a time of growing interdependence. Within the USA, the single-interest groups have multiplied and become more assertive against a setting where there is relatively less surplus to distribute and less enthusiasm about having this surplus allocated by central government. Cutler rightly treats the choices implied by these pressures as political rather than economic—he calls the process of balancing them 'a kind of political triage'—and sees in them the reason why it has become 'far more important in 1980 than it was in 1940, 1900 or 1800' for the US government 'to have the capability to formulate and carry out an overall program' (Cutler, 1980, pp. 132-3).

The historian Otis L. Graham identifies the mid-1970s as the crest of the US pro-planning movement, the twin shocks of oil and wheat shortages in 1973/4 having brought home to American policy-makers the need to look at the economic situation in its entirety and to do so on a longer time-scale. The practical reflection of the changed attitude was described above (pp.49–51). However, the reaction against interventionist government which manifested itself in taxpayers' revolts, and turned many ex-liberals into anti-regulationists, naturally also extended to the rejection of most forms of government planning. The anti-interventionist mood was exploited by Reagan on his election platform, and continues to be at the centre of his declared policy. Will it last? There are signs that the higher echelons of government will hesitate to destroy what has been painstakingly built in the 1970s, and that, moreover, big business is not necessarily averse to some delicate planning activity emanating from the centre, for it is difficult to plan within a large enterprise if the national situation remains veiled in speculative darkness.[17]

Does a corporatist setting make planning more acceptable and effective? Is this why the Germans plan effectively (even though they give lip-service to anti-planning)?

Leontief favours 'offering labor leaders the opportunity to take a responsible and effective part in the design and implementation of a national economic plan'. His view is that by this means 'the power of organized labor would . . . be applied where it counts, instead of being dissipated or absorbed by inflation' (Leontief, 1976, p.11). This presupposes a functioning corporatist situation, in which informed and fully-briefed union leaders, who know themselves to be backed by the grass-roots movement, take their seat round the debating table with government planners and the representatives of private business (and, ideally, with those who safeguard the consumers' interest). If this appears impossible to achieve, so did the German and Austrian *Mitbestimmung*.

To quote Leontief again, writing about palliatives for technological unemployment:

> In fact, the success of Chancellor Schmidt's anti-inflation policies is built on the firm foundation of institutionalized joint labor–capital participation in the management of German industry. The by-law requires that one-half of the Boards of Directors of large corporations represent the shareholders while the other half be elected by labor. Among the latter, most are elected by that corporation's own labor force; but some—the outside labor directors—represent essentially the national trade union movement. . . . This means that employers and employees maintain a working contact at the very grass roots of German industry. (Leontief, 1979, p.50. See also Shonfield, 1965, p.251, n.32, p.261, n.55, and Crouch, 1980, pp. 100–2.)

Leontief goes on to say that in Austria 'the institutional set-up is very similar to the German one except that the government plays a greater role in across-the-board negotiations between trade unions and employers' organizations . . . by contributing rather detailed input–output types of projections of the economic outlook for some years ahead'.[18]

All this brings us back to the subject of incomes policies: these are, as we have said previously (p.139), the key issue, the test that the French and the British and the Americans fail, and the Germans by and large pass. We have asserted that it was in the obtaining of consensual support for incomes policies that corporatism's chief function lay, and that without some kind of incomes policy planning is doomed to fail. The answer to the question about the compatibility of corporatism and planning is in the affirmative. Not only are they compatible, but indicative planning cannot function effectively without the consensus which comes from smoothly running corporatist institutions.

Notes to Chapter 10

1. For an exposition of this view, see the writings of Bernard Cazes on L'Etat-Protecteur, in particular 'The Welfare State: A Double Bind' (September 1980) and 'La Crise de l'Etat-Protecteur dans les économies occidentales' (1980–1).

2. On the growing cost of the inefficiencies of the welfare distributing bureaucracy see above, pp.27–8, and Wildavsky (1980). Bernard Cazes suggests that there has been a fundamental deterioration in public services, in large part due (he thinks) to the decline of the attachment to the principle of *noblesse oblige* among lower grade public servants. If his assumption is correct (Cazes, September 1980, pp.8–9), the fact that, owing to changes in values, public services are no longer in a position to rely on an abundant supply of 'conscientious and low-cost' labour may explain in part the deterioration in the quality of these services. Or is it simply that the pace of expansion has been too rapid?

3. Oliver Williamson (1975) emphasizes that, *in business*, hierarchical situations, where people collaborate under the command of some recognized leadership, are more efficient than real or simulated market situations. Does the same apply to political decision-making?

4. Schmitter (1979, pp.26–30) has interesting things to say about the reasons why societal corporatism is so unevenly distributed across countries—and across types of proprietary interest within countries.

5. In an interesting essay on 'Corporatism Without Labor? The Japanese Anomaly', Pempel and Tsunekawa (1979) claim that an anomaly in Japanese corporatism is that it is only two-sided, consisting of business (plus agriculture) and government, with labour not represented. Is it not rather that labour's participation in the corporate processes is not overt? Some of the corporatist process in fact takes place at enterprise level—between the management and the single enterprise union. The way in which organized labour in fact acts in unison (see the spring wage offensive) surely makes it an integrated force which counts in the dialogue? [*Ed.*]

6. This does not account for the fact that German trade unions were also co-operative in the early post-war period, with no access to formal political power. On 'encompassingness' see Olson, 1978, pp.38–9, and also the extended version of this essay, circulated in photocopied form in the same year (see note 7 below).

7. The phrase is Mancur Olson's. He originally wrote, in the context of UK's damped-down growth rate, of 'institutional arthritis' in a paper.

'The Political Economy of Comparative Growth Rates', which was circulated in 1976 in photocopied form. It was later printed as part of a US Joint Economic Committee exercise (1978), and republished in *Portfolio*, vol.7, no.1. In the form 'institutional sclerosis' the phrase first saw light in an expanded version of the original paper, circulated in 1978; it also was used in a slightly different context in a 'Main Issues' paper of the OECD Interfutures project, dated 2 February 1979, and again, in July 1979, in the Interfutures report, *Facing the Future*. A definitive restatement of the ideas contained in these works is to be found in Olson's 1982 book, *The Rise and Decline of Nations*. [*Ed.*]

8. Why so much veto power?—does it reflect, in part, the move to a service economy: the dependence on continuously provided central services, such as electricity, garbage collection, transport, etc., where the workers have in practice gained physical control over enormously expensive pieces of capital equipment, or are organized to maintain the effective monopoly of a particular service?

9. Olson does not explain why lots of interest groups with lots of status, on the Swedish model, should necessarily be of such good behaviour. They *are*, but for deeper reasons—perhaps to do with long-standing preferences for openness, transparency, accountability and consensus-seeking.

10. The author referred to a number of articles by Okun, published from the mid-1970s on, of which Okun 1975:2 is the key one. *Prices and Quantities*, which came out posthumously in 1981, is a useful amplification and development of the argument. [*Ed.*]

11. [*Editor's note, based on comments by David Shonfield*]: See Shonfield, 1982, p.107. The phrase 'suppressed civil war' is François Duchêne's. The end of the 1974-9 Labour government's 'social contract' experiment was not just the result of the alienation of the TUC from the process of economic management. The unions in fact tried to rescue the government by reformulating the terms of the agreement on two occasions. It was the CBI, representing the employers in a notable display of solidarity, which paved the way for the end of the agreement by its successful campaign against punitive sanctions in public sector contracts. The employers' resistance to being made the 'policeman' of a social contract originally devised by government and TUC meant the government had only exhortation to back up its unilateral declaration of a low limit for pay rises. As soon as the limit was defied by an *employer*—as it was by the Ford Motor Company under the pressure of a strike in November 1978—the policy was destined to collapse.

In retrospect it is remarkable that the social contract in the UK endured for so long—from mid-1975 to the latter part of 1978—and the reasons it collapsed were at least as much to do with the failure to construct or evolve agreed institutions to supervise the terms of the bargain. The policy was agreed in an extremely *ad hoc* manner at a time of mounting concern about the political impact of sustained record inflation levels. Its failures were patched up with an eye to short-term solutions (notably the agreement to a special permanent pay formula for the fire service after a long strike at the end of 1977). And its only institution, the Price Commission, inherited from the previous administration, failed both to command the confidence of business and to convince trade unionists that the policy was working for their benefit.

Personalities were to a large degree responsible for the initial success. The Director-General of the CBI, John Methven (later to lead the co-ordinated opposition to the perceived unjust methods of policing the pay limit), had previously been in charge of the Office of Fair Trading. On the union side, Jones and Scanlon were, uniquely, union leaders who commanded a wide personal following (and political loyalty) among the members of the layer of local union officers and full-time work-place representatives, whose assent was critical to the remarkably smooth transition from rapidly escalating wage demands to acceptance of a cut in real wages in the summer of 1975.

12. A separate Directorate General for consumer and environmental protection was set up at the European Community's Commission headquarters in Brussels in 1981. [*Ed.*]

13. The story of this phase of US institution-building is relevant and fascinating, but too detailed to summarize here. The reader is referred to Cappelletti *et al.*, especially the essay by Marc Galanter (1981). [*Ed.*]

14. A number of experiments started in the early 1970s. An account of the first six or seven years will be found in an essay by George Applebey (1979).

15. The quotations are from Shonfield, 1965, pp.336 and 222 respectively. I am indebted to J. G. Ruggie, who focused on them in his essay on 'Complexity, Planning and Public Order' (1975, p.143, n.57). [*Ed.*]

16. Lloyd N. Cutler is a Washington lawyer deeply involved in the governmental process, who became Counsel to President Carter in 1979. In his article in *Foreign Affairs* he proposes a series of constitutional changes, which would, among other advantages, 'diminish the power of single-interest groups to veto balanced programs for governing' (Cutler, 1980, p.142). [*Ed.*]

17. Large American firms have of course for a long time recognized the function of long-term planning in the conduct of their own business operations, and their planning techniques—especially those of

multinationals, such as IBM—developed markedly during the last ten or fifteen years. The logic which connects efficient planning in the private sector with the setting of longer-term guidelines by government was, however, only patchily apprehended.

18. The German or Austrian type of *indirect* corporatism may be what we have to settle for—with the workers' voices heard round the company board table. Certainly, the German record of industrial peace is impressive—and its reasons are not fully understood; among the large Western democracies the Germans have by far the lowest number of work days lost through industrial action per 1,000 employees—their five-yearly averages are in line with those of Scandinavians and the Dutch. The Japanese alternative, of worker docility bought at the cost of protective policies by individual employers, is not realistic in the foreseeable future, when the whole long history of Western organized labour emphasizes conflictual stances. Nor is it likely to be acceptable to employers whose profits are squeezed in conditions of slow growth.

It is perhaps not just a matter of chance that both Germany and Japan have cultural features which are not commonly found in other Western-style democracies. We have, for many years, been aware of the importance of national characteristics in the pursuit of advantage in international trade. It is increasingly obvious that such characteristics are becoming more important as a function of comparative advantage in the successful management of industrial relations, in spite of the social and psychological downgrading (especially in American comment) of 'mere' national traits as sources of politico-economic behaviour. They certainly figure large in the successes and failures of consensus-seeking.

Germany for instance *is* different, especially different from other European nations, in a sense that Britain and France, for all their particularities, are not. It is not only the extraordinary capacity of the Germans for sustained collective effort, illustrated in the spectacular economic rebounds from deep defeat after two lost wars within the space of thirty years. There is also the striking ability of individuals to rise to the occasion, and to do so promptly as if the whole business of initiative—and the qualities of imagination which are integral to it—had been routinized. This runs counter to the stereotype of the German bruited around the world by their two great historic opponents, the British and French. The popular image of the German in warfare as a species of armed sheep—useless when deprived of flock or shepherd—was found deeply deficient during the Italian campaign in the last stages of World War Two. The stubborn (and murderous) retreat with its huge casualties among the German officer class was only possible because of that unlooked-for capacity of individual members of German units, in hierarchical order as one after another got killed, to take immediate and pretty effective command of the situation. These men, right down to the NCOs who took over when none of the officers was left, acted as if they had known all along what it would be like to take command. The qualities of initiative and enterprise were striking at all levels.

After that experience, one should not really have been surprised at the way in which Germans as individuals and in groups proceeded with such extraordinary rapidity from the reconstruction of their economy (which had been torn apart by the deliberate assault on it conducted by the Western allies both during and immediately after the War) to the conquest of world markets.

11

PRESSURES ON FIRMS AND GOVERNMENTS

WE have grown accustomed to the commonplace arguments about the conventional, doctrinal reasons for intervention—the ones rooted in strong *political* convictions about exercising control over the capitalist economy for the sake of public benefit (however defined). But under present conditions a great part of the complex armour of state intervention—from, say, the limited objective of control over retail prices, through various degrees of participation in private enterprise, to outright nationalization—is not based on political (and more or less arbitrary) initiatives of the interventionist state. Rather, it is the typical modern enterprise that goes to the public authorities to solicit their aid.[1]

The new big firm is no longer the untrammelled autocrat which the radical stereotype of the first half of the twentieth century had portrayed as a permanent feature of capitalism. It has had to accept an increasing degree of 'outside' interference in management from three main sources: from workers' participation (particularly strengthened in Germany, Sweden and the Netherlands); from reinforced anti-trust measures in certain countries: Germany, the UK and generally throughout the EEC (in the US, however, the original thrust of anti-trust legislation has recently become enfeebled); and from the assertion of consumer interests—represented, as well as by consumer associations, by regulatory agencies and public pressure bodies.

Such a firm now caters for much larger markets, and makes its policy decisions against a background of heterogeneous, often divergent or contradictory national economic objectives of innovation and restructuring; frequently it is also subject to transnational pressures, because, besides selling and investing abroad, it may depend on foreign capital markets for some of its resources. While its investment needs are growing, the motivation of private investors to commit funds in such a complex business often remains slack. The basic problem is almost invariably traceable to the perception that profitability—after innovation and restructuring—will remain low, at least over a long initial period.

When the marginal product of capital is falling, the possible remedies are twofold: a fall in the share taken by wages; or subsidies to increase the rate of return on capital. (A disguised underwriting of losses through nationalization can of course serve the same purpose.) The liquidity of innovators is squeezed by slow growth: the saving of high real labour costs by capital deepening (substitution of labour by capital) is reduced and it takes longer to amortize the capital costs of displacing the (costly) labour. Increasing the rate of profit is now seen as of overriding priority, since it is the paramount condition for more investment (and less unemployment).

Good timing has in fact become crucial: many bankruptcies result from delays in realizing the earnings of sensible investments, which were made on the basis of generally correct predictions but which had overestimated the speed of market acceptance.

Low investment is now recognized as the most serious obstacle to growth, in contrast to the 1960s and early 1970s when the constraint appeared to lie almost exclusively in prospective labour shortages. Belatedly, after years of lowered ratio of fixed investment to GNP (a trend which dates from the late 1960s), economists have recognized that the shortage of fixed capital was going to be the chief constraint of the 1980s. This is why, to meet growing investment requirements—especially the needs for inputs of indivisible sums for innovation and restructuring on which returns will be long-delayed and profitability may remain low for many years to come—industry requires and actively solicits the support of public funds.

Possibly the lengthening of lead-time (and the enlarging of indivisibilities) makes the proceeds of investment especially sensitive to any mistiming of the moment when production comes on stream. Public funds are required to bail out those firms—some of them 'national champions'—which have proved incapable of withstanding the pressures of the business cycle or of competition (and which need to be safeguarded, if only with the aim of salvaging the greatest number of jobs). Guarantees by government against the effect of business cycle risks also become necessary.[2]

Investing public funds in private enterprise and, more generally, the growing variety and scope of public intervention arising out of the new economic circumstances and increasingly extending beyond national boundaries, give rise to new formulas for the mixed economy, and require new or strengthened means of asserting the public interest.

Is it possible to exercise sufficient 'social control' to ensure that the necessary investment gets done? In principle, in conditions where the constraint on growth comes not through any shortage of savings but from a lack of incentives to invest, it should be readily possible for the public authorities to collect up capital and syphon it into the activities where it is short. In fact, governments do this in the present business cycle without deliberate policy, simply because more enterprises have fallen into the hands of the state (in the UK, Italy, Sweden and elsewhere). The state is willing to accept a lower rate of return on capital (or, in the case of the UK under the Thatcher government, cannot at times avoid doing so), in order to ensure the social return of higher employment. It is then faced with the need to restructure these industries and invest in them to raise productivity—and so increase long-term profits.

Rescue operations

The ways in which governments intervene to bail out firms which have fallen on hard times have been examined at various stages in this book (see pp.8–9 and 75–7). Drawing some of these methods together we can distinguish several different philosophies of aid to unprofitable (usually high-employment) big business, especially those enterprises which perform a 'national champion' role.[3]

1. Straightforward government aid (as in France, Sweden and the UK), sometimes with equity or other participation rights, initially as an employment-supporting, anti-cyclical measure. Towards the end of the 1970s this was increasingly made conditional on structural adjustment; medium-term profit targets are usually set.

   Perhaps the purest example of this form is Italy's investment in the Istituto per la Ricostruzione Nationale (IRI), a public venture now half a century old. There, precisely because the investment in the early 1970s was deliberately intended to be anti-cyclical (in the expectation of a later pick-up in general economic activity and the resultant possibility of bottlenecks in basic industries, such as steel), the problem of over-capacity and over-employment became acute by the late 1970s. There followed strong demands for reform, to ensure that IRI would not be cast simply as a 'hospital for lame ducks'.[4] The National Enterprise Board formula in the UK (see below pp.162–3) also falls into this category.

2. Conditional aid, as in the Chrysler US case in late 1979 when Congress agreed 1.5 billion dollars aid if the banks supplied several hundred million and the union agreed to contribute around 500 million dollars by accepting wage increases below the going rate. The conditionality was partly designed to curb wage costs; it was also intended to activate private sector financial support.

3. A purely bank-financed rescue, coming to the aid of a company which has been making consistent large losses, as in the first (1975) rescue of the German firm AEG. This was said to be possible only because the German private sector (and notably the banks) is so ideological—that is, sufficiently opposed to public intervention on principle to be willing to put up its own money rather than ask for public assistance. The other banks clubbed together behind AEG's main support, the Dresdner Bank.[5] There are parallels here with Japanese rescues, for example the case of the Ataka rescue (p.77).

Governments, on the whole, grow increasingly reluctant and discriminating in assenting to direct involvement. For example in the US Chrysler rescue case, there was readiness on the part of the state to lend and/or give money, but not to accept management responsibility.[6] Meanwhile the trade unions try to drive social democratic governments into a job preservation exercise through direct ownership. In Britain for instance the Amalgamated Union of Engineering Workers demanded that the government take an ownership stake and therefore a seat on the board of Chrysler UK.[7] In the event, the government resisted the trade union pressure. The public authorities, anxious to retain the advantage of the multinational connection, gave Chrysler money, and guaranteed loans on a large scale, but no equity was acquired. Instead the technique of 'planning agreement' (Benn's chosen instrument of remote control) was resorted to, the only instance in which this method was actually used. The technique of the 'planning agreement' eventually proved inadequate to secure effective control when the company was taken over by Peugeot. Direct equity participation through the National Enterprise Board might well have been a better means of asserting public interest in the private sector.

In Britain as elsewhere there is growing emphasis on formulas which use different types of public/private mix and which can be used as an instrument of more sophisticated bargaining. The example of British Leyland illustrates the point. The government tried to make investment funds, which the market would have been loath to supply, dependent on the firm's productivity performance—above all on fewer work stoppages—at a time when inadequate domestic output was pushing up car imports into the UK. In the then prevailing circumstances, the blackmail turned out to be not really credible. There were political reasons why a Labour government would not want to let this nationalized industry decay, as well as economic grounds, directly related to the balance of payments, why Britain chose to keep a domestic car-making capacity to meet a large proportion of home demand.

New styles of state enterprise in the UK

Another type of instrument of intervention is exemplified by an episode relating to the British National Oil Company (BNOC). In 1976 BNOC acquired Burmah's North Sea subsidiary, at what appeared to be a high price, in order to be able to pose a credible bargaining threat to the international oil companies which operate in the North Sea. The aim of the operation was to try to induce them to accord to BNOC a first option on 51 per cent of their production (which might be called a pseudo-nationalization at market prices). By capturing Burmah's team of oil explorers, BNOC was, moreover, able to emphasize its ability—and intention—to exploit the new North Sea blocks to be offered for auction, if the international oil majors fulfilled their threat to hold off from bidding (Krapels, 1977, p.32ff.).

The BNOC North Sea case is altogether one to dwell on as it

illustrates a number of the new aspects of nationalization and especially the narrowing of the borderline between nationalized and private industry aspirations (see below, p.168). For instance BNOC insisted on the right of first refusal to buy North Sea oil at market prices (no different from the position taken by ordinary international oil companies in the Middle East or in Venezuela). Through entering the North Sea business as an operator with the status of a 'real' (i.e. privately owned) company, BNOC's views—on operating and depletion rates, on appropriate profits—were based on hard experience. BNOC demanded a seat on the boards of operating companies in which it was interested, so that it was involved in business decisions from the earliest stage—again in order to make effective the national views on long-range depletion.

This degree of initiative was possible in the UK under the Labour government of the late 1970s. The Tories, since their electoral victory in May 1979, have been trying to roll back state enterprise activity, but they find it difficult to deal with *potential* big lame ducks without a more active policy of public intervention. This was emphasized by Arthur Knight, chairman of the National Enterprise Board in the years 1979–80: the formula of some moderate pump-priming only for risky 'high technology industry' is too simplistic. For one, high technology is usually intertwined with medium and low technology, particularly in the field of public utilities; you often cannot isolate the activity in a particular enterprise. Furthermore, what about declining enterprises or industries, potentially profitable in parts, which the capital market (thinking only in terms of company units) is ill-equipped to sort out?

Knight had a hard time working out the new 'terms of reference' for NEB with the Tory ideologues, who were especially leery of anything resembling Labour's Industrial Reorganisation Corporation—a publicly-owned merchant bank with a national purpose. Knight insisted that a nationalized holding company must have the function of 'picking some winners', as well as nursing the losers.[8]

The NEB at its inception in the mid-1970s was a forcible assertion of the new style of public intervention. The emphasis from the first (see National Enterprise Board Annual Report, 1976) was on the exercise of 'commercial judgment' in the same way as in any other business, and on an adequate return on its investments;

its overall target was 15 to 20 per cent on capital employed. It was intended to function not just as a provider of funds but, like BNOC, as an operator, and was given access to the sort of business information from the companies under its purview ('regular monthly' reporting on one-year targets) which would be demanded by a US bank from its corporate borrowers. This entrepreneurial approach consciously rebutted the suspicion that this form of national ownership is a soft option.

In particular the access to systematically collected business information gave the NEB leverage in the key sectors in which it was interested (rumoured to have been initially eight or nine) and which it selected for the main policy aim of 'promoting industrial restructuring'. The 'aims and functions' set down for the Board made it clear that this new style of state entrepreneur had a general brief which gave it very great commercial freedom to go in and bid for takeovers etc.—even aggressively, without the consent of the company to be taken over (NEB, pp.5, 45). The NEB's business orientation was further emphasized by the compartmentalization of commercially unattractive firms, acquired at the direction of the Secretary of State for Employment or for reasons of national expediency. Such 'lame ducks'—British Leyland and Rolls-Royce were two examples—could be excluded from the NEB's target profit rate.

British inhibitions and foreign pragmatism

After earlier disappointments (see Part One, pp.6–7), outright nationalization, except in so far as it provides a home for lame ducks, grows less credible as a means of expressing the public interest. Its attractions are few. Japan and the US were in any case never in this game, but the disillusionment with nationalization applies throughout Western Europe, with the possible exception of France. There it is a live political issue in Mitterrand's and other left-wing programmes.

But the Left is not necessarily 'anti-market', even in France and Italy. In fact Italian communists are disappointed with the effects of nationalization and wary of its use as a soft option. In deciding in 1980 to support Alfa Romeo's (Alfa Sud) proposed deal with Nissan, they opted to incorporate market pressures to keep this nascent bi-national company on its toes.[9]

Moreover, as has been stressed before (Shonfield, 1982, p.111), outside the UK the Right does not treat nationalized industry policy as a major ideological issue. The Thatcher government does, even if many of its plans to denationalize may be frustrated (see p.7). As far as the UK Left is concerned, besides continuing to be a favourite topic of Bennite platform speeches, nationalization appears to offer a soft option when trade unions are faced with plant closures. The Conservative opposition to the public sector in the UK is in part a simple ideological fixation, in part the result of a re-examination in the late 1970s of the record of nationalized industry, whose poor performance in the UK was analysed in some detail by Eltis in an article (Eltis, 1979) which appeared shortly before the Thatcher government took office.

Eltis's essential argument is that because of a certain slackness in the thinking by managers—in particular, a tendency to be excessively responsive to science-based arguments for technical innovation—the 'surplus' in the form of 'marketed goods' turned out by public enterprise is relatively very small, compared with private enterprise performance. The growth of public enterprise, at the expense of private, means that the resulting tendency to fail to satisfy from domestic sources the demand for marketed goods has the effect of stimulating excess imports; balance of payments deficits follow. 'In the case of Britain, a few extra industries are nationalized after each return of a Labour government. . . . The financial crises . . . that follow this [i.e. low pricing, low productivity, excessively high investment]—and other government policies such as large increases in public expenditure on social services in the non-market sector—have then led tough Labour Chancellors to restore the financial and economic balance of the economy'—by setting higher profit performance criteria, etc. (p.20). All this relates to a familiar argument from Bacon and Eltis in their 1976 book; here, too, Eltis points to the lesson that 'if a society wishes to have extensive nationalization and social services as well—and the Left invariably wants both—it must run the nationalized industries prudently and to a large extent commercially' (1979, p.20).

This simplistic view of the Left's imperatives is not true of social democrats in Sweden or Germany, from whom there has been no great demand for nationalization; in fact in Sweden there is now a tendency towards de-nationalization. In the UK the question of more nationalization as such is only an intermittent political issue on the left of the Labour Party.

The argument also ignores the fact that nowadays additional industries come into public ownership often *because* they are low profit-earners and have an employment problem with grave social consequences; the French steel industry in 1978; Swedish shipbuilding in 1977/8; and in the UK, shipbuilding, also in 1977/8, and the long story of British Leyland are all examples of this new manifestation. The Eltis analysis does not take account of instances when the purpose of nationalization is precisely to ease the social cost of a necessary rundown of employment—a result which cannot be achieved by most profit-seeking private enterprises. In such cases a lower-than-normal surplus is of the essence. Nationalization can also be counter-cyclical: again maintaining investment (in particular) when private industry collectively rushes for cover. (The emphasis in Eltis's 1979 article on *1975* figures in UK—showing a huge discrepancy between public and private investment costs—wilfully obscures this point.) Sometimes counter-cyclical public investment is useful in the long term: the Swedes made a feature of it, though the policy in fact failed them in the mid-1970s. Finally, there is the aspect of long lead-time investment with a high component of technological innovation. This is clearly the purpose of nuclear energy development which is given by Eltis as a prime example of waste. (Would not the railways development costs in, say, the *1840s* have shown a similar discrepancy between high net demand on national resources and low immediate rate of return?)

If the Eltis sequence of the failure to satisfy domestic demand, leading to excessive imports and thus to balance of payments deficit, always applied, Italy, with its large public enterprise sector and heavy social burden (curbing prices; maintaining employment) should have shown especially heavy balance of payments deficits in the second half of the 1970s. In fact, its balance of payments, after the first shock effects of the oil crisis and the worldwide slump, bounced back sharply in 1977/8, into high surplus in 1978. There must have been some powerful offsetting factor of entrepreneurship (no North Sea oil!) at work here.

The point about the lack of professional managerial control over public enterprise investment decisions is, however, well taken. There is evidence of gullibility on the part of governments and managements. But there is also evidence of an ability to manage structural change while reducing social costs—for instance the rundown of coal mines and railways—and of management skill, for example in the UK steel industry, which tries to manage necessary rationalization and loss of employment, but has at times been prevented by governments afraid of political consequences. Such governments do, in fact, also interfere with private industry, by subsidies (regional and other); but it must be said that this is *not* on the scale of the interference in highly exposed public enterprises (often especially in utilities, where price-sensitiveness is high in periods of inflation). However, this does not prevent government employers from confronting (and sometimes winning) major strikes in important sectors such as transport and coal.

What lies behind the categorical positions of Right and Left in the UK? Can it be that the formula of British Petroleum or, earlier, the East India Company has left a heritage of lasting distrust? Is it because UK ministers are such powerful controllers and full ministerial control inhibits entrepreneurship, so that public enterprise becomes less like private venture (in contrast with, for example, Salzgitter in Germany and Renault in France)? Firms of this type are identified in the guidelines laid down for the National Enterprise Board (p.46) as subsidized enterprises. They are not to be confused with others in which the NEB invested because of longer-term commercial reasons. On occasion these are sold off at a profit, after having been helped out of trouble over a relatively short period. The 1977 sale of NEB's 30 per cent stake in Reed & Smith, the paper manufacturers (*Financial Times*, 8 December 1977, p.26) was an early example of this.

However, such quiet profit taking was exceptional; the emphasis in the guidelines was on long-term profitability (NEB, p.46)—intervening in cases where the market, through private companies, sets an excessively high rate of discount on future profits and therefore writes down the present value of assets which have substantial value from the national point of view, or simply fails to set sufficiently high value on the industrial opportunity for changing the structure of the economy. The latter obviously involves higher risks than companies making judgments on the basis of anticipated incremental change would be inclined to take. The NEB, just as much as the private sector, has to acquire its funds at going market rates of interest—and must show prospects of good profit. But it had a lot of money and could afford to wait.

It came as no surprise that the private sector watched the NEB's new style of interventionism with trepidation. The first major row happened in 1977 over the Board's successful takeover bid for parts of Fairey Aviation, in competition with a commercial rival, Trafalgar House. Conservative politicians, forgetting for a while their usual grouch about the deficit trading of nationalized industry, were especially loud in their denunciations of this type of public enterprise as altogether too entrepreneurial.

Yet another function laid down in the NEB's objectives was providing the critical mass required for putting together a large-scale export deal with a long time-scale and big risks—e.g. contracts for construction in developing countries. This is less controversial: governments everywhere are in any case already heavily involved in it (through export credit guarantees, ExIm bank loans, etc.) so that this cannot be seen as an extension of interventionist activity.

The question is: Will the occasional use of the public shareholding by government destroy private business, because it raises the permanent threat of policies with objectives that do not maximize profits?

Compare and contrast the British resistances with the experience in the 1970s elsewhere. The French, despite Barre's strong ideological preference for private investment, seized the opportunity offered by the prevailing low level of investment during the period of the VIIth Plan (1976–80) to intervene with productive public investment channelled through the *Grandes Entreprises Nationales* (Shonfield, 1982, p.101; also above, pp.44, 45).[10]

Also in contrast with the UK, Germany, for all its anti-interventionist discoursing, has been particularly lavish in subsidies, both to support current operating costs and for investment purposes. The German operating subsidy to the railways is a much higher proportion of total receipts than the UK one. The German coal subsidy is huge. And industrial subsidies to overcome 'competitive disadvantages' in industry, allocated under the 1978 *Finanzplan* to be spent in the one year 1979, reached the enormous sum of 14.5 billion D-Mark (well over £3,000 million). In the financing of all this, the role of *publicly owned* banks (including the *Landeszentralbanken*) is important.

Certainly the history of collaboration between interventionist government and private enterprise is quite different in countries like France or Germany or Japan. In these countries the partnership is natural. One hypothesis could be that the hostility in the UK is against the *whole* public sector. Public enterprise is the exposed flank which the government attacks first. Could the UK adopt a different stance, making public enterprise feel less unloved (by Tories) or exposed (under Labour)? On the Left there has been the 'commanding heights' rhetoric. Gaitskell's failure in 1959–60 to abolish Clause Four, the Labour Party's pronouncement on public ownership, still lingers. Yet throughout the 1970s Labour governments as well as Tory were most pressing in the deliberate policy of cutting subsidies.

But why the special Tory ferocity against public enterprise? In part, it stems from the reaction to Left rhetoric and weak Labour leadership which led to such unnecessary assertions as the acquisition of aerospace and resisted the well-established formula of mixed enterprise. More fundamentally, the weakness of public enterprises (by no means uniform) is a symptom of a more widespread economic malaise—of general weakness and low profitability in British industry. With the malaise comes an insistence on short-term shareholders' rights; the long-term corporate planning needs are ignored. The widespread anti-planning ethos of the Tories and the fact that they have not forgotten that public enterprise investment played a large (and unhappy) role in the Labour's National Plan of the 1960s may also have added to the general hostility.

Nationalized firms are moreover seen as powerful rivals by private firms, who grumble about the competitive power of businesses with ready access to cheap public funds. In fact state-owned firms are now involved in many partnerships with private ones, and even those which are fully nationalized are most anxious to prove that they are really part of the private enterprise system.

While the instrument of nationalization is, without doubt, effective as a means of exercising useful day-to-day pressure and regulation, as was shown in the account (pp.161–2) of the BNOC episode, does it continue to be so effective once the nationalized firm has become part of the wider system, is fully established, and tries to show that it can make profits like anyone else? Profits and the independent capacity to borrow—BNOC has both—make the nationalized enterprise less vulnerable to day-to-day political interference on the part of government. Perhaps this is part of a more general experience about the state's involvement as entrepreneur: that the state-owned organizations—once established—develop autonomy and behave much like other entrepreneurs.

Multinational firms and national governments

What will be the future of the relationship between firms and national governments, as the firm becomes increasingly part of an international economy? For example, the mixed enterprise becomes a difficult formula when a substantial proportion of the equity of the home company is in foreign hands. Major problems arise in guaranteeing the national attachment (seen as essential in the case of 'national champions') of companies which have spread abroad. It is not sufficient for a 'national champion' just to be domiciled in the mother country: it needs to be more firmly attached. Is the formula by which the government holds a portion of the equity of such a 'champion' with international dimensions a sufficient guarantee of a solid national foothold in the company?

The very flexibility of multinational companies makes it difficult for governments to control them. The American experience in trying to curb the export of capital by US multinationals simply led them to raise more of their capital abroad. This is another example of the economies of scale: an established international firm has access to capital markets *anywhere*.

Vernon points out in his excellent mid-1970s survey[11] that, when faced with governmental restrictions, MNC networks could to a considerable degree 'substitute one type of asset for another. If money could not be sent, then credit guarantees could. If goods could not be sent, then blueprints or experts could take their place. With international transportation and communication so greatly improved the network was flexible in what it moved across international boundaries. For the United States or any other country to control the spread of such enterprises, its measures would have to be draconian' (Vernon, 1977, p.364). This is true: the costs of blocking access to any given market are very high for the blocker.

The power of traditional instruments of national policy—

exchange rates, interest rates, even tariffs and (locational) subsidies—declines, according to Vernon, owing to the unresponsiveness of MNCs to these kinds of pressures (Vernon, pp.364, 369). This is because in a multiplant system long-term considerations dominate. And long-range planning has to be reconciled with the growth of future uncertainties. By the mid-1970s big American MNCs were said to be investing with a maximum time horizon of five years, treating returns on capital beyond this five-year period as not coming within their calculation of the rediscounted value of the investment.

Vernon also stresses that the factor of size grows increasingly important as firms become more flexible and widen their range of options about what they will shift across national frontiers: goods, money, technical know-how, highly skilled management. Above all size, with a variety of outlets for products and of sources of input, gives a firm an enviable stability in the conduct of its business. It can therefore plan ahead—in terms of long-range indivisible units of investment, which under present conditions have also grown much larger (p.158 above)—with more confidence. It has an advantage which helps it to maintain a technological lead over smaller competitors.

But what in the end is probably more significant is the fact of the considerable growth of intra-company international trade, which amounted by the mid-1970s to between one-quarter and one-third of total trade in manufactures and industrial raw materials (Vernon, 1977, p.368).[12] These transactions within the ambit of single MNCs are highly insensitive to short-term governmental policy changes.

Once an investment has been made, staff recruited etc., a change in exchange rates is not important because the MNC has to compare the full cost of operating in the newly created system against the marginal cost of operating in the old. However, this particular argument needs qualification. If the multinational company is, for example, operating at less than full capacity, it may respond to favourable changes of exchange rates—or to short-term tax concessions and subsidies—by marginal shifts in the location of its operations. The important factor is that the long-term view on the world-wide distribution of a production programme makes you loath to shift in response to short-term policy changes.

As we have said, the effect of tariffs and subsidies can to some extent be mitigated (say by internal transfer pricing). Short-term shifts in exchange rates are offset by super-efficient foreign exchange hedging, so efficient in fact that MNCs may often succeed in bringing about exchange movements through the act of anticipation.[13]

All this does not mean that it is necessarily too costly (or too unproductive) to exercise *some* measure of public control over the operations of MNCs, for example on such matters as transfer pricing. The very publicity attaching to the operations of highly visible MNCs and the readiness with which published information is communicated from one country to another (as well as the influence of the efforts progressively being made to standardize the presentation of company accounts and other kinds of information) put a significant curb on the freedom of manoeuvre of the MNCs.

A great deal of this pressure is most effectively applied through the instrument of international regulation—by the OECD, the EEC—usually in exchange for extending a protective umbrella over the operation of the MNCs in their host countries. Thus the 'Guidelines' accepted by member countries of the OECD in 1976 (OECD, *International Investment and Multinational Enterprises*) insist on 'national treatment' for foreign enterprises. The intention is to afford MNCs in the host countries treatment, which so long as it is not inconsistent with the protection of the host's 'essential security interests', is not less favourable than that given to domestic companies; any departure from the principle of 'national treatment' must be notified to the OECD within sixty days of the decision being made. In exchange, the OECD demands a degree of transparency, placing each MNC under the obligation to provide complete information on its whole corporate activity to all the host governments for tax purposes. The need for joint international surveillance of transfer pricing is emphasized. The bargain also stresses that the research and development undertaken by multinationals should be available to help host countries to innovate.

A later OECD document issued in April 1978 adumbrated the machinery for continuing consultations on the elaboration of government policy in member countries on such matters as investment incentives and disincentives.

So far, such international measures have done little to mitigate the widespread negative attitudes to MNCs. Is the very intense phobia about MNCs on the left, and also in some right-wing parties, for instance in France, simply due to the fact that this is how resistance to the loss of autonomy implied by growing interdependence most readily expresses itself? Or is there something more: are MNCs seen as the instrument of a change in the balance of power, a change of which the already mentioned substantial and increasing proportion of intra-company trade is symptomatic? But the autarkic option is not a realistic one for affluent society (Chapter 4 *passim*); international agreement of a limited functional kind, for instance over MNCs or banks, is indispensable. So public power can only reassert itself, say, over the international capital market, by the surrender of sovereign national power. This happens to some extent in the EEC, which should be seen not as a regional phenomenon, but as a 'joint-interest group'—an important experiment in bringing the new footloose 'barons' of international business under control.

Clear rules must also be established in a wider international framework (as Vernon points out, 1977, p.370ff.) to govern the MNCs' behaviour in order to reduce conflicts, in particular between Europe and the USA (and also between Japan and the rest of the developed world). To repeat the concluding words of *The Use of Public Power*: 'In the conditions of slow growth prevailing in the 1980s the openness which is one of the great achievements of the years since 1945 will be under constant attack. To maintain this openness it is essential to give, throughout the OECD, the greatest degree of priority to matters of international industrial policy' (Shonfield, 1982, p.115).

Notes to Chapter 11

1. One is tempted to speculate that the changing vocabulary of the theoretical concepts of how best to intervene is a deep-seated source of the new, more accepting attitudes to intervention. This vocabulary has become more modulated, more discriminating, less alarming. See, for instance, the 1975 *Kyklos* article, and the Ely Lecture (published in May 1976) by Assar Lindbeck, whose thinking exemplifies this modified approach to 'selective' interventionism.

2. Is there in addition a more general attempt to reinsure against *adverse* government intervention—making the effects of public rule-making predictable and favourable to the firms in question? [*Ed.*]

3. Typically, other methods are required in regulating industries such as textiles, where there are often large numbers of small producers (Japanese problems in this connection were described on p.95 above). [*Ed.*]

4. The phrase is Arthur Knight's.

5. The cure was to prove inadequate and AEG, merged with another problem company, Telefunken, continued to limp ever more markedly. The combine was eventually put into receivership and a new rescue plan was then put into action with some conditions attached of a similar nature to the 1979 Chrysler package. Indeed the government was required to put up guarantees because the banks could no longer handle matters. [*Ed.*]

6. This had also been the case with the French steel companies in 1978. [*Editor's note based on comments by William Diebold*]: However, there is some surveillance of Chrysler's performance by a US government committee at a quite high level, and certain criteria have to be met before successive tranches of aid are made available. Also, before the 1979 public aid scheme was finalized, some changes were made in the company's top management, though exactly how these fitted into the rescue operation remains obscure.

7. Chrysler UK was by then no longer attached to US Chrysler; it had been sold off, alongside its French fellow company, as part of the American company's bid to save itself before it needed government help. [*Ed.*]

8. Knight regarded the Institut de Développement Industriel in France as a proper parallel for the NEB.

9. The Italian effort to limit open-ended state commitments, by appointing an independent 'commissario' to oversee the management of ailing companies coming for assistance, is also noteworthy.

10. The Japanese used their FILP (see p.87, n.5) in a similar way.

   While the French are not particularly strong on co-ordination (only in the VIIth Plan was there a serious attempt to co-ordinate objectives), comparing the two nationalized sectors, there is by and large much more co-ordination in France than in UK. What is most striking is that there are, in the British nationalized industries group, no common assumptions about the future of the economy, or the trends that will bring that future about and (as a survey of management in state undertakings, including the Post Office, shows) no attempts even to communicate with one another and arrive at some sort of consensus.

11. Andrew Shonfield's notes on this survey, prepared by Vernon for the Commission on Critical Choices for Americans in 1977, have been used extensively in this section. [*Ed.*]

12. G. K. Helleiner's *Intra-Firm Trade and the Developing Countries*, 1981,

has useful data on the amount of international trade that is intra-firm. [*Ed.*]

13. Other advantages accrue to multinationals, on the insurance principle, from being spread over a number of markets. There are conversely clear *disadvantages*—by way of greater exposure—in being a multinational in times of recession. [*Ed.*]

12

CONTENDING WITH THE 1980s

THE pressures from business, unions and other interests that have made corporatism such an important element in the contemporary economy have also led to theories of the ungovernability of democratic societies. These may be peculiarly relevant to political conditions in the US: the separation of powers, the frustration of party politics and of any attempt by the Presidential executive to found its power in the legislature, make it increasingly difficult—as Lloyd Cutler points out (1980, p.132)—for American government 'to formulate and carry out an overall program'. Compare this with the 1950s, when L. B. Johnson as majority leader could form a stable Democratic Congressional majority. The reasons for the change are thought by Cutler to be in part institutional: the breakdown of the élitist principle of appointing a committee chairman according to the rules of seniority. There is for the present no manageable group of notables to rely on. Then there is the increasingly 'allocative' function of a state with limited resources; so that its decisions to favour any one group have a zero-sum outcome: 'if the losers on each item are given a veto . . . a sensible balance cannot be struck' (p.133). The third type of reason which Cutler identifies is to do with international interdependence which does not allow policy issues to be voted on as separate questions. It makes US government unreliable as an international actor.

Not for the first time (see the effect of US attitudes to bureaucratic politics and especially to regulation) a phenomenon which affects the American style of running things has been converted by doom merchants into a problem about governability, purporting to involve us all. There is no cause to expect this particular contagion to spread; there are in any case other systems of federal government which are designed to cope with problems of making programmes work (for instance in Germany, where an important role is performed by party power).

In Western Europe, the changing character of social democracy reflects the rehabilitation of market forces for certain social purposes. The social democrats (in the wider sense) are the only policy-makers who try to provide the doctrinal basis for the further development of the mixed economy. They were successful in providing the background against which some of the economies of Northern Europe could reach North American per capita incomes, and do so while improving the welfare of the majority. Eliminating poverty—or at least most of it—within one's national boundaries was a natural and highly popular objective after the terrible insecurity of the 1930s and 40s, and in view of the immense technological advance and the possibilities of affluence derived from sustained growth. But we have seen (above, p. 129) that by the second half of the 1970s there had been a shift in the emphasis of welfare policies, and one does not have to postulate the continuance of the backlash to foresee further changes in objectives.

There are those who criticize the prevailing liberal philosophy of the 1960s (which put the key notion of equality at the base of the social and political changes), and who claim that it was the distrust of politicians and the belief in the perfectability of politics through the participation of broader groups which eroded the authority of the state. The counter-argument points to the fact that the changes engendered by this philosophy enhanced public power at the expense of over-mighty subjects, such as the white supremacists in the US or the big business community.

How is the personal use of an American-scale income likely to develop in Europe? It will not, we think, foster the stereotype transatlantic type of energy-intensive, materials-crunching mass culture of the third quarter of the twentieth century. But how will Europeans use the capacity to produce? By directing it into the provision of more leisure with the consequent slowing down of growth? Into the larger-scale financing of services which would have a collective character?

Would the social democracies be less good at creating the circumstances for continued reasonable growth rates in the changed conditions, which make it necessary to control inflation, restructure production and come to terms with high unemployment? How would we cope with pressures from competing (and often equally deserving) interest groups for shares of public expenditure, when this could no longer increase in relation to the national product? The contradiction between wanting less taxation, less regulation and less interference, while at the same time wanting a larger and fair share for all, better value for what the consumer spends, and more control over the strategic instruments of the economy, will have to be reconciled.

It is not clear how to subject major strategic instruments of the economy—the big banks, and also the insurance and pension funds which in the UK, the US and Japan are increasingly the guardians of the individual citizen's savings—to the guidance of public interest while retaining the advantages of a free-ranging investment policy in search of security and maximum profit. We have argued that a corporatist system has proved to be the most effective framework for such planning in a democratic society. Productive industry and commerce should be in principle not owned by the state, but still subject to much more aggressive inspection for price collusion, as their structure becomes steadily more oligopolistic. Governments taking measures to reinforce the competitive impulse in an essentially oligopolistic situation, by anti-trust legislation (such as in the most active days of the American drive of the 1960s) and by insistence on the transparency of pricing (a weapon contributed by the European social democracies), are likely to remain an enduring feature of our economies. At the same time there are distinct pointers to the more extensive use of 'market techniques' in the established fields of public services. The object is dual: to give more choice to the consumer, and to limit the rate of growth of both taxation and public expenditure by returning to some form of consumer responsibility through making the purchasers pay directly (at least in part) for the goods or services they wish to acquire.

Public goods in the market place

We have already made the point (p.130) that the favoured means of effecting this reconciliation is to push as much as possible of public expenditure (especially on welfare) back into the market, while controlling the market for the sake of public interest.

Public regulation can take a variety of forms, and the texture of a society is deeply affected by the form that is chosen. We may continue to depend mainly on what Charles Schultze in his discussion of the problem calls 'command-and-control techniques'—the direct exercise of bureaucratic power—or we may opt for the increasing employment of incentives which make use of the normal pursuit of private gain with a systematic shift in its direction to serve the aims of public policy.

Whether it is to buy public goods more cheaply, to have more choice of what gets bought, or to encourage the consumers of public goods (by some direct involvement of their pocket or cheque book) to make more economical choices, or simply to give these consumers too a wider range of choices—or indeed for any combination of these reasons—returning to the market seems, after the reputed extravagances of services bought out of rapidly growing public expenditure, a very sound idea. But it is full of snags and it is a piece of good fortune that the early debate on the subject has been handled with subtlety and foresight of the complexities implied in practice. The three outstanding theoreticians who explore the complexities of the market for public goods are, among the Americans, Charles Schultze and Arthur Okun and, among the Europeans, Fred Hirsch.

Schultze (1977) argues strongly for the increased use of market mechanisms for the distribution of public goods. He accepts fully the argument that there must be—in the United States—more public provision of services such as medical treatment and also more public control over the use of the natural environment. His concern is how to make more extensive use of 'market-like' arrangements, i.e. *'buy/sell relationships'*, in the pursuit of legitimate social objectives. He wants less detailed regulation of the behaviour of individuals by means of prohibitions and penalties; more reliance on decentralized decision-making (analogue of the market) with the state intervening continuously to set the terms of the buy/sell transaction, essentially altering the market price of the goods and services in question to achieve such aims as more equal education, better health services, less pollution.

He maintains that a more efficient method of allocating scarce resources is to arrange matters so that consumer choice, as well as—whenever possible—rational business calculation, operate on the result.

The consumer option must be a real one, assured, when

necessary, by more public regulation. One condition for this must in fact be that no other monopolistic or oligopolistic features are built into the system, which would make it altogether too inconvenient to shop around for a suitable school or hospital because, for instance, only those in the immediate vicinity are reasonably accessible. That in turn means that profits from the supply of such services must be large enough to elicit the creation of some surplus capacity. Otherwise there will always be a tendency for a reversion to rationing. It is indeed probable that this is one of the ways in which the demand for higher quality of public services, which is surely going to be one of the features of increasing consumer affluence, will assert itself during the coming decades. It will undoubtedly be more expensive than the rationed, or quasi-rationed, type of public service which most Western societies have today.[1]

Schultze has an impressive series of examples of how this might be done. Health services can be provided to all by a system of universal health insurance, with contributions graduated according to the level of income down to zero, while leaving patients free to shop around among doctors and hospitals for what they want. In similar fashion, it can be made appropriately expensive to add to the pollution of natural resources or to the congestion of roads and other forms of communication by forcing the individual to recognize that he has to sacrifice personal income to indulge his comfort or his fancy. Some of Schultze's proposals, e.g. on making hospitals and universities charge the market price and compete with one another (always postulating complete health insurance for the individual and a comprehensive education voucher system) are regarded as shockingly right-wing by many Europeans. On other matters—such as work safety, where he recommends an 'injury-rate tax' on the employer and higher compensation for the injured worker—he leans towards radicalism. His intention here is to find substitutes, in the shape of a system of money rewards and penalties, for the inadequacies of the industrial safety inspectorate and for the lack of incentives to apply new technology to the matter of accident prevention. But one is bound to ask if other means would not reduce the secondary economic costs of this kind of operation and perform the business of meeting performance standards more efficiently.[2]

How does he propose to create the market-like institutions

which will compete with one another? He wants the state to provide 'seed money' for new health centres and schools—to act as a kind of entrepreneurial banker. Then, once the institution has been established, the public authority is to opt out and confine itself to income transfers to individuals whose payments would sustain the entrepreneurial providers of welfare services.

Schultze may, however, stretch his case excessively when he suggests that the interposition of a market, e.g. in education, would have the advantage of reducing the need for hard-to-get information (Schultze, 1977, p.19). He contrasts education with the recreation industry to the detriment of the former; in neither case, he says, do we know the 'production function', but it does not matter because the buyers of recreation signal directly the things to which they attach value and the producers respond. With some qualifications, says Schultze, it should be the same for education.

This is surely an over-simplification. He misses Hirschman's important point about the significance of 'voice' precisely in those situations in which information is scarce and uncertain; this often arises in the case of new products, or new services such as day-care for pre-school children, where the demand has arisen prior to a clear formulation of what it is one wishes to buy—or to supply (Hirschman, 1981, pp.219ff.). Schultze is arguing precisely that 'exit' will do in the place of 'voice'. It won't. Here is the kind of case with a more general implication for social and individual choice:

—the customer must be involved in joint exploration of the facts with the producer; the data which the producer needs can only come in this way—the clinical, experimental, approach is of the essence (at least at this stage of education, mental health care, etc.);
—there also must be a long-term commitment by the customer, a service contract, otherwise the institution with its consensual assumptions cannot function. Schultze is insensitive to this point. The fact is that the scope for 'exit' has to be closely constrained. This severely limits the *buy/sell* relationship.

Many of Schultze's ideas are in fact about methods of creating institutions which provide wider scope for 'exits', i.e. competing bodies which will have no incentive (because of the concurrent establishment of comprehensive—and presumably, by implication, equal—insurance rights), to treat the welfare of rich and poor differently. At present, the rich can choose and therefore exercise pressure; the poor cannot.

Here, one's conclusion is that the real necessity is to reinforce the 'voice' in the running of organizations producing welfare services because the buy/sell relationship is not powerful enough to shape institutional structures in line with public needs. Sometimes the availability of 'exit' reinforces 'voice'; sometimes, however, it is the commitment—the blocking of 'exit'—which is essential to the effective exercise of 'voice' in an institution with a collective purpose.

In contrast with Schultze, Arthur Okun explores which areas necessarily involve public policy to such an extent that they must be withdrawn from the straightforward market process and subjected to regulation and control (Okun, 1975, pp.19ff.).[3] His point is that just as we do not allow electoral votes to be bought and sold—we in fact arrange that the bargaining for individual votes is sharply circumscribed, though the more general political bargaining has some of the quality of chaffering with groups of voter interests—so minimum wages, for instance, should not be subject to market forces. A change in the demand or supply of labour should not reduce the living standard of the marginal worker. If the result is more unemployment, the community must pay for this. Similarly, people's minimum food wants should be withdrawn from any form of bargaining about behaviour; Okun therefore gives strong support for food-stamp types of programmes which pursue *specific* welfare purposes (1975, pp.112ff.).

In consequence, his formula is to expand 'the domain of rights and help keep the market in its place' (Okun, 1975, p.112). And this naturally involves more direct government intervention in setting minimum standards over a growing range of social life.

Fred Hirsch's arguments start from the premise that the growth phase of capitalism was essentially transient: it was the stage when the multiplication of ordinary private goods went forward and the whole of society enjoyed the benefits of the economies of scale. Capitalism was made legitimate to the citizens of Western countries by the promise that all could in time, as a result of the process of growth, enjoy the standard of living of those who were at present the richest members of society. But in fact the goods that people want to have once their discretionary income becomes large are 'positional goods', whose enjoyment depends on capturing a privileged share of an essentially scarce resource.[4] Having this kind of benefit depends, in some measure, on depriving someone else of it. And, as he puts it: 'If everyone stands on tiptoe, no one sees better' (Hirsch, 1976, p.5).

The argument is that the competition for such positional goods is necessarily very wasteful and frustrating. It leads to inflation because (a) people who spend their private incomes in trying to obtain these things find that they need more and more money, and still do not achieve their object, since the prices of these essentially limited items rise much faster than those of goods which can be readily produced; (b) the general demand for such positional goods as education leads to a vast expansion of public expenditure. Hirsch's contention is that the only effect of the latter is to establish excessively high standards of performance for certain sought-after jobs, simply as a filter for the excessive numbers of people competing for them.

The outcome of the greatly intensified competition is a general 'commercialization' of all social transactions. The situation moreover tends to be aggravated as people who previously felt secure in the possession of their positional goods find that they have to struggle for more and more income simply to defend the place that they had previously acquired for themselves. His argument is that to reverse the process of commercialization requires a deliberate act of political will. It amounts to a negation of the whole capitalist ethos. Early capitalism, he says, benefited from the restraints on people's behaviour derived from a pre-capitalist morality. Competition for certain goods and services was restrained because the mass of the population had low expectations. Moreover, their aims as consumers could be and were satisfied by the provision of a lot of things as collectively enjoyed goods; they were not so keen on the privatization of goods providing enjoyment.

Essentially it is the lapse of the old hierarchy and the arrival of the mass-consumption society which creates the conflict from which there is no escape, according to Hirsch, except by the enlargement of the range of publicly provided goods, not subject to the competition of personal consumption. The money economy has to be withdrawn from a large area of activity. The essential meaning of the reform which he proposes is that people should assume that there are considerable inherent constraints on personal consumption and choice, and therefore accept some other, non-monetary, principle as the basis for the share-out. This seems to come close to the argument advanced by Heilbroner (1976, ch. 5) about the need for imposed austerity in the society of the future. The formula which Hirsch proposes is to reduce the incomes of people in the most favoured jobs, on the ground that the most intense positional competition is for jobs themselves. If the money were less, then the intensity of the competition might be reduced. His formula really amounts to a systematic reduction of net disposable income, in order to recreate the earlier situation in which people did not have the resources at their disposal with which to compete for positional goods. (In the job market, competition is to be reduced by making high-grade jobs, in themselves attractive, pay less.)

It would seem that Hirsch assumes that public provision must necessarily go with the reduction of personal choice, because the latter leads to competition which is bound to be frustrating. By contrast Schultze, as we have just seen, wants to enlarge the area of competition in the sphere of public goods. Although they are publicly provided, he sees no reason in principle why the individual should not choose between different sources of public provision. The condition for achieving this is simply that there should be enough supply of the service to allow all the customers to receive it without rationing. There is no reason why pricing should not be a filter, so long as the public welfare arrangements provide insurance or some other method to allow everyone to pay the suppliers of these services, on the same footing as those who pay their fees directly out of private income.

The answer may well be that social arrangements must be such as to avoid any *gross* inequalities of income—by heavy taxation of the very rich and by heavy social security payments to the poor which brings their paying capacity up to a level where they can compete on approximately equal terms with the more favoured members of society. This in essence seems to be the principle governing social welfare service and taxation in a country such as Sweden. It does not imply a removal of the decision about the supply of such services from the area governed by individual consumer choice to another area where decisions about the allocation of a public good or service are made as a result of a collective political choice. (Hirschman deals with this matter—the use of political 'voice' as opposed to market 'exits'—much more subtly than Hirsch. It is surprising that Hirsch did not include Hirschman in his bibliography.)

Schultze cites a number of examples to support his assertion that 'social intervention has almost always been output-oriented, giving short shrift to the process-oriented alternative' (1977, p.29). The latter is, as he puts it, to try to isolate the causes of the failure of the market process to produce the desired result and then to endeavour to restore 'as nearly as possible, an efficient market process'—i.e. one which will respond to a set of signals which truly reflect what people want. Because of the bias in favour of outright regulation and the setting of standards by public authority, he says, the ability of government has been 'taxed, well beyond its limit, . . . to make complex output decisions. And it has stretched thin the delicate fabric of political consensus by unnecessarily widening the scope of activities it must cover' (Schultze, 1977, pp.28–9).

He also argues that there is no need to lay down an absolute 'non-degradation approach' to the environment. There is room for manoeuvre here: absolute beauty does not need to be absolutely preserved, in view of what has happened to the rest of the landscape. He proposes instead a nationwide tax on each unit of noxious gas emitted and similarly on each unit of input of pollutant into water and other commonly enjoyed substances (Schultze, 1977, pp.35, 50f.).[5]

On the critical issue Hirsch and Schultze agree: there should be more collective provision; however, their formulas for collective provision differ. To make it efficient, says Schultze, it needs to be individually 'purchased'. But that cuts across Hirsch's point about the capitalist ethos. He wants to reduce net disposable income, in order to re-create the earlier situation in which people did not compete for positional goods. In practice, can the two things be separated? 'Voice' or 'exit' must predominate.

Hirsch's remedies involve a lot more tax, at a time when the limit of taxability is in sight: does this make them entirely impractical?

It should also be noted that Hirsch makes it sound as if a capitalist mode of production and exchange was universally accepted. But in fact the high period of Western capitalist prosperity, in the 1960s and up to the early 1970s, was also the period of the great advance in publicly provided social welfare, designed specifically to remove certain goods—including some 'positional goods' like access to natural beauty spots, the sea shore and so on—from the straightforward capitalist mode of competition.[6]

One is inclined to settle on Okun's and Schultze's picture of the future as the more realistic one. It is one of a market economy which is more regulated than today but which may well be wider in its extent, since it is likely to encompass, in some modified form, considerable areas of the public sector.[7] In fact, many of the old polemics between the left-wing and right-wing parties, which have provided much of the stuff of political debate in the democratic societies of the Western world about the respective roles of the market and of the state in the mixed economy, will have little relevance for the future. There may be differences about the appropriate instruments of public intervention that are by common consent required to give a strategic direction to one or another sector of the economy. But in the state's day-to-day business a common logic of government is likely to assert itself, pointing to the maximum decentralization of authority consistent with some broad measure of economic efficiency. The latter-day evolution of the welfare society, with its characteristic demand for consumer participation in the making of all public decisions affecting the lives of identifiable individuals or groups of people, imposes a formula of this kind. Some of the consequences are already visible. It is striking how the European social democrats, the extreme centralizers who were also the pioneers of welfare-state politics, have been learning (admittedly at different rates: Britain more slowly, Scandinavia and Germany faster) the wisdom of delegating responsibility for detailed economic decisions about what is to be produced, at what price, and how it is to be sold, to other mechanisms than the central apparatus of government.

As regards the regulation of private enterprise, there are a variety of ways in which the public interest can be effectively asserted without either a direct takeover of business or the imposition of a detailed set of rules subject to legal penalties. In some cases it will suffice to establish effective 'price transparency', with a detailed breakdown of costs and earnings, subject to regular publicity, under the surveillance of an independent public agency. In other cases, the public authorities may set maximum rates of profit for certain goods and services, and tax the excess on an ascending scale. Similar arrangements for steeply progressive taxes could be applied to industrial pollutors of the environment or businesses which threaten to make excessive use of scarce national resources. The point is that this type of arrangement which avoids detailed regulation of the industrial process itself but applies financial disincentives to certain kinds of industrial activity is likely to be both more efficient and less obnoxious in political terms.

International concertation and the EEC

'The international constraints on independent national action were not by any means always clearly perceived in our period': in 1965 this author argued as if international integration were still only an optional element in the system of modern capitalism, without clear awareness that interdependence would in a matter of a few years alter the character of the system irretrievably, or that autarky could deeply change the calculations of growth policies. 'The trend nevertheless was towards a growing recognition of the reality of such constraints on national autonomy, and that has continued to be so during the 1970s' (Shonfield, 1976, p.166).

As we have asserted, the autarkic option is no longer adequate and some sovereignty has to be relinquished in exchange for international control over those factors of our economic system which are no longer bound by national frontiers. This is of course only one of the reasons why we West Europeans have acquired the will to enter into a formal economic alliance with our partners in the European Community. When openness has come under attack from national interest groups in the search for employment opportunities, it is a good time to remind ourselves that what we were, in the first instance, aiming to achieve through the EEC was a customs union which would enlarge the international market for our manufactures.

Looking back on the years when this customs union was being formed, and indeed on the whole quarter of a century following the end of World War Two, the outstanding feature of the time was an unprecedented and practically uninterrupted boom in world trade in manufactured goods. The Europeans were able to overcome their reluctance to take the risks involved in dismantling their tariff barriers with one another, because their exports were growing so rapidly and the world offered them vast and varied opportunities for earning foreign exchange.

We have seen in the first part of this book that during the 1970s the Europeans faced markedly less favourable international circumstances and a more confusing external environment—and reacted in a confused fashion. They were embarrassed by the continuing flood of unwanted dollars emerging from the United States, but proved unable to create an alternative form of international money which offered them comparable convenience. Their capacity for collective decision-making has been insufficient for this kind of demanding task, the more so as the national economic performance and interests of the member states of the Community have increasingly diverged: in fact a high degree of interdependence between nations does not necessarily make them complementary. In the light of this situation it is a matter for wonder that, in spite of the economic divergence in the 1970s and the pressures generated by the business slump in the middle and the strains of the end of the decade, the essential structure of the European Community has not suffered more dramatically.

Indeed, it is increasingly clear that the second stage of European integration, which began at the end of the 1960s, expresses a quite distinct principle from that which provided the impulse for the first stage. The Europeans, having taken advantage of the sustained world prosperity of the post-war period to establish a customs union, were prompted during the 1970s, by the economic slowdown and the new pressures on international markets, to experiment with fresh forms of international co-ordination, which are designed essentially to defend the gains already secured through the establishment of their partial economic union. It seems unlikely that they would have begun their enterprise merely in order to protect common economic interests; but having moved forward together when times were easier, they were ready at the end of the 70s to engage in policies of collective self-defence in economic matters. The chief aim is to safeguard free trade *within* the Community.

Governments, especially when they attempt to bring about structural changes in production and employment, need to secure the active assent of employees, or for that matter consumers, affected by their policies. For some countries withdrawal from international co-operation for the purpose of short-term national gains may seem an attractive option. Indeed, a country faced with the prospect of continuing high unemployment during a prolonged period of structural adjustment—such as the UK for example needs to contemplate—may regard the policy of selective protection of vulnerable industries as a rational option (a variation of the classical infant industries argument).

Nevertheless, even the governments of the weaker national economies of the West, such as the UK and Italy, have managed thus far to resist the powerful populist call for import controls as a remedy for rising unemployment. In the UK, the Labour government of 1974–9 especially was under strong political pressure from its trade union allies, whose support was crucial for its anti-inflationary policies, to slap on a variety of import controls. Yet its desire not to break ranks with the other Western nations and defy the consensus, expressed in the formal OECD pledge not to seek remedies for domestic economic recession at the expense of the trade of other industrial countries, triumphed over the tactical temptations of national politics.

External policy becomes readily capable of co-ordination when it is clearly seen to relate to some aspect of internal Community policy. A restrictive external trade policy, for example on steel or on textiles, requires internal measures of control in the Community countries over such matters as pricing, investment, and even volume of output. This, in the circumstances of economic recession, means that collective EEC decisions are, in practice, being made on such delicate national issues as the level of unemployment in a particular industry in a given country, which have hitherto been regarded as belonging exclusively to the sovereign control of national governments.

Why does the European Community survive? The question is not why it does not advance faster, but why it continues to go forward at all. Why is there no fundamental defiance by its disaffected members? Is what ultimately holds it together the perceived task of coping with the results of the decline of US economic power? Or is it its ability to manage with reasonable skill the highly interdependent politico-economic system? Or is it perhaps both these factors? And do they depend on the present composition of the Community, with its relative homogeneity, and might they no longer manifest themselves when the group is enlarged to take in the Southern Mediterranean countries?

The EEC is most particularly useful for managing transnational relations during a period in which states and their apparatus have—partly through interdependence, partly for other reasons—become weaker in relation to organized interest groups.

There are many instances when the EEC countries find themselves pitchforked into the making of common policies long before they are ready for the exercise, simply because of external pressures. Once this happens, the 'linkage effect', i.e. the tendency to involve quite disparate issues not directly connected with the subject originally proposed for negotiation, makes itself felt. This is not so much because of a tendency on behalf of the various interest groups affected to press for the extension of joint policies in new directions, but more because governments and officials find it increasingly inconvenient to be saddled with piecemeal measures deriving from particular contingencies, which make it difficult in practice to conduct national policies which are coherent or predictable.

The upshot is that the Community sometimes has to involve itself in laborious discussion of longer-range objectives on which the views of member states are often very diverse, essentially because the outsiders demand to know what they can expect as the probable framework of European policy beyond the immediate tactical issue under negotiation. Sometimes the outsiders are frankly hostile, as for example the Soviet Bloc countries in the early and mid-1970s' dispute about geographical fishing limits in their respective areas and the sizes of the permissible catch. The EEC, in order to defend itself, was compelled somewhat reluctantly to force the pace of its own internal bargaining on this highly contentious matter, because of the much greater risk of loss which would be run by individual Community countries negotiating with the Soviet fishing interests on their own.

But there are other cases where the Community's initial posture is by no means defensive. Nor are the outsiders engaged in any hostile initiative. They are simply wanting assurance about where the Community is likely to be going on some subject which is of particular interest to them, over a period stretching some years ahead. If the individual European nations reply by saying that these are matters which concern them individually and are not formally subject to joint decisions, the nations outside are still likely to persist in their queries. They see the Community as a dynamic organization which may progressively absorb certain functions which are now exclusively the responsibility of national governments. They therefore think it wise to obtain a clear assurance about the direction collective policies are likely to take in the future, even if collective action is absent at present. If external pressures of this kind are indeed met to any large extent by the European Community, integration will of necessity have progressed a good deal further forward by the year 1990—while the Europeans will no doubt continue to complain and criticize themselves for their own lack of 'political will'.

To some extent, we are the victims of our own enormous success in expanding international trade during the past thirty years. Foreign trade is now so significant a factor in the economies of many Western countries that we all feel ourselves more vulnerable, and have become more nervous about the effects on us of the way in which other nations conduct their domestic economic policy.

The forces tending to erode a liberal international trading system are going to be considerably strengthened during the 1980s. There will of course at any time be some countries which feel that their economies are at a relative structural disadvantage compared with those of their competitors, either because of the accidents of timing in their industrial development, or the historical circumstances which influenced its composition, or because of wrong or stupid political decisions made in the past. All these are grounds for active intervention by governments to eliminate a real, or imaginary, handicap.

Government intervention of this type is likely to be more dangerous for the management of the international trading system in the conditions of the 1980s because:

1. there will be many more instances in which the case for deliberately engineered structural changes in productive industry can be persuasively made out. Whether it is to save or to cheapen energy, or to increase the long-term opportunities for employment, governments will be impelled to intervene more powerfully and more frequently. They will do so either because they feel the need to change the structure of their

economies faster than market forces are capable of doing the job or, more fundamentally, because they do not believe that market forces on their own would necessarily push in the required direction;

2. whereas in the past such intervention has mattered little, so long as it was not directly applied to international transactions, today the issue of 'fair trade'—the exchange of goods and services produced under more or less equal conditions—has acquired a prominence equal to or greater than that of the traditional liberal objective of free trade. This is, again, partly because governments have so many more ways of intervening than in the past. And when they do so in such a way as to improve conditions for their own national producers, that may be enough to cause other countries, which feel themselves in consequence placed at a competitive disadvantage, to block the channels of trade.

These strains coincide with the relative decline of US economic performance. In the late 1970s American domestic expansion policy was conducted as if external constraints were insignificant, but it is open to question whether this will be true of the 1980s when the realities of interdependence have been taken on board. This is not tantamount to forecasting a return to the isolationist spirit. It would be difficult to find an easy way back from the United States' international involvement. But there is likely to be much greater caution in the future about undertaking the risks and economic costs of international leadership—and that just at the time when such leadership is going to be badly needed. We must also learn to expect a tendency for Americans to look in the future for a new and more favourable political–economic return from bargaining with Europe and Japan.

On permissiveness and the recognition of social authority

Throughout the 1960s and the 1970s we have been faced with the paradox of the state which is on the one hand cast in an ever more demanding, powerful role, mobilizing an increasing proportion of private incomes for public purposes (note, from the mid-1960s on, the increasing proportion of social expenditures and social transfers in the service of 'equalizing' the treatment of minorities:

the old, the young, blacks, women—who of course are a 'minority' only in terms of not having had, before the 1960s, recognized equal rights); and on the other hand suffering from the evident enfeeblement of its coercive capacity in facing 'veto groups' of various kinds.

This enfeeblement is the result of the increasing importance of active assent in our societies, which in turn is due, at least in some measure, to the fact that the social welfare impulse demands the avoidance of coercion (whether the coercion is directed at consumers or at producers is immaterial in this context).

Enforcement of law by armies and police grows more difficult with the spread of permissiveness, increased assertion of legal rights and the ease of organizing protest movements (through better communications, more leisure, more income for discretionary spending). But after the scares of the mid-1970s (of which the Baader–Meinhof terrorist activities were a major focus) Italy stands out as the exceptional case; Germany is nearer the norm. Yet even in Italy there is no real breakdown of governability.

The movement towards a reinforcement of human rights continues waxing strong. Capital punishment is the touchstone of attitudes to liberalism: the occasional outbursts of clamour for its return are not sustained. There is at the beginning of the 1980s little sign of a growing resort to coercive power. There are, on the other hand, many pointers—especially from the societies which were not unduly battered by the shock waves of the 1970s—that government and the inevitable mixed economy function best in conditions where a network of processes has been established which helps along the smooth adjustment of the balance of countervailing forces.

The 1960s and 70s saw a flowering of movements aimed specifically at reinforcing the countervailing power of consumers. This was achieved in part through anti-trust legislation—especially in the United States—and also, increasingly, by means of improved 'access to justice' arrangements, which allowed the consumers to press their claims against the manufacturers or suppliers of unsatisfactory goods and services (see above, pp. 144–9).

In reaction to the explosion of veto groups it was asserted that these special claimants will tend to win out against government and other public authorities purporting to represent the mass of consumers and taxpayers, and that therefore the *only* way to secure the public interest is to enforce a resistance to interest group demands by the institutional limitation of the financial responsiveness of government.

How significant are the signs of the reaction against the liberal state? In the 1970s we witnessed a number of distinct symptoms of reaction against the permissive, open-handed stance of government which we had come to take for granted in the first quarter-century after 1945; these have been discussed at some length in this book, see pp.26–33. Surprisingly, in view of its initial impetus and pervasiveness, as well as of the political signals of the Thatcher and Reagan elections, this anti-liberal backlash does not appear to have taken strong hold of public opinion.[8]

The sum total of its measurable effect amounted to some slowing-down of the rate of growth of that portion of public expenditure which went into social welfare. On the more elusive doctrinal side a spate of new pressure groups threatened to submerge some of the achievements of the permissive society. Minorities sometimes behave like this—reacting against the very aspect of the libertarian culture which has earlier sustained the assertion of their own minority rights. This is all part of a tendency, after the first flush of liberation, towards a second phase, which is the assertion of populist authoritarianism.

In his *Zero-Sum Society* (1980) Lester Thurow argues that societies have become permanently more difficult to govern because previously passive minorities have become active and organized. In the past, adjustments to economic change have always exacted the compliance of a victim class or victim group; traditionally, before the First World War, recession involved cuts in wages. In our own time, inflation could also be cured, at the cost of the redistribution of income to the disfavour of some weak group. He goes on to argue that as all the potential victim groups now have power to resist, conflicts about the redistribution of income become more acute, and government is paralyzed.

Thurow's remedy is to obtain consent from the newly enfranchised groups by means of a programme of guarantees of minimum standards. He would for instance guarantee the right to work by the creation of a 'socialized sector of the economy designed to give work opportunities to everyone who wants them' (p.206).

What he does not take into account is that this too would probably be at the expense of some existing group of workers—typically, in the West, of adult white males of prime working age. It is they who will have to foot part of the extra bill—the addition to unemployment pay which is given to workers brought into employment by non-market means. Why should they agree?

What of the alternative of 'repressive solutions' (Appelbaum, 1980), especially when the old-established groups, in coalition, make up a powerful, unassailable majority? This raises the question of minorities in conflict with majorities. The 1960s movement in favour of disadvantaged groups went forward and was often prompted and actively sustained by majorities of non-beneficiaries. But what if, as we have asked in an earlier context (Shonfield, 1982, p.115), the mood changed when the majority—and also some of the exposed minority groups—became dominated by the need to defend existing gains? Would openness and tolerance survive? Would the provisions for the welfare of weakly organized minorities survive?

It is very doubtful if our societies would tolerate embattled minorities with a power to do harm to other, weaker groups. What could however occur easily is the combination of a government unsympathetic to the long-term interests of, say, a racial minority group with the erosion of welfare benefits directed to that group. And there are many who are vulnerable to this type of treatment: pensioners, the physically handicapped, heads of large families, all unorganized or too loosely organized for effective counter-action. A tentative conclusion might be that the first potential victims of a recurrence of authoritarian spirit are the beneficiaries of public welfare at the margin—those that suffer from no clear 'group disadvantage' and are merely handicapped by circumstances.

Is there a cycle of the permissive and the authoritarian, repeating in the late twentieth century the pattern of the shift from the permissive mores of the 1920s to the authoritarian politics of the 1930s? Having achieved its political aims, the second generation of activists is often chiefly concerned with closing ranks within the liberated group, asserting its collective rights at the expense of others: in the first phase, at least, the outcome of the game is a zero sum. However, the theory of alternation between the permissive and the authoritarian is quite different from the view that the revolution devours its own children. *If* Burke's law holds, what it governs is the behaviour of factions after liberation from a traditional authority: the victors usually divide into competing groups, and if one of these gains an advantage then it uses it violently, the inhibition of customary legal constraints having been removed by the revolution.

It is a commonplace of history that consensus authoritarianism—the Bonapartism of the mid-nineteenth century—has been at the foundations of the totalitarian state. And yet, as we have argued some years ago in a polemic about the long-term future management of capitalist institutions (Shonfield, 1978), the 'reinforcement of a more unitary public authority' required to make efficient use of public intervention 'does not in itself imply a bias towards despotism. . . . It is a mistake to imagine that tyrannies, at any rate in modern industrial states, believe themselves to have a blank cheque to carry through unpopular measures'.

There is in fact no necessary connection between the reinforced authority at the centre of society and increased restrictions on minority rights. But in practice populism, used to appoint a dictatorial government, moves this way: the rights of minorities *are* restricted, and there is generally less tolerance for novelty in ideas and in personal behaviour.

Looking back into the history of this century, it is in its denial to groups, such as national or racial minorities which claim collective identity, of recognized legal rights that the authoritarianism of majority rule, the descendant of Bonapartism and popular Caesarism (the word is Halévy's, 1965, p.312), is at its most characteristic. It is totally conformist in spirit: homogeneity enhances the collective will. The attitudes dominating the politics of the second half of this century are the opposite of this, with collective strength deriving from social structures which accommodate diversity.[9]

Towards a new labour market?

If we return here to developments in the labour market, it is because in this sphere there are signs of a new tolerance for diversity and innovation. If this is sustained it will modify for the better the bleak outlook for the 1980s. Why be quite so despondent when, by a lucky coincidence, many of the elements which are most important for a realignment of our economies have combined in our favour? To begin with, we should keep a sense of proportion about the decrease in the rate of growth. Even if there is no foreseeable return to the high rates of growth which prevailed for some thirty years after the end of the war, an achievable rate—say, of 3 per cent—is, we ought to remember, much higher than the growth rates of past centuries. It still leaves room for both individual and public consumption to expand. (To be satisfied with such a low level of performance may of course be a peculiarly British aberration.)

To come now to the positive factors: Among these we count increases in productivity—through restructuring and innovation—and demographic trends which move to our advantage. Now, there would be room for real pessimism if what we were facing was a demographic upsurge in conjunction with stagnant productivity. While it is true that in the medium term we have to adjust both to lower rates of growth and to the entry of ever-increasing cohorts into the labour market, the long-term prospects are more favourable. In the OECD, by contrast with other countries, we can expect an ageing population, and this is by no means a necessarily negative phenomenon. Already under present conditions, those who are getting on in years are very different from their like some time ago: they are more flexible, more capable of adjustment to two or three different careers in the course of their working lives.

What gives grounds for some optimism is above all this change in the psychological stance, this profoundly altered attitude to work—to work sharing, to re-training for new careers, to being entrepreneurial on one's own behalf. We are in fact witnessing the growth of a sort of deproletarianization, above all of the young, but which also gains ground among the older people.

It needs to be emphasized that what should, indeed, give us cause for concern is our tardiness in taking advantage of the coming opportunities: the very long delays in making new investment, particularly in technical innovation, pay off. The danger is the greater because our current decisions control over a period of some thirty years—a whole generation—the outcome of the investments we make now. We must hope that these delays in the return on new investment can be cut short—and should try not to fall into the common error of expecting the future to hold no improvement on the present.

We have learnt to take for granted the gains of the period since 1945, and also the political attitudes which went to their making. Those of us who approved the past changes think that tolerable existence will not be possible—in affluence or out of it—if we do not continue to strive towards consensus about objectives which seemed self-evident in the 6os, but which now risk being displaced by immediate economic strains.

Firstly, we must maintain openness in international economic relations; our joint decisions about industrial policy must secure it. This becomes of paramount importance as impaired growth starts eroding our incomes.

Secondly, we want to reinforce the acceptance of heterogeneity in social policy, according *legitimate* equal status to groups hitherto unrecognized: such as homosexuals, 'young people'; or treated as marginal—among them women, the old, blacks, other 'foreigners'.

In third place—last but not least important—we wish to continue with the active pursuit of the welfare of classes or sub-classes of people with an identifiable social/economic disadvantage—the old, the low paid, the physically handicapped.[10] The guiding principle here is not the pursuit of greater equality of opportunity for people already equally endowed, but an attempt to make good, in some measure, the inequalities stemming from natural and environmental conditions.

Notes to Chapter 12

1. [*Editor's note based on comments by Wolfgang Hager*]:
   This approach to problems of distributing public goods on the voucher system may be too negative: for one thing, greater choice need not necessarily entail greater expense. It may be made available through having a variety of smaller (and more accessible) units—smaller neighbourhood hospitals, smaller institutions of higher education. In theory, at least, we would stand to lose on the economies of scale; but the extra competition might well improve both the cost and the quality of the service on offer. This would however imply that small is beautiful after all—a view which the author did not hold.
2. Not all of Andrew Shonfield's criticisms of Schultze's Godkin

Lectures have been located. In this instance it is not clear whether the more efficient methods he had in mind were to do with more or better legislation, or with the enforcement of existing regulation, or both. [*Ed.*]

3. Among the themes Andrew Shonfield intended to write about more fully was this whole matter of public goods which could not be left to the market, for instance the expense of the individual's access to justice in cases where the other party was a powerful public body or a rich—and also powerful—business enterprise. For the experiments aiming to redress the balance, see the last volume of the Access to Justice Project series (Cappelletti, 1981), and especially the essay 'Justice in Many Rooms' by Marc Galanter. [*Ed.*]

4. The term 'positional' is applied by Hirsch to goods which 'are either (1) scarce in some absolute or socially imposed sense or (2) subject to congestion or crowding through more extensive use' (1976, p.27).

5. The techniques to be used in following this kind of approach, as an alternative to the continuing promulgation of standards which are bound to be changing all the time, are spelled out in the essay on 'Safety Regulation' by Nina W. Cornell, Roger G. Noll and Barry Weingast (Owen and Schultze, 1976).

6. [*Editor's note: The following preliminary notes by Andrew Shonfield are also relevant*]:

   According to Hirsch, 'measured' growth can continue. But much of it represents an aggregation of 'positional goods' i.e. real growth of mass consumption was a transient stage.

   Clearly the argument depends crucially on *how much?*—what proportion consists of *positional goods*? He gives no guidance on this point. Also can the general enjoyment of 'positional goods' or their near-substitutes be increased? Yes.

   The character of the different limits on the supply of positional goods needs to be defined. E.g. (1) highway space to relieve congestion can be extended in the *long run*, but in the short is infinitely inelastic. (2) The paradigm of *absolute* limit on supply is used as type to describe the whole problem. But it *is* possible to reproduce near-substitutes of great pictures; or see them through mirrors in crowded galleries; or look at them from a greater distance. (3) New forms of sharing out the sea shore and other beauty spots in danger of over-crowding, say, visiting on different days, while still using 'money entrance fees'.

   Hirsch wants to *reverse* the process of 'commercialization'; less individually determined consumption: you reduce choice—'the market mode'—and get what is offered at random. Schultze believes the opposite of this.

   Hirsch and Heilbroner agree that a change from the capitalist *ethos* is required. But don't we now need—with an even greater degree of urgency—risk-taking innovation? Therefore big prizes *are* necessary even more—to combat diminishing productivity of capital, as more externalities are 'internalized'.

To Schultze, the *buying* of public goods should be done individually (e.g. medicine); however, the *provision* of public goods must be subject to a collective act of will. In contrast to Hirsch, he thinks that the political mode (of provision) can be mixed with the market mode of purchasing. (Not, however, for pure positional goods.)

7. If one were looking for some analogue to these markets of the future, one might find it today in the highly regulated money markets of Western Europe. There is still quite a lot of room for initiative, but the system operates under surveillance and those who are successful have to have a very close understanding of the rules. It is worth observing, by the way, that this situation does not deter recruits to the profession of banking.

8. More recent American evidence from public opinion surveys indicates that on most 'social issues', on which there had been 'an approximately linear shift towards the liberal pole from the end of World War Two to the early 1970s, the '70s seemed to show a plateau (but not a reversal)'. See US SSRC *Social Indicators Newsletter*, 1982, p.2, quoting James A. Davis and Tom W. Smith. [*Ed.*]

9. USSR stands against this whole trend: its aim is conformity with minimum concessions to the traditional national minorities.

10. It is, one should note, this aspect of modern society—the desire to pursue actively and effectively the abolition of gross inequalities—which is ignored by the partnership of Milton and Rose Friedman; they claim that 'a society that puts freedom first will, as a happy by-product, end up with both greater freedom and greater equality' (Friedman, 1980, p.181), but do not go on to explain how, with market forces untrammelled, this is to come about.

APPENDIX

by Niels Thygesen

INTERNATIONAL MONETARY ASPECTS OF THE MIXED ECONOMY

ANDREW SHONFIELD's concern with the gradual erosion of international economic co-ordination of macro-economic policies in the decade of the 1970s emerges clearly in several places in *The Use of Public Power* (1982) and in the present volume.[1] His general theme is that the governments of the main industrial countries had from the mid-1970s withdrawn to an unnecessary degree from active management of their economies, thereby removing the foundations of international economic co-operation. In particular, the central banks could not be relied upon to maintain the required efforts of co-ordination after they had turned inwards and concentrated their attention on the pursuit of their domestic monetary targets. Indeed, he writes:

> The role of central banks in inhibiting the process of international co-ordination needs to be taken on board in this connection. . . . They were bastions of national sovereignty and did not want to spell out in detail, let alone attempt to co-ordinate with others, the varied devices which they use to manage their own domestic situations (p.60 above).

This critical appraisal seems even more apt in the 1981–2 period, when governments and central banks have tended to give minimal weight to the international consequences of their domestic measures, than it was in the 1970s and it is not difficult to guess what Andrew Shonfield would have had to say on these recent examples of the abdication by governments in international monetary affairs. But it may be more useful to bring out what he did have to say, in largely unpublished contributions to official or more academic study groups, on three important illustrations of the inadequacies of international monetary co-operation in the 1970s: the reactions to the consequences of the first oil price shock, the disarray in the intra-European exchange rate relationships and policy co-ordination in 1976–7 and the early experiences with the European Monetary System.

A European Community Balance of Payments Fund

Andrew Shonfield was one of the two UK members (the other was Sir Donald MacDougall) of the Study Group on Economic and Monetary Union 1980 set up by the EC Commission in early 1974 and presided over by Robert Marjolin. As a well-known critic of the approach to Economic and Monetary Union in the Werner Report (European Commission, 1970)—he regarded a locking of intra-European exchange rates as premature and poured scorn on the Werner Report as 'a scheme for European integration by central bankers instead of governments' (Shonfield, 1973, p.76)— he recognized the need for differential responses by EC member countries to the oil price shock and the inevitability of some flexibility in intra-EC exchange rates. But he was deeply concerned that the emergence of a collective EC-deficit on current account would foster strong centrifugal tendencies in the Community as member countries scrambled to reduce their share of the unavoidable deficit and/or to attract (directly or through the Euro-markets) longer-term financing from the new surplus countries. In a contribution to the Marjolin Report he wrote:

The new situation of collective balance-of-payments deficit on current account will almost inevitably produce a different mood among the members' governments. The mood is likely to be averse to the additional risk-taking attendant on the removal of still more barriers to the movement of goods and money across the national frontiers of the Community. The key problem therefore is how to reduce the risks of big deficits in the overall balance-of-payments of members' countries during the period ahead. The proposal to mobilize the collective creditworthiness of the nine member states for the borrowing of large amounts of funds, both from the Middle East oil producers directly and from intermediaries handling the oil producers' surplus in the Eurocurrency market, is designed to meet this end (Shonfield, 1975, pp.143–4).

This proposal to put the Community's capacity to borrow at the service of member countries in an exposed position, thereby improving their ability to sustain demand and avert part of the collective recession of the mid-1970s, was formulated at a time when the more global, but less cohesive, international organizations such as the IMF and the OECD were stirring to put into place financing mechanisms with a similar purpose. The IMF reached agreement on an Oil Facility in early 1974 and extended its scope in 1975; however, this scheme was largely seen to serve the interests of those Fund members whose economies were less developed. The OECD started in the autumn of 1974 an intensive round of negotiations to set up a much larger 'Safety Net' at the instigation of the US Secretary of State Henry Kissinger, but the agreement of March 1975 was never ratified by the US Congress. Constructive use could clearly, in retrospect, have been made by the Community of a separate facility with the authority to borrow annually something like half of the collective deficit induced by the rise in the oil price, which Andrew Shonfield conservatively estimated at 20 billion dollars in 1974.

The snag was obviously the degree of conditionality to be attached to such a scheme. To extend medium-term loans of, say, five to seven years' maturity, unconditionally was clearly not on, given the divergent policies and performances of the EC countries in 1974–5; in particular, Italy and the UK were beginning to diverge dramatically from Germany and the Benelux countries with respect to both inflation rates and external deficits. Policies in both Italy and the UK were clearly, in Shonfield's view, unsustainably expansionary. He was therefore ready, when challenged by the more cautious members of the Marjolin group, to elaborate in later versions of the proposal on the type of conditions to be attached to loans by the Balance of Payments Fund. For someone keenly aware of the reluctance of governments in the larger European countries to be seen to surrender parts of their economic sovereignty (however illusory that notion might have become as a result of increasing interdependence) he in fact went rather far in the direction of outlining the independence and discretion to be vested in the European institution—a reinforced Monetary Committee—functioning as an intermediary lender.

Before the proposal had been fully elaborated, the Group's discussion was overtaken by the authorization by the Council of Ministers in October 1974 of the raising of an EC Joint Loan of up to 3 billion dollars for much the same medium-term purposes as those outlined by Andrew Shonfield. The Marjolin Group therefore in its Report of March 1975 (European Commission, 1975) confined itself to asking for a substantial increase in future authorizations and left the details of the Shonfield proposals to the Annex volume of individual contributions. Although the EC's oil-induced deficits proved more short-lived than anticipated in 1974–5—the Community was back in substantial current surplus by 1978, by which time UK resources in the North Sea were also being exploited—the Community went through a disastrous patch in 1975–6 when inflationary divergences reached a peak and sterling and the lira plummeted in the exchange markets. In the end it was the package of conditions attached to IMF loans which served to stabilize the UK and Italian economies. The EC played a marginal role by extending medium-term loans to Ireland and Italy, but no mechanism for a serious independent assessment was developed in the EC itself; the Monetary Committee contented itself by tagging its terms to those set by the IMF. Contrary to what Shonfield had hoped, there was insufficient understanding in the EC that the stakes were so much higher in keeping goods, services, and capital moving as freely as possible inside the EC where interdependence was so strong.

The period of disarray in Community monetary and exchange-rate policies and in policy co-ordination: 1976–8

The year 1976 was in some respects the low point in the Community's performance in the 1970s. Sterling and the lira depreciated with unprecedented speed and far beyond what even their past high inflation could justify. France left the 'Snake'[2] again, since the '*relance Chirac*' of 1975 had undermined confidence in the franc's refound parity. Germany had to intervene more heavily to sustain the remaining smaller currencies of the 'Snake' and German public opinion was visibly getting tired of its obligations to intervene and import inflation. Economic growth was resuming in most countries, but in a disappointing way after two–three years of recession; policy co-ordination was at a low ebb in the Community as in the more global councils.

In these unpropitious circumstances Andrew Shonfield was active in setting up a discussion group of officials and academic economists to consider the next steps in European integration. With Giovanni Magnifico of the Banca d'Italia he brought together a group—named the Villa Pamphili Group from the hotel in Rome where most of its meetings were held—which comprised two successive chairmen of the Monetary Committee of the EC, the chief economists of the Bank for International Settlements and the OECD, a past chairman and a member of the German *Sachverständigenrat* and some academic economists. The group met about three times a year between mid-1976 and mid-1978; by that time its ideas were overtaken by the negotiations that led to the launching of the European Monetary System. Shonfield's contributions left a significant mark on the two public statements of the Pamphili Group (*The Times*, 26 July 1976, p.21 and 28 June 1978, p.20)[3] as well as on several papers prepared by members of the group under their own name (e.g. Balassa, 1978 and van Ypersele, 1977).

Shonfield's ideas at this stage were pragmatic and yet daring. They were pragmatic not only because the situation seemed to require a hard-headed analysis of costs and benefits of taking the next steps, but also because he wanted to distance himself from a revived monetarist approach to EC integration which some of his former colleagues from the Marjolin group had taken in publishing the so-called All Saints' Day Manifesto for European Monetary integration (*Economist*, 1 November 1975, pp.33–8). The Manifesto argued that monetary integration could be most efficiently achieved by issuing a new parallel European currency of constant purchasing power; this indexed currency would gradually outcompete national EC-currencies and thus bring about monetary integration through a market process. Shonfield objected to this blueprint, not only because his confidence in the ability of markets to perform a complicated selection of this type was limited; he also was convinced that governments would be unwilling to engage in the experiment once they had perceived its radical nature, and that they deserved some more constructive advice for the short-term future. His instinct was therefore to ask what could be done on the one hand to restore some order to the intra-EC exchange rate structure and on the other hand whether the role of the European Unit of Account (EUA)—the basket later used in the European Currency Unit—could be gradually extended towards a currency role.

These two themes and the need to develop more concerted macro-economic policies formed the agenda for the Pamphili Group. Andrew Shonfield was strongly in favour of introducing target zones for those European currencies which were individually floating at the time (sterling, French franc, lira). These zones would be formulated in terms of the European average expressed by the EUA; they would not be sustained by intervention obligations, but by consultations to adjust policies once a currency crossed the threshold of its zone.

It is very characteristic of his attitude to European monetary integration that he always regarded it as only a partial solution until relations with the main world currency had also been put firmly on the agenda. In his draft of the 1978 statement by the Pamphili Group he wrote:

> While the EUA target zones for the individual EC currencies would form the central first tier of a reformed exchange-rate system, the EUA/$ relationship which forms the second tier would also be crucial. Time is hardly ripe for a high degree of fixity. But the floating of the European currencies *vis-à-vis* the dollar needs to be better managed in a way that turns this onerous responsibility into a Community concern rather than leaving it as the task for essentially only one member country, viz. Germany.

And on the closely related issue of the enlarged role of the EUA in both official and private transactions he wrote in the same draft:

> While a European-based international reserve asset seems a desirable long-run supplement to the dollar, great care must be taken in introducing it not to further upset the precarious state of exchange markets. We therefore see this initiative, not as a part of any aggressive—and futile—strategy to dislodge the dollar from a major part of its international role, but as a useful complement to the closer management of European exchange rates which we have proposed.

These views were fully reflected in the published statements of the Pamphili Group, as was some of Shonfield's analysis of the need to implement a differentiated and internationally co-ordinated expansionary strategy in 1977–8, but since this analysis and the author's regret that this important phase was wasted 'mainly in wrangling between the strong and the weak economies about who should do what first' (p.59 above), is developed earlier in this text, there is little reason to return to it here.

Early experiences with the European Monetary System

The series of negotiations leading to the European Monetary System (EMS) in the course of 1978 was obviously an evolution which Andrew Shonfield followed closely and with special attention to the political implications and motivations of the rather technical economic arguments brought forward by the negotiators.[4] He contributed to the debate on the EMS and on UK participation therein on at least three occasions in 1978–9: in his evidence to the House of Commons Select Committee in late 1978 (Shonfield, October/November 1978) and in statements at conferences in Bologna and Geneva in November–December 1979.

Although the EMS did in several respects correspond to the proposals he had helped to develop in the Marjolin and Pamphili Groups, Shonfield was less than enthusiastic about the launching of the new initiative. While he deeply regretted the lack of UK interest in the negotiations and the consequent loss of influence on the outcome, he also felt that some of the participants had failed to think through the full logic of membership and that several countries were still too inward-looking in their policy design to make the new exchange-rate commitments sustainable. One important example may illustrate this point of view.

In his comment on a paper by Tommaso Padoa-Schioppa (1980) covering a wide range of topics for discussion in the further evolution of the EMS, Shonfield returns to a basic problem of the international monetary system: can several national currencies coexist harmoniously as international reserve assets, and what could European monetary co-operation do to improve the prospects? A major problem in the 1970s and early 1980s has been the emerging reserve role of the main European currency, the D-Mark. At times when that role was developing rapidly, the

D-Mark tended to be pushed upwards, away from the other EC-currencies, while in periods of cyclical weakness in the Germany economy, such as the period of current account deficit in 1980–1, downward pressure on the D-Mark was reinforced by reserve switches back into the dollar. The creation of the EMS was to some extent a response to this special time bomb under the intra-EC exchange structure; by linking the D-Mark more firmly to a wide group of EC-currencies an opportunity arose to Europeanize the reserve currency role of the D-Mark by pushing the ECU into an increasingly important position. 'The logic of what the Germans originally wanted to achieve through the establishment of the ECU requires them to take a new and radical view of their own existing administrative habits', wrote Andrew Shonfield (1980).[5] He did not get much of an answer at the Geneva conference or since then, maybe because German attitudes were already changing from what he (and others) presumed to be the official position of protecting the D-Mark against becoming an international reserve currency.

The example suggests that Andrew Shonfield's analysis was typically aimed at what was the most constructive European response to a complex global situation. The dialogue with the United States was an essential element and he did not see the EMS or earlier initiatives primarily in a perspective of antagonism or even defensiveness *vis-à-vis* the United States.

His attitude to UK participation in European monetary initiatives was not without ambiguity. While he was strongly in favour of an active UK role, he recognized on several occasions in 1979–80 that sterling could not have been a constructive participant in the EMS, given the 'monetary extremism' of the Thatcher government—by which he meant that 'monetary measures are made to bear too heavy a load of economic policy at large, and that they are used as a substitute for other actions, e.g. in the field of fiscal policy, which ought to complement monetary policy'.[6] He further argued that the deliberate upheaval undertaken by the new UK government in the framework of policy-making—in taxation, foreign exchange controls, wages and other incomes policies etc.—would make the United Kingdom resemble 'a restless elephant difficult to contain without discomfort in a European bed'.

In short, he deplored the UK policies of 1979–80 not only for their domestic effects, but because they made the United Kingdom a prime example of what could go wrong when interdependence through the exchange market was neglected. He quoted with approval the observation by the then Governor of the *Bundesbank* that Germany could afford to be less strict in its internal money supply policy when it received the incidental benefits of an appreciating D-Mark (Emminger, 1979), and regretted that no comparable reaction was forthcoming from UK policy-makers. Under these circumstances he saw little prospect and little purpose in advocating the inclusion of sterling in the EMS exchange-rate arrangements.

The common element in Andrew Shonfield's thinking about the international monetary aspects of the mixed economy was clear: the industrial countries will neglect their strong financial inter-dependence at their peril. They are likely then at the same time to produce undesired side-effects on their own economies through their domestically-oriented policies and to destabilize the interna-tional economy. They will aggravate these problems further by abdicating from any direct responsibility to influence their capital flows and their exchange rate. His vision that there is a need to reassert government responsibility over these magnitudes of great importance for national welfare, and to do so in close co-operation with other governments committed to the management of the mixed economy, could hardly have found stronger backing than the disappointments he was spared in the international economy of 1981–2.

March 1983

Notes to Appendix

1. See in particular *The Use of Public Power*, pp.47–55, 77–81 and 107–9, and this volume, pp.58ff.
2. The 'Snake': an exchange rate system, in which participating countries undertook to keep their currencies within predetermined margins. The original (1972–3) participants were Belgium, Denmark, France, Germany, Ireland, Italy, the Netherlands, Norway, Sweden and the UK.
3. Published by four leading European newspapers—*The Times*, *Le Monde*, *Die Welt* and *La Stampa*—on 26 July 1976 and 28 June 1978 respectively.

4. His keen interest in this area was a major inspiration in the most thorough study on the EMS negotiations, Peter Ludlow's *The Making of the EMS* (1982).
5. Incidentally, this theme was familiar to the author from the time in the late 1960s when he had advocated a possible Europeanization of the reserve currency role of sterling, then being frantically upheld through various international agreements and an exchange-rate guarantee. In his contribution to 'Sterling—European Monetary Co-operation and World Monetary Reform' (see Shonfield, 1968), he recommended a funding operation in which a European monetary institution was to buy up parts of official sterling balances by selling longer-term European reserve assets, a proposal reminiscent of the Substitution Account negotiated in the IMF in 1979–80, as well as of the present (1983) idea of substituting D-Marks for EUAs.
6. Private communication, 22 November 1979, following the Bologna conference.

BIBLIOGRAPHICAL REFERENCES

ALBERT, Michel
Article on the French VIIth Plan, *Le Figaro*, Paris, 24 April 1976

APPELBAUM, Eileen
Review of *The Zero-Sum Society* by Lester C. Thurow, *Challenge*, vol.23, no.4, White Plains, NY, September–October 1980

APPLEBEY, George
'Small Claims in England and Wales', in *Access to Justice*, vol.II, Promising Institutions, Book II, Mauro Cappelletti and John Weisner, eds, Giuffrè–Sijthoff, Milan–Alphen aan den Rijn, 1979

BACON, Roger, and ELTIS, Walter
Britain's Economic Problem: Too Few Producers, Macmillan, London, 1976

BALASSA, Bela
'Resolving Policy Conflicts for Rapid Growth in the World Economy', in *Banca Nazionale del Lavoro Quarterly Review*, no.126, Rome, September 1978

——'L'économie française sous la Cinquième République 1958–1978', in *Revue Economique*, vol.30, no.6, Paris, November 1979

BALLON, R. J., ed.
The Japanese Employee, Sophia University, Tokyo, 1969

BANK FOR INTERNATIONAL SETTLEMENTS (BIS)
Annual Report, 1979–80, Basle, 1980

BECK, Morris
'The Expanding Public Sector', in *National Tax Journal*, vol.XXIX, no.1, National Tax Association—Tax Institute of America, March 1976

BUCHANAN, James M., and WAGNER, R. E.
Democracy in Deficit: The Political Legacy of Lord Keynes, Academic Press, London, 1977

BURNS, Arthur
'The Anguish of Central Banking', Per Jacobson Lecture, IMF Annual Meeting, Belgrade, September 1979

CAPPELLETTI, Mauro, assisted by WEISNER, John, and SECCOMBE, Monica, eds
Access to Justice and the Welfare State, Sijthoff, Klett-Cotta, Bruylant, Le Monnier—Alphen aan den Rijn, Stuttgart, Brussels, Florence, 1981

CAZES, Bernard
'La Crise de l'Etat-Protecteur dans les économies occidentales', paper for the second Atalaya Colloque, Mexico, November 1979, published in revised form in *Commentaire*, no.12, Paris, Winter 1980–1

——'The Welfare State: A Double Bind', paper for the OECD conference on Social Policies in the 1980s (photocopied, Paris, September 1980). Published in OECD, *The Welfare State in Crisis*, Paris, 1981

CORNELL, N. W., NOLL, R. G., and WEINGAST, Barry
'Safety Regulation', in *Setting National Priorities*, see OWEN and SCHULTZE, *below*

CROUCH, Colin
'Varieties of Trade Union Weakness: Organised Labour and Capital Formation in Britain, Federal Germany and Sweden', in *West European Politics*, vol.3, no.1, London, January 1980

——'The conditions for trade union restraint', in *The Politics and Sociology of Global Inflation*, Leon N. Lindberg and C. S. Maier, eds, Brookings, Washington DC, 1981

CURTIS, Gerald L.
'Big business and political influence', in *Modern Japanese Organization and Decision-Making*, Ezra F. Vogel, ed., University of California Press, Berkeley, 1975

CUTLER, Lloyd N.
'To Form a Government', in *Foreign Affairs*, vol.59, no.1, New York, Fall 1980

DAVIS, James A.
'Conservative Weather in a Liberalizing Climate', in *Social Forces*, no.58, University of Carolina Press, Chapel Hill, June 1980

ECONOMIST, The
'A Currency for Europe—The All Saints' day manifesto for European monetary union', 1 November 1975

——'Proposition 13, California's Lucky Number', London, 5 January 1980

——'Taxes, atoms and cigar smoke', London, 8 November 1980

212 Bibliographical references

'The Swedish Complaints Board: Its Vital Role in a System of
Consumer Protection', in *Access to Justice*, vol.II, Promising
Institutions, Book II, Mauro Cappelletti and John Weisner, eds,
Giuffrè–Sijthoff, Milan–Alphen aan den Rijn, 1979

ELSTON, C. D.
'The Financing of Japanese Industry', in *Bank of England Bulletin*,
vol.21, no.4, London, December 1981

ELTIS, Walter
'The True Deficits of the Public Corporations', in *Lloyds Bank
Review*, no.131, January 1979

——*see also* BACON *above*

EMMINGER, Otmar
'The Exchange Rate as an Instrument of Economic Policy', in
Lloyds Bank Review, no.133, July 1979

EUROPEAN COMMISSION
Werner Committee: Report to the Council and the Commission on
the realisation by stages of economic and monetary union in the
Community, in *Bulletin of the European Communities* (Supplement),
Brussels, November 1970

——Report of the Marjolin Study Group—'Economic and Monetary
Union 1980', Brussels, March 1975

——Annex II to the Marjolin Study Group report (*as above*),
Brussels, March 1975

EUROPEAN ECONOMY—Special Issue 1979
'Changes in industrial structure in the European economies since
the oil crisis', Brussels, 1979

FINANCIAL TIMES
'Chemical industry in a new era', by David Fishlock, quoting
Robert Malpas, Technical Director, ICI, 28 January 1977

——'Reed & Smith forecast second half loss', 8 December 1977

——'Ambassador [Nicholas Henderson] Praises Thatcher', 15
September 1979

FRANCE, VIIIth PLAN
Proposals submitted by the Government to the Economic and Social
Council for its opinion (photocopied), Paris, April 1979

FRIEDMAN, Milton
In evidence before the US Congress Joint Economic Committee,
89th Congress, 2nd Session, 1966: Congressional Committee Prints,

JO424 89/2/66, microfiche card 1, pp.30–6; this also reproduces Friedman's 1963 evidence before the JEC

——'The line we dare not cross', in *Encounter*, vol.47, no.11, London, November 1976

——, and FRIEDMAN, Rose
Free to Choose—A Personal Statement, Penguin Books, Harmondsworth, 1980

FUTATSUGI, Yusaka
'The Measurement of Interfirm Relationships', in *Industry and Business in Japan*, Kazuo Sato, ed., Croom Helm, London, 1980

GALANTER, Marc
'Justice in Many Rooms', in *Access to Justice and the Welfare State*, *see* CAPPELLETTI *above*

GALENSON, Walter, with the collaboration of ODAKA, Konosuke
'The Japanese Labor Market', in *Asia's New Giant*, Hugh Patrick and Henry Rosovsky, eds, *see* PATRICK *below*

——'The Japanese Labor Market', in *Recent Developments of Japanese Economy and its Difference from Western Advanced Economies*, Hisao Kanamori, ed., Japan Economic Research Center, Tokyo, 1976

GERMANY
Annual Report of the Council of Economic Experts (*Sachverständigenrat*) 1975/6; December 1975; September 1978

——*Der Finanzplan des Bundes 1978–1982*, September 1978

GRAHAM, Otis L., Jr
'Toward a Planning Society', in *Dialogue*, vol.12, no.4, International Communications Agency, Washington DC, 1979

HALEVY, Elie
The Era of Tyrannies—Essays on Socialism and War (Original edition: *L'ère des tyrannies: études sur le socialisme et la guerre*, Gallimard, Paris, 1938). English translation in paperback: Anchor Books, Doubleday, New York, 1965

HARTMAN, Robert W.
'Multiyear Budget Planning', Appendix B in *Setting National Priorities: The 1979 Budget*, Joseph A. Pechman, ed., Brookings, Washington DC, 1978

HAYEK, Friedrich A.
'The New Confusion about "Planning"', *The Morgan Guaranty Survey*, Guaranty Trust Co. of New York, January 1976

HECLO, Hugh
'Frontiers of Social Policy in Europe and America', in *Policy
Sciences*, vol.6, Elsevier, Amsterdam, 1975, quoting the report of
the US Council of Economic Advisers, 1974

——'Public Expenditure in Sweden', Paper for the Conference on
Political Liberty and Collective Welfare, Konrad Adenauer
Foundation, Bonn, 9–11 December 1976 (photocopied)

HEILBRONER, Robert L.
Business Civilization in Decline, Marian Boyars, London, 1976

HELLEINER, G. K.
Intra-Firm Trade and the Developing Countries, Macmillan, London, 1981

HIRSCH, Fred
Social Limits to Growth, Harvard, 1976, Routledge, London, 1977

HIRSCHMAN, Albert O.
*Exit, Voice, and Loyalty—Responses to Decline in Firms,
Organizations, and States*, Harvard, 1970

——'Exit, voice, and loyalty: further reflections and a survey of
recent contributions', 1973, republished in *Essays in Trespassing:
Economics to Politics and Beyond*, Cambridge University Press, 1981

HOUT, Thomas M., *see* MAGAZINER *below*

HOWARD, A. E. Dick
'The Supreme Court under Warren and Burger: Of Activism and
Restraint', in *Wilson Quarterly*, vol.1, no.3, Smithsonian Institution,
Washington DC, Spring 1977

INDUSTRIAL REVIEW OF JAPAN, 1980
Japan Economic Journal, Tokyo, March 1980

INSEE—Institut National de la Statistique et des Etudes Economiques
Economie et Statistique, no.115, Paris, October 1979

JAPAN
EPA (Economic Planning Agency), *New Economic and Social
Seven-Year Plan*, Tokyo, August 1979

——Ministry of Labour, *Year Book of Labour Statistics, 1980*,
Tokyo, 1982

——*White Papers of Japan 1978–79*. Annual abstract of official
reports and statistics of the Japanese Government, Japan Institute of
International Affairs, Tokyo, 1980

KIYONARI, Tadao, and NAKAMURA, Hideichiro
'The Establishment of the Big Business System', in *Industry and
Business in Japan*, Kazuo Sato, ed., Croom Helm, London, 1980

KRAPELS, Edward N.
'Controlling oil: British oil policy and the British National Oil
Corporation', paper for the US Committee on Energy and Natural
Resources, Government Printing Office, Washington DC, 1977

LEHMBRUCH, Gerhard
'Liberal Corporatism and Party Government', in *Comparative
Political Studies*, vol.10, no.1, issue on 'Corporatism and
Policy-making in Contemporary Western Europe', Philippe C.
Schmitter, ed., Sage Publications, Beverly Hills, Calif., April 1977

LEONTIEF, Wassily W.
'National Economic Planning: Methods and Problems', in
Challenge, vol.19, no.3, White Plains, NY, July–August 1976

——'Is Technological Unemployment Inevitable?' in *Challenge*,
vol.22, no.4, White Plains, NY, September–October 1979

LINDBECK, Assar
'The Challenging Role of the National State', in *Kyklos*, vol.28,
no.1, Basle, 1975

——'Stabilization Policy in Open Economies with Endogenous
Politicians', 1975 Richard T. Ely Lecture in *American Economic
Review*, vol.66, no.2, Nashville, May 1976

LUCIER, R. L.
'Gauging the strength and meaning of the 1978 tax revolt', in *Public
Administration Review*, vol.39, no.4, Washington DC, July–August
1979

LUDLOW, Peter
The Making of the European Monetary System, Butterworth, London,
1982

MAGAZINER, Ira C., and HOUT, Thomas M.
Japanese Industrial Policy, Policy Studies Institute, London, 1980

MIYAZAKI, Yoshikazu
'The Japanese-type structure of big business', in *Industry and
Business in Japan*, Kazuo Sato, ed., Croom Helm, London, 1980

MODIGLIANI, Franco
'The Monetarist Controversy or, Should We Forsake Stabilization
Policies?', American Economic Association presidential address,
September 1976, published (with revisions) in *American Economic
Review*, vol.67, no.2, Nashville, March 1977

NAKAMURA, Hideichiro, *see* KIYONARI *above*

NAMURA RESEARCH INSTITUTE
Annual Report, 1978, Kamakura City

216 *Bibliographical references*

NATIONAL ENTERPRISE BOARD
Annual Report, 1976, London

NOLL, R. G., *see* CORNELL *above*

ODAKA, Konosuke, *see* GALENSON *above*

OECD (Organization for Economic Co-operation and Development), Paris

——*International Investment and Multinational Enterprises*, June 1976

——*Japan* (annual economic survey), July 1976

——*Public Expenditure on Income Maintenance Programmes* (Studies in Resource Allocation no.3), 1976. See also companion studies: *Public Expenditure on Education*, June 1976; *Public Expenditure on Health*, September 1977; and *Public Expenditure Trends*, June 1978

——*Manpower and Employment Problems and Prospects*, August 1978

——*Facing the Future—Mastering the Probable and Managing the Unpredictable*, Report of Interfutures Group, July 1979

——*Controlling Public Expenditure*, seminar papers (photocopied), May 1980

——*Economic Outlook*, no.27—Occasional Study 'Incomes Policy in Theory and Practice', July 1980

OKUN, Arthur M.
Equality and Efficiency—The Big Tradeoff, 1974 Godkin Lectures, Brookings, Washington DC, 1975

——'Inflation: Its Mechanics and Welfare Costs', in *Brookings Papers on Economic Activity*, 1975:2, Washington DC, 1975

——'An Efficient Strategy to Combat Inflation', in *The Brookings Bulletin*, vol.15, no.4, Washington DC, Spring 1979

——'The Invisible Handshake and the Inflationary Process', in *Challenge*, vol.22, no.6, White Plains, NY, January–February 1980

——*Prices and Quantities: A Macroeconomic Analysis*, Brookings, Washington DC, 1981

OLSON, Mancur, Jr
'The Political Economy of Comparative Growth Rates', 1976 paper published in *U.S. Economic Growth from 1976 to 1986: Prospects, Problems and Patterns*, vol.2, The Factors and Processes Shaping Long-Run Economic Growth, Studies Prepared for the Use of the Joint Economic Committee of the United States, Government Printing Office, Washington, 10 November 1978. Reprinted in

Portfolio, International Communications Agency, Department of
Economics, University of Minnesota, vol.7, no.1

——*The Rise and Decline of Nations*, Yale University Press,
1982

OWEN, Henry, and SCHULTZE, Charles L., eds
Setting National Priorities—The Next Ten Years, Brookings,
Washington DC, 1976

PADOA-SCHIOPPA, Tommaso
'The EMF: Topics for Discussion', part of the proceedings of the
Second International Seminar on European Economic and Monetary
Union, Geneva, 7–8 December 1979, in *Banca Nazionale del Lavoro
Quarterly Review*, no.134, Rome, September 1980

PATRICK, Hugh, and ROSOVSKY, Henry, eds
Asia's New Giant—How the Japanese Economy Works, Brookings,
Washington DC, 1976

PECHMAN, Joseph A.
'The Budget Outlook', in *Setting National Priorities: The 1979
Budget*, Joseph A. Pechman, ed., Brookings, Washington DC, 1978

PEMPEL, T. J., and TSUNEKAWA, Keiichi
'Corporatism Without Labor? The Japanese Anomaly', in *Trends
Towards Corporatist Intermediation*, Philippe C. Schmitter and
Gerhard Lehmbruch, eds, Sage Publications, Beverly Hills and
London, 1979

RIVLIN, Alice
'A Guide to the Congressional Budget Process' (interview) in
Challenge, vol.18, no.3, White Plains, NY, July–August 1975

ROSOVSKY, Henry, *see* PATRICK *above*

RUGGIE, John G.
'Complexity, Planning, and Public Order', in *Organized Social
Complexity*, Todd R. LaPorte, ed., Princeton University Press, 1975

SCHMITTER, Philippe C.
'On Organizing Interests: Speculative Exploration in the Political
Economy of Modern Associability', photocopied paper for
conference on The Social and Political Challenges of the New
International Economic Order in Comparative Perspective, Villa
Serbeloni, Bellagio, Italy, 24–8 April 1979

SCHULTZE, Charles L.
'Federal Spending: Past, Present, and Future', in *Setting National
Priorities*, Henry Owen and Charles L. Schultze, eds, 1976, *see*
OWEN *above*

——*The Public Use of Private Interest*, 1976 Godkin Lectures,
Brookings, Washington DC, 1977

SECCOMBE, Monica, *see* CAPPELLETTI *above*

SHONFIELD, Andrew
British Economic Policy Since the War, Penguin Books,
Harmondsworth, 1958

——*Modern Capitalism—The Changing Balance of Public and Private
Power*, Oxford University Press, 1965

——Contributions to discussion at Federal Trust Conference on
'Sterling—European Monetary Co-operation and World Monetary
Reform', London, 16–17 January 1968, published as Federal Trust
Report, Special Series no.3, London, 1968

——*Europe: Journey to an Unknown Destination* (1972 Reith
Lectures), Penguin Books, Harmondsworth, 1973

——Letter to *New Society*, London, 24 October 1974

——'A European Community Balance-of-Payments Fund', in
Annex II to the European Commission's Marjolin Report, 1975
(q.v.)

——'Can the Western Economic System Stand the Strain?' in *The
World Today*, vol.32, no.5, Royal Institute of International Affairs,
London, May 1976

——'Can Capitalism Survive Till 1999?' in *Encounter*, vol.48, no.1,
London, January 1977

——'Between Intervention and Multiplicity—A Reply', in
Encounter, vol.50, no.1, London, January 1978

——Memorandum [dated October 1978] by Professor Sir Andrew
Shonfield of the European University, Florence, in the *First Report
from the Expenditure Committee of the House of Commons*, 'The
European Monetary System', minutes of 3 November 1978, Session
1978–9, HMSO, London, 20 November 1978

——Letter to Niels Thygesen, 22 November 1979, following the
Bologna conference

——Comments on Tommaso Padoa-Schioppa's paper (q.v.),
September 1980

——'Innovation: Does Government have a Role?' in *Industrial
Policy and Innovation*, Charles Carter, ed., Heinemann, London,
1981

——*The Use of Public Power*, Oxford University Press, 1982

SMITH, Tom W.
'General Liberalism and Social Change in Post World War II America', in *Social Indicators Research*, no.10, Washington DC, March 1982

STREECK, Wolfgang
References in this text are to the photocopied draft, 'Union Structure in the German Car Industry', the material from which has been divided between Streeck's *Industrial Relations in West Germany: A case study of the car industry*, Heinemann Educational Books, for Policy Studies Institute, London, 1983, and a PSI research paper, *Industrial Relations, Trade Unions and Works Councils in the German Car Industry*, Policy Studies Institute, London, 1983

SUNLEY, Emil M., Jr
'State and Local Governments', in *Setting National Priorities*, Henry Owen and Charles L. Schultze, eds, 1976, *see* OWEN *above*

TAIRA, Koji
Economic Development and the Labor Market in Japan, Columbia University Press, 1970

TANAKA, Yonosuke
'The world of the *Zaikai*', in *Politics and Economics in Contemporary Japan*, Hyoe Murakami and Johannes Hirschmeier, eds, Japan Culture Institute, Tokyo, 1979

TAYLOR, Allen, ed.
Perspectives on US–Japan Relations, Ballinger, New York, 1973

THUROW, Lester C.
The Zero-Sum Society: Distribution and the Possibilities for Economic Change, Basic Books, New York, 1980

THYGESEN, Niels
'International coordination of monetary policies—with special reference to the European Community', in *New Approaches to Monetary Policy*, F. L. de Juvigny and J. E. Wadsworth, eds, Sijthoff & Noordhoff, Alphen aan den Rijn, 1979

TIMES, The
'Three steps towards European harmonization', 26 July 1976

——'Call for expansion of EEC unit of account', John Earle, Rome, 28 June 1978

TSUNEKAWA, Keiichi, *see* PEMPEL *above*

UEKUSA, Masu
Sangyo soshiki-ron (The theory of industrial organization), Chikuma-Shobo, Tokyo, 1982

220   Bibliographical references

US CONGRESSIONAL BUDGET OFFICE
Budget Options for Fiscal Year 1977, Washington DC, 1976

US SSRC, Center for Coordination of Research on Social Indicators
Social Indicators Newsletter No.17, Washington DC, August 1982

VERNON, Raymond
'Critical Choices: The Structure of Industry', in *Western Europe: The Trials of Partnership*, Critical Choices for Americans, vol.VIII, David S. Landes, ed., Lexington Books, D. C. Heath, Lexington, Mass., 1977

WAGNER, R. E., *see* BUCHANAN *above*

WALLICH, Henry C., and WALLICH, Mable I.
'Banking and Finance', in *Asia's New Giant*, Hugh Patrick and Henry Rosovsky, eds, *see* PATRICK *above*

WEIDENBAUM, Murray L.
Business, Government, and the Public, Prentice-Hall, Englewood Cliffs, 1977

WEINER, Nan
'The Japanese Wage System', in *Compensation Review*, American Management Review, New York, January–March 1982

WEINGAST, Barry, *see* CORNELL *above*

WEISNER, John, *see* CAPPELLETTI *above*

WILDAVSKY, Aaron
'The Theory of Expenditure Limitation', March 1980 paper in OECD, *Controlling Public Expenditure*, May 1980, *see* OECD *above*

WILLIAMSON, Oliver E.
Markets and Hierarchies, Free Press, New York, 1975

van YPERSELE, Jacques
'A Central Position for the Special Drawing Right in the Monetary System', in *Banca Nazionale del Lavoro Quarterly Review*, no.123, Rome, December 1977

ZUSHI, Saburo
'Case Study: How to Go Bankrupt and Still Stay Afloat—The Ataka Affair', in *Politics and Economics in Contemporary Japan*, Hyoe Murakami and Johannes Hirschmeier, eds, Japan Culture Institute, Tokyo, 1979

INDEX